# AUTONOMY

# AUTONOMY

## FLEXIBLE SOLUTIONS TO ETHNIC CONFLICTS

### Ruth Lapidoth

UNITED STATES INSTITUTE OF PEACE PRESS
Washington, D.C.

The views expressed in this book are those of the author alone. They do not necessarily reflect views of the United States Institute of Peace.

United States Institute of Peace
1550 M Street NW, Suite 700
Washington, DC 20005-1708

First published 1997

Printed in the United States of America

The paper used in this publication meets the minimum requirements of American National Standard for Information Sciences—Permanence of Paper for Printed Library Materials, ANSI Z39.48-1984.

**Library of Congress Cataloging-in-Publication Data**
Lapidoth, Ruth Eschelbacher, 1930–
      Autonomy / Ruth Lapidoth.
        p. cm.
      Includes bibliographical references and index.
      ISBN 1-878379-63-1 (hardback). — ISBN 1-878379-62-3 (pbk.)
       1. Minorities—Civil rights. 2. Minorities—Political activity. 3. Autonomy.
    4. Autonomy—Case studies. I. Title.
JF1061.L36 1996
323.1—dc20                                         96-42468
                                                      CIP

In memory of our son Michael, 1959–1982

# CONTENTS

# FOREWORD

Across the globe—from Sri Lanka to northern Iraq, Chechnya to Bosnia—minority groups are asserting their distinctive ethnic, religious, or national identity and demanding greater control over the expression of that identity, not only in cultural and social matters but in political and economic areas as well. Much of that assertion is based on "the right of self-determination of peoples." Heard less often are pleas for accommodation and self-restraint. Indeed, such pleas are more typically heard from those whose authority is being challenged—the governments of ethnically heterogeneous states—but all too frequently such official declarations of restraint seem intended to support an embattled status quo or even at times to disguise government attempts to repress dissent.

This disdain for give-and-take and accommodation is usually counterproductive, spawning only greater antagonism and leading frequently to bloodshed. Those minorities that insist upon seceding from the states within which they find themselves almost always fail in their ambitions, unable either to overcome the opposition of the state or to sustain themselves as an independent entity. Those states that dismiss the notion of compromise must usually reckon with prolonged and violent opposition from the dissaffected minority. The erroneous assumption that the right of self-determination of peoples includes within it the right of secession serves to confuse the dialogue and interfere with the process of accommodation.

There is reason to believe that those minorities and governments willing to negotiate in good faith with one another may find that by not insisting on their maximum demands, they can actually secure significant gains. For such parties, "autonomy" rather than secession can be an invaluable means of institutionalizing and enshrining mutual accommodation. Indeed, as Ruth Lapidoth demonstrates in this innovative and authoritative volume, flexibility and compromise are the very hallmarks of success when it comes to resolving ethnic differences peacefully through the establishment of autonomous regimes. "Autonomy," Professor Lapidoth emphasizes, "is not a panacea, but only a tool or a framework that can constitute an adequate compromise if the parties are looking for one. . . . Autonomy cannot create the wish for compromise, but it can help shape its content. Like any tool, it must be used in accordance with the special circumstances of each case." Obviously, the term "autonomy" is a flexible one, whose details must be ironed out in the negotiating process.

The American experience has historically minimized the role of group rights. Our emphasis has been on individual rights. Individuals are free to assemble in groups as they wish (or not to do so) and can as individuals or within groups publish, speak any language they wish, attend any church they wish, express their cultural and ethnic loyalties, participate in or form political movements, or engage in any other non-violent activities that do not strongly offend community sensibilities. In this manner, we have as a nation generally avoided the divisiveness that has characterized other areas of the world where the concept of group rights has been dominant.

Indeed, the sum total of individual rights for the group seeking respect and identity is no less than can be achieved by the group when it emphasizes group rights. This is particularly true once it is clear that secession is not an alternative without violence or the consent of the existing government.

Minority groups that are seeking greater political identification and acknowledge their limitations can thus achieve modest but nonetheless concrete gains by opting for autonomy—for gaining control over their own affairs in some areas while remaining subject to the authority of the state in other matters. From the perspective of the state, the granting of autonomy may be the only workable, peaceable solution to the problems posed by a minority whose demands for secession must be rejected because they threaten the unity and well-being of the state, yet whose aspirations for cultural or ethnic respect and even self-government cannot be silenced or satisfied within the existing system of governance. Within this context, Professor Lapidoth's study is of immense service to stability and respect for law.

With a scholar's attention to analytical precision, factual accuracy, and scrupulous objectivity, and with a policymaker's appetite for useful knowledge and practicable options, the author details and explores the protean character of autonomy as both a concept and a practice. Autonomy inhabits a famously imprecise area of international law and international relations, one in which there is little or no agreement on the meaning of even such basic terms as "peoples" and "minorities." With welcome clarity, Ruth Lapidoth lays out the conceptual landscape, presenting the diversity of scholarly opinion, distinguishing among autonomy's subtypes, contrasting autonomy with other arrangements for the diffusion of power within heterogenous societies, and offering her own definition of the concept.

These theoretical insights are then applied to concrete situations. Convinced that autonomy has the potential to help in the peaceful resolution of ethnic conflicts, the author examines more than a dozen case studies—some of which have rarely been dealt with before—to assess the circumstances, terms, and development of these autonomous arrangements. Although the cases she investigates are extremely varied—ranging from Greenland to Eritrea, from the Baltic States to the West Bank—Professor Lapidoth makes clear that they do not illustrate all the relevant situations in which autonomy in one form or another has been, or might be, contemplated. However, the cases are more than varied enough to exemplify her contention that "one of the great advantages of autonomy is its flexibility. It includes a wide range of possibilities—from a minimum of competence, on the one hand, to a great number of powers just short of full independence, on the other hand."

The last part of the book spells out a host of issues to be considered when establishing an autonomous regime and identifies those factors that may increase the chances for success. The author is both pragmatic and precise; her detailed recommendations are likely to prove invaluable in stimulating the inventiveness of negotiators on both sides of the table and of policymakers from interested third parties.

Professor Lapidoth's ability to address the concerns of policymakers and practitioners as well as academics and analysts is very much in keeping with the United States Institute of Peace's interest in bridging the gap between the policymaking and scholarly communities. In terms of subject matter too, there is a clear correspondence between *Autonomy* and the work of other Institute authors: among the Institute's more recent publications are Ted Robert Gurr's *Minorities at Risk: A Global View of Ethnopolitical Conflicts*, Patricia Carley's *Self-Determination: Sovereignty, Territorial Integrity, and the Right to Secession,* and Timothy Sisk's *Power Sharing and International Mediation in Ethnic Conflicts.*

In addition, the Institute sponsored a conference on U.S. responses to self-determination movements in 1996, and two recent grants deal directly with autonomy: John McGarry of King's College, Ontario, and Brendan O'Leary of the London School of Economics are assessing a range of options for regulating ethnic conflict, and Paul Williams of the University of Cambridge is investigating the legal and political consequences of state breakup and issues of secession.

In more general terms, it seems entirely fitting that Ruth Lapidoth should have begun writing *Autonomy* during her tenure as a peace fellow in the Institute's Jennings Randolph Program for International Peace, for the author's hope "that this study may assist policymakers and practitioners in the search for ways to settle disputes and to ease tensions by compromise" reflects an important dimension of the mandate conferred on the Institute by Congress.

Max M. Kampelman
Vice Chairman, Board of Directors
United States Institute of Peace

# ACKNOWLEDGMENTS

This study is largely based on research conducted while the author was a Peace Fellow at the United States Institute of Peace in Washington, D.C., during 1990 and 1991. I am grateful to the Institute and to Ambassador Samuel W. Lewis, who was the Institute's president at that time. At a later stage, I benefited from the assistance and the encouragement of the Jerusalem Institute for Israel Studies; I am very grateful to the head of the Institute, Professor Rami Friedman, as well as to its director, Ora Ahimeir. I also wish to thank Dr. Alan Stephens for having suggested the subject to me, as well as Professor Donald Horowitz, the Honorable Herbert Hansell, and Dr. Shavit Matias, for their good advice. Special thanks are due to Dr. Phoebe Kornfeld and Jocelyn Nieva, as well as to Gideon Rottem and Rotem Giladi for their great assistance at various stages.

The section on attempts to solve the Palestinian problem with the help of autonomy as an interim measure is partly based on a larger study of the 1978 Camp David process, which was supported by a grant from the Ford Foundation received through the Israel Foundations Trustees and by the Harry and Michael Sacher Institute for Legislative Research and Comparative Law; I am grateful to both institutions. In fact, the introduction to that study was the nucleus out of which grew the present one. I also thank the Leonard Davis Institute for International Relations for its support.

In the preparation of chapters 3–6 and 12, I relied to some extent on certain articles I had published earlier: "Some Reflections on Autonomy," in *Mélanges offerts à Paul Reuter: Le droit international—Unité et diversité* (Paris: Pedone, 1980); "Autonomy" (in Hebrew), *Mishpat Umimshal* 1 (1992); "Autonomy: Potential and Limitations," *International Journal on Group Rights* 1 (1994); "Sovereignty in Transition," *Journal of International Affairs* 45 (1992); and "Redefining Authority: The Past, Present, and Future of Sovereignty," *Harvard International Review* 17 (1995).

Part of the study was written while the author was a Visiting Professor at Georgetown University Law Center (1993); I offer my deep thanks to Dean Judy Areen, as well as to the colleagues, staff, and librarians—particularly Ellen Schaffer and Barbara Rainwater—who did their utmost to help me.

In my study of specific cases, I benefited from the advice of many colleagues and friends to whom I will refer in the relevant sections. I am indebted to Professor Hurst Hannum and to Selma Hoedt, who allowed me to use the proofs of the collection of *Documents on Autonomy and Minority Rights* (published in 1993 by Martinus Nijhoff), and to Professor Daniel Elazar, who permitted me to use the manuscript of *Federal Systems of the World: A Handbook of Federal, Confederal, and Autonomy Arrangements,* since published by Longman (1991; second edition 1994).

The manuscript has greatly benefited from the very helpful comments of Dr. David Stewart, Professor Anne Bayefsky, and Ambassador Max Kampelman, who read it in its entirety. To all of them I am very grateful.

Many thanks are due to Alicia Rosov, who copyedited the manuscript, to Mrs. Aliza Argov-Shirion and Ms. Mary Ann DeRosa for the excellent typing, and to Frances Bowles, who prepared the index.

Last but not least, my thanks go to the paradise-like Bellagio Study and Conference Center, in whose Santa Caterina study the manuscript was rethought and the conclusions were written.

# AUTONOMY

# INTRODUCTION

Autonomy is a means for diffusion of powers in order to preserve the unity of a state while respecting the diversity of its population; it has been successful in some cases and failed in others.

Because of its growing relevance, the subject deserves close examination and analysis. The object of this study is to analyze the concept of autonomy with special consideration of its possible role as a method of relieving tensions resulting from the heterogeneity of a great number of states. Special emphasis will be given to its potential to address the aspirations of minorities, of indigenous populations, and of peoples striving for self-determination.

With the rise in ethnic consciousness, there is growing interest in the subject of autonomy in many parts of the world. Autonomy is increasingly suggested as a method of resolving certain conflicts, and it is not uncommon for regions to demand it. Thus, some have proposed to solve the Chechnya conflict by granting autonomy to its inhabitants; autonomy may also contribute to the solution of some of the ethnic problems in parts of the former Yugoslavia. In the Middle East, the most famous cases where autonomy is on the agenda are the areas of Iraq inhabited mainly by Kurds and the territories administered by Israel that are inhabited by Palestinian Arabs. In the Far East, autonomy has been proposed for Hong Kong and Macao once they are returned to China. Efforts have also been made in the Philippines to establish autonomy for the Muslims in the island of Mindanao and for the indigenous population in the Cordilleras. In the Western Hemisphere, Puerto Rico enjoys autonomy. Regimes of autonomy for indigenous populations have also been established or are foreseen in other countries, for example, Nunavut in northeast Canada and Yapti Tasba on the Atlantic coast of Nicaragua. These examples demonstrate the widespread resort to autonomy and the hopes attached to this notion.

That interest and those hopes probably stem from the fact that autonomy has been successful in some cases, such as in the Åland Islands, South Tyrol/Alto Adige, the Faroe Islands, West Berlin before the reunification of Germany, Greenland/Kalaallit Nunaat, the Spanish provinces, Puerto Rico, and certain areas inhabited by indigenous populations. However, in other cases autonomy has failed to solve problems, for example, in Eritrea (where autonomy was followed by full annexation, a long and bloody war, and independence in 1993); in the southern Sudan (where the abolition of autonomy led to a resumption of the civil war); and in the former Soviet Union (where ethnic conflict has intensified and has led to armed hostilities in the wake of the break-up of the state).

The interest of the international community in certain regimes of autonomy depends on the nature of the group that enjoys or requests it. Sometimes an ethnic group has a historical or linguistic affinity to another country: the inhabitants of Åland speak Swedish; the majority of the inhabitants of South Tyrol speak German; a considerable number of citizens of Slovakia speak Hungarian; the Muslims in Xinjian in China have an ethnic link to the inhabitants of eastern Russia; and the Tamil Hindus in Sri Lanka have links with the Tamil Nadu in India. Sometimes an ethnic group is dispersed among several countries, such as the Sami in northern Europe or the Kurds, who are dispersed among Iran, Iraq, Turkey, Syria, and Armenia.

This research was initially begun with the hope that it would lead to a model or some models of autonomy, but the author soon realized that due to the great diversity of the various cases, it would not be feasible to formulate a practical general model. Therefore it appeared to be more useful to highlight the main features of autonomy and to indicate the principal options that are open to those who contemplate the establishment of a regime of autonomy.

The study is based on an examination of opinions of writers, as well as on an analysis of actual cases. In part I, we examine the problems autonomy is intended to solve. Autonomy serves to secure the rights of minorities, of indigenous populations, and of peoples seeking self-determination; it aims to ease ethnic tensions. In addition, it may be used to solve problems related to other sources of heterogeneity, such as economic diversity.

Part II analyzes the concept of autonomy, with special consideration of the difference between territorial and personal autonomy; the latter is sometimes called cultural autonomy. Similarly, an attempt is made to study the relationship between autonomy and sovereignty. In addition, territorial autonomy is compared with other arrangements for the diffusion of powers: federalism, decentralization, self-government, associate status, and self-administration.

One might expect the analysis of the notion of autonomy to precede the examination of the problems that it is intended to solve. However, the author has decided to change the natural order of the discussion and start with a study of the problems to be solved, because the notion of autonomy is still somewhat vague. A prior understanding of the aims of the system will help in analyzing the concept.

Whereas the first two parts address more theoretical aspects of autonomy, in the third part actual cases are studied, including past and present ones. It was not easy to choose among the many cases of autonomy that the author has studied. The choice was made in accordance with certain considerations, including keeping the book to a reasonable length. It was also thought preferable to examine a small number of cases in depth rather than to summarize many instances without going into details. Finally, the cases should be as varied as possible, from all points of view: geographic location, period of establishment of the regime, cases of success and of failure, differences in the origins of the regime, and the powers and structure of the autonomous authorities as well as their relationship with the center.

After much hesitation, the author decided to limit the discussion of instances of autonomy of indigenous populations—or aboriginals, or "First Nations"—to the case of Greenland/Kalaallit Nunaat (hereafter referred to simply as Greenland). In most other countries, the right to self-government of indigenous peoples and its implementation are still in flux and therefore difficult to evaluate. The basis of the requests for self-government of indigenous peoples is a claim to "original sovereignty"; because the indigenous tribes were independent nations before the occupation by Europeans, they claim to have an "inherent right" to self-government, a right which does not derive from the state. The request for self-government is often linked to claims to property rights, such as title to land, and to rights to hunt, fish, and trap on traditional lands. In federal states, the claims of aboriginals often clash with the rights and powers of the federal units.

The requests for self-government of indigenous populations and those cases where such autonomy exists in practice certainly deserve a thorough examination, but this would go beyond the modest aims of the present study. However, the general claim of aboriginals for self-government is discussed, as well as the case of Greenland.

Finally, an attempt is made to analyze the typical issues and the possible alternatives that have to be considered when establishing an autonomous regime, as well as factors that may contribute to the success of the regime. Some of these are objective features not controllable by the parties, while others may be more subjective and could be influenced by the relevant actors.

The author hopes that the present study will contribute some new ideas to the literature on autonomy, in particular in three respects: the attempt to understand the concept of autonomy and to compare it with other means of diffusion of powers; awareness of the practical issues to be considered when establishing a regime of autonomy; and the enumeration of elements that may enhance the chances of success.

It is the author's earnest hope that this study may assist policymakers and practitioners in the search for ways to settle disputes and to ease tensions by compromise.

# PART I

# THE ROLE OF AUTONOMY

*The heterogeneity of most states has often been a source of friction and conflict. Several means have been used to try to solve the problem. On the one hand, attempts have been made to achieve homogeneity by imposing assimilation; on the other hand, ways have been sought to accommodate that heterogeneity, in particular by a diffusion of powers. One of those means is autonomy. In this part an attempt is made to review the relevance of autonomy to the status of minority groups, to indigenous populations, and to peoples striving for self-determination. We also consider the potential of autonomy to manage situations of economic heterogeneity.*

# EASING ETHNIC TENSIONS

1

Ethnic awareness and the ensuing tensions have definitely been on the rise during the last quarter of the twentieth century, both in Europe (east and west) and in Third World countries. This development may be related to the swift progress of modernization, urbanization, decolonization, and even democratization (as explained in detail in chapter 10). In addition, groups of indigenous populations have increased their demands for recognition of their special rights. The various claims are based on four conceptual frameworks in the area of human rights: (1) the right to equality and nondiscrimination; (2) the right of minorities to preserve and develop their own culture, religion, and language; (3) the right of indigenous populations to preserve their traditions, as well as their special rights to land and its natural resources; and (4) the right of peoples to self-determination. In some of those cases in which ensuring equality and minority rights does not satisfy the aspirations of the group, and in which full self-determination is not an option, autonomy is granted in order to settle the conflict or ease it.

The following examples demonstrate the dimensions of the problem: the demand for independence in Corsica, the acts of violence carried out by some Basques in Spain, the fate of Gypsies (Roma) and of migrant workers, the ethnic mosaic in the republics established on the ruins of the USSR, the atrocities perpetrated in what used to be Yugoslavia, the secession of the Slovak Republic from Czechoslovakia, and the ethnic tension between Romanians and Hungarians in Transylvania. In South Asia examples include hostile acts performed in Sri Lanka (between the Tamil Hindu minority and the Sinhalese Buddhist majority) and in India (such as by the Sikhs in the Punjab and among Muslims and Hindus in the wake of the destruction of the Babri Masjid mosque in Ayodhya), and the tension between China and Tibet. Among the numerous conflicts in the Middle East, one may mention the problem of the Kurds who are scattered in five countries (Turkey, Iraq, Syria, Armenia, and Iran); the tension between Turks and Greeks in Cyprus; the interethnic and interreligious tension in Lebanon; and the Arab-Israel conflict. In Africa, acts of violence occur daily against the background of ethnic tensions in Sudan, Somalia, Burundi, and Rwanda. In the Western Hemisphere, the demands of Quebec and of indigenous populations such as the Indians and the Inuit (Eskimos) stand out.

The goals and aspirations of minority groups may be classified under six major headings:

- a basic demand for equal rights and integration (or full assimilation) into the predominant group;
- an aspiration for group rights for the minority;
- an aspiration to institutionalize group rights in the framework of personal autonomy;
- a demand for either territorial autonomy or federalism;
- a quest for self-determination and the right to secede into full political independence; and
- a desire to become the dominant power in the country.

Autonomy, in its various forms, would seem to be relevant to some of these goals and aspirations. A distinction should be made among the three groups of potential beneficiaries: ethnic minorities (including national, linguistic, and religious groups), indigenous populations, and other peoples. Before considering the relevance of autonomy to these groups, it may be useful to mention that a primary aim of all individuals, including members of minority groups, is to achieve equality and non-discrimination. However, reaching this goal does not require autonomy.

## AUTONOMY AND MINORITY RIGHTS

Surprisingly, there is no generally accepted definition for the concept of either a minority or a member of a minority.[1] According to a definition proposed by an expert in the field, Francesco Capotorti, "a minority is a group which is numerically inferior to the rest of the population of a

State and in a non-dominant position, whose members possess ethnic, religious or linguistic characteristics which differ from those of the rest of the population and who, if only implicitly, maintain a sense of solidarity directed towards preserving their culture, traditions, religion or language."[2]

Before World War I, minorities were only rarely protected: They often suffered from discrimination, and only a small number of laws and treaties granted them equality and protection of their special status (for example, by allowing them to practice their own religion). After World War I, the rights of minorities were guaranteed in various countries— in the newly established states, in states whose territory had been considerably increased, and in defeated states (except Germany)—either by international treaties or by declarations made at the time of the admission of the state to the League of Nations. A supervisory mechanism related to the League was also established.[3] In some states, minorities were granted not only the substantive rights for the preservation of their identity, but also personal autonomy, which enabled them to ensure their rights by acting themselves within the framework of their own institutions.

After World War II, the emphasis shifted to the protection of individual rights; consequently many of the new human rights treaties did not deal with minorities. This neglect of minority rights apparently had its origin in three considerations: First, one presumed that minorities' rights would be adequately guaranteed by general human rights, in particular by the principle of nondiscrimination; second, between the two world wars there were cases in which certain minorities were not loyal to their country of citizenship and instead assisted a foreign country to which they had an ethnic affiliation; third, because many minority groups were expelled at the end of World War II to those countries with which they had an ethnic affiliation, it was commonly thought that the problem of minorities had largely disappeared.

However, it soon became apparent that the minorities problem had not disappeared and that the general rules in the field of human rights were not sufficient for ensuring special minority rights. As a result, the international community again addressed the subject. The first development in this direction was the provision included in Article 27 of the 1966 International Covenant on Civil and Political Rights: "In those States in which ethnic, religious or linguistic minorities exist, persons belonging to such minorities shall not be denied the right, in community with other members of their group, to enjoy their own culture, to profess and practise their own religion, or to use their own language."[4] Although the right ensured in this article is fairly limited, it constitutes a proper beginning. Other instruments also provided a certain protection of the rights of minorities, either directly or indirectly.[5]

The development of human rights, including those of minorities, was hampered during the Cold War. Once the political climate changed, a big step forward in the recognition of the rights of members of minorities was made in the framework of the Conference on Security and Cooperation in Europe (CSCE; the organization was renamed the Organization for Security and Cooperation in Europe [OSCE] in 1995).[6] The most relevant development in this process was the adoption in June 1990 of the Document of the Copenhagen Meeting of the Conference on the Human Dimension of the CSCE.[7] Although this document is not legally binding, it certainly is of great political importance. It affirms that questions relating to national minorities "can only be satisfactorily resolved in a democratic political framework based on the rule of law" (Article 30); that persons belonging to national minorities have the right to enjoy human rights without discrimination (Article 31); that "[t]o belong to a national minority is a matter of a person's individual choice and no disadvantage may arise from the exercise of such choice" (Article 32); and that members of a minority have the right to establish their own institutions and maintain contacts among themselves within their country, as well as with members of the same group abroad (Article 32). The document adds that states have a duty to protect the identity of national minorities (Article 33), stating further that the minority's history and culture should be taken into account at "educational establishments" of the state (Article 34). Moreover, members of a minority must be allowed to effectively participate in the public affairs of the state (Article 35). The document also requires members of the minority to respect the territorial integrity of the state (Article 37).

The Copenhagen document specifically indicates that granting autonomy is one possible way of attaining the aforementioned objectives: "The participating States note the efforts undertaken to protect and create conditions for the promotion of the ethnic, cultural, linguistic and religious identity of certain national minorities by establishing, as one of the possible means to achieve these aims, appropriate local or autonomous administrations corresponding to the specific historical and territorial circumstances of such minorities and in accordance with the policies of the State concerned" (Article 35, Paragraph 2). This reference to autonomy is fairly modest, as there is no clear recommendation to establish autonomy.[8]

Minority questions were again discussed in the framework of the CSCE at a Meeting of the Experts on National Minorities convened in Geneva in July 1991.[9] The experts were of the opinion that "[i]ssues concerning national minorities . . . are matters of legitimate international concern and consequently do not constitute exclusively an internal affair of the respective State." They further stressed that "[i]n areas inhabited mainly by persons belonging to a national minority" the human rights of all persons have to be protected, including those of members of the group that is the majority in the whole state and members of another minority (Section III). Again, there is a noncommittal reference (in Section IV) to autonomy:

> Aware of the diversity and varying constitutional systems among them which make no single approach necessarily generally applicable, the participating States note with interest that positive results have been obtained by some of them in an appropriate democratic manner by, *inter alia:*
>
> — advisory and decision-making bodies in which minorities are represented, in particular with regard to education, culture and religion;
> — elected bodies and assemblies of national minority affairs;
> — local and autonomous administration, as well as autonomy on a territorial basis, including the existence of consultative, legislative and executive bodies chosen through free and periodic elections;
> — self-administration by a national minority of aspects concerning its identity in situations where autonomy on a territorial basis does not apply;
> — decentralized or local forms of government.

It is interesting to note that this text refers to both territorial and personal autonomy (discussed in chapter 4). The provisions of the Report of the Geneva CSCE Meeting of Experts were endorsed by the Document of the 1991 Moscow Meeting of the Conference on the Human Dimension of the CSCE (by Article 37).[10] The 1992 Helsinki Decisions have foreseen the appointment of a High Commissioner on National Minorities who should provide "early warning" and, as appropriate, recommend "early action" in response to tensions involving national minority issues.[11]

Minority rights were also the object of the 1992 UN Declaration on the Rights of Persons Belonging to National or Ethnic, Religious and Linguistic Minorities,[12] as well as of the 1995 Council of Europe Framework Convention for the Protection of National Minorities.[13] However, autonomy was not mentioned.

Problems of minorities have been discussed extensively in the framework of the Yugoslav crisis. On 27 August 1991 the European Community established a peace conference (which convened in The Hague) and an arbitration commission (the "Badinter Commission"). Several proposals discussed at the peace conference, in particular the Carrington Draft Convention of 4 November 1991, included provisions on the protection of minorities; the participants also recommended establishing autonomous structures having legislative, executive, and judicial functions in regions where members of a national minority form a local majority.[14]

Moreover, at an extraordinary European Political Cooperation (EPC)[15] ministerial meeting in Brussels on 16 December 1991, an outline on a common position on Guidelines on the Recognition of New States in Eastern Europe and in the Soviet Union was adopted, including, inter alia, the condition that the new state shall guarantee "the rights of ethnic and national groups and minorities in accordance with the commitments subscribed to in the framework of the CSCE" and in accordance with the Carrington Draft Convention.[16] The European Community's insistence on a constitutional commitment to granting autonomy to certain regions is rather interesting. Perhaps autonomy was intended to permit the parties to be quite separate, while remaining in one state—a separateness needed because relations had so drastically deteriorated.

The arbitration commission—composed of five members chosen from the presidents of the constitutional courts in the member-states of the European Community—also had to deal with questions relating to minorities. Although the commission did not mention autonomy expressly, it referred to it indirectly by basing some of its conclusions on the Carrington Draft Convention.[17] The arbitration commission also stated that problems of state succession should be solved in accordance with international law, "with particular regard for human rights and the rights of peoples and minorities."[18] The commission further stated that ethnic, religious, and language minorities "have the right to recognition of their identity under international law."[19] Moreover, the Badinter Commission expressed the opinion that the norms of international law requiring states to respect the rights of minorities are peremptory rules. The commission even mentioned the possibility, where appropriate, of allowing members of minority groups (in this case, Serbians living in Croatia) to adopt the nationality of their choice, thus exercising their right to self-determination on an individual basis.[20]

Autonomy was to play an even greater role at a later stage, in the Vance-Owen proposal of 20 October 1992. Under this proposal, Bosnia and Herzegovina was to be divided into seven to ten autonomous provinces. The text included relatively detailed provisions on this regime of autonomy, with special emphasis on human and minority rights.[21]

The Carrington Draft Convention, the Guidelines on Recognition, the opinions (avis) of the arbitration commission, and the Vance-Owen proposals certainly have great bearing on the notions of succession, self-determination, minority rights, and autonomy. In fact, the states that had formerly been a part of the Socialist Federal Republic of Yugoslavia adopted provisions on the protection of minorities in their constitutional texts.[22] Moreover, two of them—Croatia and Slovenia—have specifically provided for regimes of autonomy.

Croatia's Constitutional Law of Human Rights and Freedoms and the Rights of National and Ethnic Communities or Minorities of 1991, as amended in 1992, foresees not only the protection of minorities but also their cultural autonomy and even territorial autonomy: "[m]unicipalities (regions) with special self-governing (autonomous) status" are to be established in areas where the minority constitutes more than 50 percent of the population.[23] In Slovenia, on the other hand, autonomy has been foreseen only for the "autochthonous Italian and Hungarian national communities."[24]

However, in later attempts to solve the conflict in Bosnia and Herzegovina, autonomy has not been mentioned. Thus, in the Dayton Accords concluded in December 1995 with the mediation of the United States, human rights are prominent but autonomy is not.[25] The new constitution of Bosnia and Herzegovina approved by the Republic of Bosnia and Herzegovina and by its two "entities"—the Federation of Bosnia and Herzegovina (that is, the Muslim-Croatian Federation established in 1994 and reinforced in 1995) and the Republika Srpska (the part inhabited mainly by Serbs)[26]—like the Agreement on Human

Rights concluded by the same parties,[27] contains detailed provisions on human rights. Not only does the text foresee the direct application of the European Convention for the Protection of Human Rights and Fundamental Freedoms including its Protocols, but the provisions of the convention are to "have priority over all other law."[28] Both documents—the constitution and the agreement—include a long list of human rights texts that are to be applied in Bosnia and Herzegovina. On this list are two documents that describe rights of national groups and minorities in detail: the 1992 European Charter for Regional or Minority Languages and the 1995 Framework Convention for the Protection of National Minorities. But there is no reference to autonomy.

Perhaps there was no need to mention autonomy as a principle because the text itself, by dividing the country into two "entities" with large powers, established a diffusion of powers in the nature of autonomy or federalism. As of the time of this writing (March 1996), it has yet to be seen whether the arrangements agreed upon at Dayton will be implemented.

## AUTONOMY AND THE RIGHTS OF INDIGENOUS POPULATIONS (OR PEOPLES)

Although much has been written about the rights of indigenous populations,[29] the term indigenous populations, like the concept of minorities, does not yet have a generally recognized definition. The UN special rapporteur, Jose R. Martinez Cobo, has proposed the following definition to the Sub-Commission on Prevention of Discrimination and Protection of Minorities:

> Indigenous communities, peoples and nations are those which, having a historical continuity with pre-invasion and pre-colonial societies that developed on their territories, consider themselves distinct from other sectors of the societies now prevailing in those territories, or parts of them. They form at present non-dominant sectors of society and are determined to preserve, develop and transmit to future generations their ancestral territories, and their ethnic identity, as the basis of their continued existence as peoples, in accordance with their own cultural patterns, social institutions and legal systems. . . .
>
> On an individual basis, an indigenous person is one who belongs to these indigenous populations through self-identification as indige-

nous (group consciousness) and is recognized and accepted by these populations as one of its members (acceptance by the group).[30]

Indigenous populations no doubt qualify as ethnic minorities and as such can enjoy the rights granted by international law to minorities. However, in recent decades the demands of indigenous populations have been growing. These groups do not consider themselves minorities because their forebears inhabited the respective territories before the arrival of those who later became the majority, and they claim rights that go beyond those recognized for minorities. In particular, they emphasize their right to traditional economic systems, to land and its resources, and to their traditional way of life within the framework of self-government or autonomy. In recent years, claims for a right of self-determination for indigenous populations have also been raised.[31]

The changing approach to the rights of indigenous populations is clearly reflected in two conventions on indigenous groups that were drafted within the framework of the International Labour Organisation. In the 1957 Convention Concerning the Protection and Integration of Indigenous and Other Tribal and Semi-Tribal Populations in Independent Countries (Convention no. 107), there is an apparent intention to ensure indigenous populations equal rights and social and economic development (for example, vocational training, social security, health, and education) and to facilitate their integration into the population. By contrast, in the 1989 text (Convention no. 169),[32] there is no longer any encouragement to assimilate; instead, emphasis is placed on granting indigenous populations the possibility of maintaining their customs, participating in decisions concerning the exploitation of natural resources within their lands, and allowing them to make decisions regarding their own institutions and their socioeconomic development. Specific provisions ensure the land rights of indigenous peoples (Articles 13–19).

Responding to the growing awareness of the need to protect and enhance the rights of indigenous populations, the UN Sub-Commission on Prevention of Discrimination and Protection of Minorities has also focused on the subject. Under its auspices, a working group has prepared a draft declaration on that subject.[33] Several paragraphs in the 1994 draft specifically address the subject of autonomy:

> Indigenous peoples, as a specific form of exercising their right to self-determination, have the right to autonomy or self-government in

matters relating to their internal and local affairs, including culture, religion, education, information, media, health, housing, employment, social welfare, economic activities, land and resources management, environment and entry by non-members, as well as ways and means for financing these autonomous functions (Article 31).

Indigenous peoples have the collective right to determine their own citizenship in accordance with their customs and traditions. Indigenous citizenship does not impair the right of indigenous individuals to obtain citizenship of the States in which they live.

Indigenous peoples have the right to determine the structures and to select the membership of their institutions in accordance with their own procedures (Article 32).

Indigenous peoples have the right to promote, develop and maintain their institutional structures and their distinctive juridical customs, traditions, procedures and practices, in accordance with internationally recognized human rights standards (Article 33).[34]

In general, the draft supports rather far-reaching claims of indigenous populations, and it may be assumed that eventually its scope will have to be reduced in order to render it acceptable to states.

In September 1991 a group of experts met in Greenland to discuss models of autonomy and self-government for indigenous populations. The meeting was held in pursuance of a UN initiative and within the framework of the Human Rights Commission's activities. Clearly, the "Conclusions and Recommendations" of that group have no binding effect; they may, however, have some impact on public opinion and on UN activities in this area. The experts concluded, inter alia, that indigenous peoples have the right of self-determination and that "[a]n integral part of this is the inherent and fundamental right to autonomy and self-government" (Article 2). Moreover, "[f]or indigenous peoples, autonomy and self-government are prerequisites for achieving equality, human dignity, freedom from discrimination and the full enjoyment of all human rights" (Article 4).[35]

In practice, several states have granted a certain degree of autonomy to indigenous populations. In the United States, for example, indigenous groups have been granted certain rights within about 280 reservations. Canada has granted self-government to various indigenous groups (for example, by establishing the autonomous region of Nunavut in northeast Canada).[36] However, a proposal to give legally binding effect to the trend to grant self-government to the indigenous populations in

Canada has so far failed. The proposal was included among others in a draft known as the Charlottetown constitutional deal, which was rejected by a referendum on 26 October 1992.[37]

Various writers have investigated the increasing recognition (or quest for recognition) of minority and indigenous rights. Some of them have suggested that these developments justify a comprehensive theory on group rights.[38]

## AUTONOMY AND THE RIGHT OF PEOPLES TO SELF-DETERMINATION

The right to self-determination has been one of the most intriguing and enigmatic notions of modern international law.[39] While many experts are of the opinion that this right exists, some deny its validity because of its vagueness.[40] Others have tried to limit it in view of its "state-shattering" effect, that is, the difficulty of reconciling it with the right of existing states to territorial integrity. Moreover, enthusiasm for self-determination has decreased since 1989 because of the acts of violence engendered by the dismemberment of the Soviet Union and Yugoslavia.[41]

Self-determination has both an "external" aspect—the right of a people to determine its international status—and an "internal" aspect—the right of the population to choose its own system of government and to participate in the political process that governs it. The principle of self-determination has gained wide recognition in the past forty years, so that some have come to regard it as an essential element of legitimacy. The International Court of Justice has recognized it as an *erga omnes* right, and as "one of the essential principles of contemporary international law."[42]

However, a closer examination of the principle of self-determination reveals that it is an ambiguous notion. As a political concept it was supported by the president of the United States, Woodrow Wilson, at the Peace Conference of 1919, where he drew the new map of Europe at the end of World War I; but the concept was applied only to a limited extent.[43] At that time, the legal aspect of self-determination was examined by two committees of experts for the League of Nations in connection with the question of the Åland Islands, and both reached the conclusion that it was not a binding rule of international law.[44] In particular, the committees expressed their opinion against the existence of a right to secede.[45] Self-determination is mentioned in the UN

Charter, not as a binding rule per se but as a purpose to be promoted.[46] The principle was confirmed in a number of UN General Assembly resolutions,[47] as well as in documents of the CSCE.[48]

The principle of self-determination attained binding legal effect in 1976, with the entry into force of the two 1966 covenants on human rights—the International Covenant on Civil and Political Rights and the International Covenant on Economic, Social, and Cultural Rights.[49] In parallel, and to a certain extent due to the influence of these texts, a customary rule developed as well.[50] The first article of both covenants states: "All peoples have the right of self-determination. By virtue of that right they freely determine their political status and freely pursue their economic, social and cultural development." The second paragraph addresses the right of all peoples to their natural wealth and resources; and the third requires states, including those having responsibilities for the administration of non-self-governing and trust territories, to promote the realization of self-determination.

However, the above provision leaves many questions unanswered and gives rise to a number of ambiguities; the following are a few examples. The first and foremost problem is the lack of a generally accepted definition of "peoples" in this context. Most definitions include two elements: the existence of objective links, such as cultural and historical ties, and a common subjective wish to belong together.[51] But these are also the ingredients of an ethnic group, and it is difficult to draw the line between people and *ethnie*. The difference is crucial since only "peoples" have the right to self-determination, while ethnic groups may merely enjoy minority rights.[52] The lack of a clear definition of the notion of "people" introduces a severe ambiguity and an element of subjectivity, often leading to a double standard in the recognition of the right to self-determination in specific cases. In the words of Thomas M. Franck, it may lead to "the gradual descent of self-determination into unprincipled conceptual incoherence."[53]

It is usually recognized that the external right to self-determination applies to colonial situations, to cases of peoples subjected to foreign or alien domination, and to the entire population of a given state.[54] But opinions are divided over the question of whether groups or "peoples" within an existing independent state may also claim it. It is generally recognized and even emphasized that all groups and all individuals enjoy the right of internal self-determination, that is, the right to political participation. But opinions are strongly divided on the question of whether that right extends to external self-determination, namely, the right to secede.

The above provision literally recognizes the right to self-determination of "all peoples." On the other hand, the international community is opposed in principle to any violation of the territorial integrity of existing states, and the Badinter Arbitration Commission expressly preferred the stability of boundaries: "[W]hatever the circumstances, the right to self-determination must not involve changes to existing frontiers at the time of independence (*uti possidetis juris*) except where the States concerned agree otherwise."[55] Similarly, according to most authors, the right to self-determination does not justify secession.[56] Only few scholars have fully recognized a right of secession as a corollary of self-determination,[57] while others have tried to strike a balance between the two norms, for example, by recognizing the right to secede only in cases of oppression (another term without a generally accepted definition)[58] or when the seceding group not only aspires for self-determination but also claims disputed territory based on a historical grievance.[59]

The practice of states is not uniform either. Whereas the secession of Katanga from Congo-Leopoldville (later Zaire) and of Biafra from Nigeria were not welcomed, the secession of Bangladesh from Pakistan was recognized and Bangladesh was even admitted to the United Nations. Most of the countries that were established on the ruins of the Soviet Union have been recognized by the international community, yet the demands for independence of some of the "autonomous republics" located within certain of these countries (particularly in Russia) have not been recognized. Similarly, the republics established after the dismemberment of Yugoslavia have been recognized, subject to certain conditions, but ethnic conflict in two of them has led to very grave violence.

Another major problem related to the question of who qualifies for external self-determination concerns minorities within the group that strives for self-determination. Does the minority that opposes secession have a right to prevent it? For instance, may the indigenous groups who live in Quebec prevent its secession from Canada? Moreover, does such a minority have the right to secede from the seceding group? Last, but not least, do indigenous peoples also have a right of self-determination? Again, opinions are divided, at least on the scope of the right.[60]

On several occasions, the UN General Assembly has determined that "[t]he establishment of a sovereign and independent State, the free association or integration with an independent State or the emergence into any other political status freely determined by a people constitute modes of implementing the right of self-determination by that people."[61] However, in recent years the General Assembly has often treated self-determination as if it were synonymous with independence.[62]

So far, we have discussed self-determination as a collective right of a people to determine its "political status." However, the Badinter Commission[63] had a quite different opinion on the notion of self-determination. It stressed the internal individual aspect of the right: "Article 1 of the two 1966 International Covenants on human rights establishes that the principle of the right to self-determination serves to safeguard human rights. By virtue of that right every individual may choose to belong to whatever ethnic, religious or language community he or she wishes."[64]

The ambiguities concerning the principle of self-determination have led some authors to conclude "that the normative status of self-determination in international law will ultimately depend on the transposition of the right of self-determination into a set of rights and obligations of states. If no such set exists, the right of self-determination will appear to be no more than a legal fiction."[65]

A discussion of the other numerous problems raised by the traditional meaning of self-determination is outside the scope of this study.[66] In any case, as has been shown, there may be a clash between the demand for self-determination and the right of existing states to territorial integrity.

An interesting balance between the two principles has been included in the UN General Assembly 1970 Declaration on Principles of International Law Concerning Friendly Relations and Co-operation among States in Accordance with the Charter of the United Nations:

> Nothing in the foregoing paragraphs shall be construed as authorizing or encouraging any action which would dismember or impair, totally or in part, the territorial integrity or political unity of sovereign and independent States conducting themselves in compliance with the principle of equal rights and self-determination of peoples as described above *and thus* possessed of a government representing the whole people belonging to the territory without distinction as to race, creed or colour. [emphasis added][67]

The plain meaning of this paragraph seems to be that if internal self-determination is properly implemented, there is no right of secession.

According to another rather innovative perspective, claims for self-determination and minority rights should be settled on a nonterritorial and nonstatist basis: In parallel with states, there should be established a system of nations, coupled with a decrease of state sovereignty, with a new allocation of powers, with functional borders, and with a distinction between citizenship—a link to the state—and nationality—a link to the nation.[68]

If one wishes to remain in a more classical framework, it should be remembered that self-determination can often be achieved before the conflict has generated strong antagonism and severe mistrust by the granting of autonomy. More and more authors seem to consider autonomy as a valid means of self-determination in a world where there is a trend toward federalization and regionalization.[69] The preference for modalities of self-determination other than independence has grown in reaction to the violence perpetrated in the name of self-determination in the wake of the breakup of the Soviet Union and of Yugoslavia.

To conclude, the rise in ethnic and national consciousness increases the need to search for solutions for the demands of minorities, of indigenous populations, and of peoples. One way to satisfy these demands while preserving the existence of the state and its territorial integrity is by establishing regimes of autonomy.

The above survey has shown that autonomy has been recognized as an appropriate means to satisfy demands of minorities, but it is still granted only in exceptional cases. As for indigenous populations, autonomy is more strongly demanded and more often granted. For "peoples," it remains a compromise solution representing a limited degree of self-determination.

# 2

## OTHER REASONS FOR
## ESTABLISHING AUTONOMY

There is no doubt that in the majority of cases the resort to autonomy is caused by ethnic tensions, but other circumstances may also call for the establishment of autonomy.

Sometimes the reason is economic. For example, when Hong Kong is returned to China in 1997,[1] there will be no considerable ethnic difference between its inhabitants and those of China; however, in order for Hong Kong to maintain its economic system, China has agreed with the United Kingdom that Hong Kong should enjoy a regime of autonomy as a "special administrative region," in accordance with Section 31 of the constitution of China. A similar arrangement was reached between Portugal and China regarding Macao, which is to be returned to Chinese sovereignty in 1999.[2]

Other situations that have prompted the establishment of autonomy have been regimes of internationalization. In various situations, certain countries have agreed to place a border region or a disputed area under an international regime. Examples include Danzig (1920–39) and Tangier (1924–56); the attempt to internationalize Trieste after World War II; and the proposal to internationalize Jerusalem at the end of the British Mandate. These regimes were often accompanied by arrangements of autonomy. For example, the municipal and local units included in Jerusalem were to enjoy "wide powers of local government and administration" under the UN General Assembly resolution of 1947.[3]

We will not study those cases in the present volume for the following reasons. As of this writing (March 1996), there is no internationalized territory in existence. For Hong Kong and Macao, autonomy has been promised in the future, but it is difficult to foresee how these commitments will be implemented.

# PART II

# THE NOTION AND ESSENCE OF AUTONOMY

*Having studied the role that autonomy is assumed and expected to play, it may be easier now to examine its meaning. The term has been used in various branches of science and with considerable differences of meaning. Therefore, in this part we begin by studying a number of definitions used by prominent authors from various countries and backgrounds. An attempt is then made to synthesize and crystallize a detailed description of autonomy. The examination, of course, takes into consideration the difference between territorial and personal autonomy.*

*The analysis of autonomy is supplemented by a comparison with other notions that are tangential to autonomy, namely, sovereignty, federalism, decentralization, self-government, associated statehood, and self-administration.*

# 3

# THE CONCEPT OF AUTONOMY

## PRELIMINARY REMARKS

Etymologically, the term autonomy derives from two Greek words: *auto,* meaning self, and *nomos,* law or rule.[1] Thus, the original meaning of the word was the right to make one's own laws. Today the concept is used in three different branches of science: philosophy and its derivatives; the natural sciences; and law, political science, and international relations. For philosophers, autonomy is a person's power to determine by oneself, through one's own rational will, "positive liberty" or "self-mastery";[2] in the natural sciences, the concept means organic independence, or the condition of a phenomenon conforming only to its own laws and not being subject to higher rules, that is, not a mere form or state of some other organism.[3] As is shown below, in the area of jurisprudence and political science autonomy has various meanings.

To avoid confusion when considering these numerous notions, it may be helpful to keep in mind the difference between concepts and conceptions.[4] While there is general agreement on the basic concept of autonomy, there are many conceptions of this concept, that is, differing views on its interpretation. The term, especially as an adjective (autonomous), is often used fairly loosely to describe the quality of having the right to decide or act at one's own discretion in certain matters.

## OPINIONS OF EXPERTS

It may be worthwhile to start this review with authors who were active at the beginning of the twentieth century. Georg Jellinek describes an autonomous entity as one based solely on its own laws, and with all the material and functional attributes of statehood: the authority to govern, to administer, and to judge.[5] Practically, this seems to be a synonym of sovereignty.

According to Paul Laband, autonomy always includes the power of legislation, but it differs from sovereignty in that it can be exercised only within the limits established by the sovereign.[6] A somewhat similar notion of autonomy is found in the writings of R. Carré de Malberg: An entity may be regarded as autonomous only when it has its own nonderivative original powers of legislation, administration, and adjudication. It should be distinguished from "self-government ou . . . décentralisation administrative (Selbstverwaltung)," a notion implying that the self-administering entity is subordinated to a superior entity that could have administered it by itself.[7] It is interesting that Carré de Malberg speaks of self-government and administrative decentralization as if the two terms were interchangeable.

For Léon Duguit autonomy implies an area protected from the legislative power of the state.[8] Henry Berthélémy uses the term as a synonym for decentralization,[9] while Maurice Hauriou uses it to describe the discretion that the laws sometimes give to the administration.[10]

Heinrich Dörge defined autonomy by referring to the regimes of autonomy established in the wake of World War I (mainly in the Åland Islands and in the Memel/Klaipeda Territory). In his opinion, those regimes have two characteristics: First, the authority of the autonomous entity includes all the significant attributes of state power (that is, legislation, adjudication, and administration); and second, those matters that are under the authority of the autonomous body are once and for all removed from the state's legislative power, unless the autonomous entity expressly agrees to a different arrangement.[11] Dörge was aware that some entities designated as "autonomous" did not, in fact, meet his definition, for example, the autonomous republics, regions (oblasti), and areas (okruga) in the Soviet Union; he denied, however, that these entities enjoyed genuine autonomy.[12]

Jacob Robinson examined the nature of autonomy, in the context of his seminal study on Memel, by comparing it with sovereignty. In his opinion, internal sovereignty assumes the supreme and unrestricted authority of the state, subject only to restrictions that are expressly specified. Autonomy, on the other hand, exists only in respect to those powers that have expressly been granted.[13]

Autonomy is also defined in Basdevant's *Dictionnaire de la terminologie du droit international* (1960). It may be of interest to note that according to that dictionary, a territory may be regarded as autonomous even when the mother state has no sovereignty over the territory—for example, in case of a trusteeship:

> Employé parfois pour désigner la liberté de se gouverner et administrer elle-même, reconnue ou conférée à une collectivité territoriale qui n'est pas investie de la souveraineté et qui est politiquement et juridiquement rattachée à un ou plusieurs Etats sans faire partie de leur territoire ni relever à ce titre de leur souveraineté.[14]
>
> [Sometimes used to indicate the freedom to govern and administer oneself, recognized or granted to a territorial community which does not have sovereignty and which is politically and legally linked to one or several states without being part of their territory or subject to their sovereignty.]

Within the context of the UN decolonization efforts, Louis Sohn sums up his conception of autonomy as follows: "The concept of an autonomous area is in between the concepts of a 'non-self-governing territory' and an 'independent' State." The autonomous territory is authorized to deal with economic, social, and cultural matters, free from interference by another government. The central government retains powers in the fields of foreign relations and international security; however, if local and international security are interlinked, the central government may also have some control over local security.[15]

It is most interesting that recent editions of the *Encyclopaedia Britannica* do not include an entry on the meaning of autonomy in the area of law and political science (the latest edition available as this study is being written is that of 1986). However, the eleventh and thirteenth editions (of 1910 and 1926, respectively) do define the concept, distinguishing among "political autonomy," "local autonomy," "administrative or constitutional autonomy," and the autonomy of certain "religious bodies, individual churches and other communities."[16]

Due to the important role that autonomy has played in the history of the Jewish people, Jewish and Hebrew encyclopedias describe autonomy extensively. The Hebrew *Encyclopedia of the Social Sciences*, for example, includes the following: "In the second half of the nineteenth century, and in the twentieth century, with the awakening of nationalist movements, . . . the concept of autonomy began to be used in order to indicate the broad or limited right to self-government which a national minority or a religious group may have—within the framework of the state and subject to its central authorities."[17]

Rudolf Bernhardt distinguishes between a broad and a narrow concept of autonomy. In its broad sense, autonomy denotes "the limits of State interference, on the one hand, and the autonomous determination and regulation of certain affairs by specific institutions on the other hand," whereas in the narrower sense it denotes "protection and self-determination of minorities." In his opinion, it is in the narrower sense that the notion of autonomy is used in modern international law.[18]

James Crawford has suggested a shorter definition. For him, "[a]utonomous areas are regions of a State, usually possessing some ethnic or cultural distinctiveness, which have been granted separate powers of internal administration, to whatever degree, without being detached from the State of which they are part."[19]

In their 1980 study on "The Concept of Autonomy in International Law," Hurst Hannum and Richard Lillich express the opinion that "[a]utonomy and self-government are determined primarily by the degree of actual as well as formal independence enjoyed by the autonomous entity in its political decision making process. Generally, autonomy is understood to refer to independence of action on the internal or domestic level, as foreign affairs and defense normally are in the hands of the central or national government, but occasionally power to conclude international agreements concerning cultural or economic matters also may reside with the autonomous entity."[20] Writing in 1990, Hannum gives a more object-oriented definition, emphasizing the purpose of autonomy: "Personal and political autonomy is in some real sense the right to be different and to be left alone; to preserve, protect, and promote values which are beyond the legitimate reach of the rest of society."[21]

The shortest description of autonomy known to this author is that of Heinrich Oberreuter (referring to R. Pohlmann): "die Möglichkeit freier Selbstbestimmung im Rahmen einer rechtlich vorgegebenen Ordnung" [the opportunity for free self-determination within the framework of a legally pre-existing order].[22] A practical definition has been adopted by Henry J. Steiner: "[A]utonomy regimes for ethnic minorities . . . amount to governmental systems or subsystems administered or staffed by a minority or its members."[23]

One may classify the above approaches into four main categories: one group includes those theories that compare autonomy to a right to act upon one's own discretion in certain matters, whether the right is possessed by an individual or by an official body; others use autonomy more or less as a synonym for independence; according to a third notion, autonomy is synonymous with decentralization; and under a fourth notion, an autonomous entity is one that has exclusive powers of legislation, administration, and adjudication in specific areas. The latter type is called "political autonomy," as opposed to "administrative autonomy," which is limited to powers in the sphere of administration.

In the literature on minorities' rights, autonomy has been used to denote limited self-rule. In private law, it expresses the power of persons to conclude contracts and perform legally relevant transactions.[24]

## AN ECLECTIC DESCRIPTION OF AUTONOMY

Having studied various theories and a considerable number of actual cases, this writer suggests an eclectic description of autonomy. It should, however, be noted that in practice there are great differences among the various cases; hence, the definition that follows does not claim to reflect accurately all the different cases. A territorial political autonomy is an arrangement aimed at granting to a group that differs from the majority of the population in the state, but that constitutes the majority in a specific region, a means by which it can express its distinct identity.

A main issue involved in the establishment of a regime of autonomy is the division of powers between the central authorities and the autonomous entity. The powers of the autonomy are usually related to matters of culture, economics, and social affairs. There are, however, different degrees of autonomy, and the extent of the powers transferred to the autonomous authorities varies accordingly, ranging from very limited to larger and up to a high concentration of major powers in the above areas. Usually, foreign relations and external security are reserved for the central government; however, in a few cases the autonomous body has limited powers with the consent of the central government to enter into international agreements and to become a member of a particular international organization. For example, Åland is a member of the Nordic Council and, with the approval of the president of Finland, is permitted to conclude agreements with the Nordic countries; Greenland left the European Community (EC), even though Denmark has remained a member, and the Faroe Islands never became a member. In some cases, the central authorities consult with the autonomous body whenever they conduct foreign affairs that may have a considerable impact on the autonomous region.

In order to avoid disputes and misunderstandings, it is important that the powers of a regime of autonomy be defined as clearly as possible when it is established. In fact, there are usually four different areas of powers to be considered: powers reserved for the central authorities, those fully transferred to the autonomous entity, parallel powers, and powers that can only be exercised jointly.

In certain cases (for example, in southern Sudan when it enjoyed autonomy), the central authorities determine a general policy in a number of areas in which the autonomous entity may act, and the local authorities are authorized to operate within the limits of this general policy. In fact, there is usually a need for cooperation, coordination, and consultation between the central authorities and the autonomous entity. This is crucial because there is likely to be a close link between their respective powers. In addition, certain powers are likely to require joint action.

Even if the transferred powers are carefully and meticulously described when the autonomy is established, future difficulties cannot always be prevented. For example, there may be differences of opinion regarding to which category of powers a certain practical matter belongs. Similarly, a question may arise in an area of powers that had not been considered beforehand; or a question may arise that encompasses different areas, one of which is within the jurisdiction of the center and the other within that of the autonomy—for example, if customs duties are within the powers of the central government and criminal law is within the jurisdiction of the autonomous authorities, who is authorized to prosecute persons suspected of having committed criminal violations of customs law?

In many cases, to ensure the cooperation that is needed for certain activities and to solve problems, the parties establish a joint organ in which both the central government and the autonomous authorities are represented (such as the Åland Delegation). In addition, they may agree upon a special procedure for settling disputes between the center and the autonomous body (for example, the documents that established the autonomy of the Faroe Islands, Greenland, and Memel contain such a procedure).

As has been noted, the powers of the autonomous entity usually include legislation, adjudication, and administration in those spheres of responsibility that have been transferred to the autonomous entity. In some cases, however, adjudication remains fully within the authority of the central government. The legislative acts of the autonomous area usually require confirmation by the central authorities, but this confirmation must be given except in severe cases defined in advance—for example, when those legislative acts amount to an excess of power or undermine the security of the state.

The assumption is that the representatives of the population in the autonomous area exercise the relevant powers. Nevertheless, coordination is often needed between the center and the autonomous authorities regarding the appointment of one or more high-ranking officials (for example, the representative of the central government in the autonomous region or the head of the local administration). In most cases, the official is appointed either jointly, or by the local authorities with the consent of the center, or vice versa. The acts of the autonomous entity in the areas for which it has jurisdiction are normally not subject to any control by the central authorities (except, as mentioned, in such cases as excess of jurisdiction).

In certain cases, the inhabitants of the autonomous region participate fully in the public life, both in their region and in the framework of the central government (for example, in Åland, South Tyrol, and in the past in southern Sudan). One may, however, also encounter different arrangements, as in Puerto Rico and in trust territories.

A regime of autonomy can be established by an international treaty, by a constitution, by a statute, or by a combination of instruments of these categories; probably it may even be established by custom. Changes in the regime of autonomy can often be introduced only with the approval of both the central and the autonomous authorities (as in Åland and Memel); in other instances, however, this is not the case (as in South Tyrol). Typically, autonomy arrangements are not rigid; they are rather flexible, allowing the introduction of changes. Moreover, at the outset autonomy is sometimes deliberately designed to be established by a gradual process (as in Greenland and in the case of the Palestinians).

An autonomy can have several types of international elements:

- It may have been established in pursuance of a resolution of an international institution; for example, the autonomy in Eritrea, 1952–62, which was established following a UN General Assembly resolution.[25]
- An international treaty may have been involved in its establishment; for example, the 1924 Paris convention concerning the Memel Territory;[26] to a certain extent, the 1921 convention between Sweden and Finland regarding the Åland Islands;[27] and the Gruber–De Gasperi agreement of 1946 regarding South Tyrol.[28]
- Autonomy may include an international machinery of supervision (such as the right that existed in Åland to appeal to the League of Nations), or a machinery for dispute resolution (such as the jurisdiction that the Permanent Court of International Justice had with regard to Memel).
- The autonomous community may have an ethnic affinity with a foreign country.

However, other autonomies do not have any international element and are established solely on the basis of internal constitutional acts (for example, the Faroe Islands, Greenland, and the provinces of Spain).

In the analysis in this section an attempt has been made to highlight the typical features of autonomy. Since actual cases of autonomy are rather diverse, they may differ in various aspects from the description suggested in this section.

# 4

## TERRITORIAL AUTONOMY AND PERSONAL (OR CULTURAL) AUTONOMY

Thus far, our discussion has dealt with a regime linked to a certain territory—powers granted to the population of a specific geographical area. There exists, however, another type of autonomy as well—personal or cultural autonomy.[1] In the words of R. Redslob, "elle sera l'apanage d'une communauté qui groupera ses membres par des caractéristiques individuelles, par exemple la conscience ethnique ou la langue, et sans égard au lieu qu'ils habitent dans l'Etat" [it will be the attribute of a community whose members are connected by individual characteristics, such as ethnic consciousness or language, and irrespective of the location of their abode in the state].[2] In other words, this type of autonomy applies to all the members of a certain group within the state, regardless of the place of their residence. Personal autonomy is normally granted to ethnic, cultural, religious, or linguistic minorities.

The concept of personal or cultural autonomy was developed in connection with the protection of minorities. During their long history, the Jews have sometimes been permitted by European rulers to administer their affairs according to their own laws and traditions.[3] A somewhat similar system, though much broader, was applied to non-Muslim communities in the Ottoman Empire—the *millet* system.[4] As has been noted, at the end of World War I an international regime for the protection of minorities was imposed on certain countries. These regimes did not involve autonomy. Some of the countries, however, went beyond their international obligation; they supplemented the rights that they were obligated to give by also granting personal autonomy, consisting of the right to preserve and promote the religious, linguistic, and cultural character of the minority through institutions established by the minority itself; these institutions were authorized to make binding decisions and impose taxes. Thus, Estonia permitted minority groups to be organized as entities of public law and to establish autonomous institutions for preserving and protecting their cultural and charitable interests.[5] To enable the institutions for cultural and religious self-rule to carry out their functions, they were granted the power to make regulations that were binding on their communities and to impose taxes. The state, however, retained certain powers of control. A minority group could neither establish nor bring to an end any regime of cultural self-rule without permission from the government of Estonia. The German and Jewish minorities used the opportunity opened to them and established their autonomous institutions. Latvia also considered granting personal autonomy to its minorities, but eventually limited it to schooling.[6] The most far-reaching provisions were included in the 1928 version of the Lithuanian constitution of 1922; unfortunately, they were implemented only partly and only for a short time.[7]

In 1991, after its secession from the Soviet Union, Latvia again enacted a law aimed at granting a certain degree of personal autonomy to its minorities.[8] (This law is discussed below, in part III, chapter 8.)

As has already been observed, the difference between protection of minority rights and personal autonomy is mainly institutional. Under personal autonomy, the state grants minorities the right to take the necessary steps through their own institutions in order to protect and implement their rights. They may act upon their own discretion, but within the limits of the laws of the state. In principle, each individual should be able to decide whether or not to belong to the minority group; however, certain groups, in particular religious ones and indigenous populations, tend to establish conditions for membership. In certain situations, it may also be difficult to leave a particular group.[9]

Any discussion of personal autonomy would be incomplete without a reference to Karl Renner's theory. At the beginning of the twentieth century, this Austrian scholar and statesman developed a theory intended to solve the minorities problem in the Austro-Hungarian monarchy. He suggested abandoning the "*atomistisch-zentralistische Schule*," which considers the state to be the sum of its individual residents; he envisioned the state as a federation of nations—"*Nationalitätenbundesstaat*"[10]—that are not attached to specific regions. Instead of being a *"Territorialver-band"* and hence a *"Gebietskörperschaft,"* the nation should be regarded as a *"Personalverband"* and hence a *"Personalkörperschaft."*[11] The latter entities, whose status should be embodied in constitutional law, would have a dual role: Having been established by the state as persons of public law, they would be free to pursue their interests in certain areas (such as education, the arts, and literature) without interference of the state, thus constituting "states within the state" (*Staaten im Staate*).[12] In addition—and this is Renner's innovation—the autonomous national entities would also have a say in the areas reserved for the state (for example, foreign affairs and security). The entities as such would thus participate in the exercise of the powers of the state, as would communities. In this manner they would take part in the decision-making processes of the state.

So far, territorial and personal autonomy have been discussed as two quite distinct notions. They are not, however, mutually exclusive; in certain cases the two may be combined. The same minority group may enjoy territorial autonomy in one region and personal autonomy in another one. For example, Atle Grahl-Madsen has proposed such a combination for the Samis (also known as Lapps) who live in the northern parts of Norway, Sweden, and Finland. In those regions where the Samis constitute a majority, he suggests that they be granted territorial autonomy, whereas in other regions they should enjoy personal autonomy in matters of culture, language, and education.[13]

Today, personal autonomy is not widespread and usually when a minority demands autonomy, that minority is striving for territorial autonomy. However, the use of personal autonomy for easing ethnic tensions should not be discarded. Quite often members of various ethnic minorities are interspersed; for example, Serbs live in Croatia (mainly in the region of Krajina), Russians live in the Baltic States, Ossetians in Georgia, Armenians in Azerbaijan, and Maoris in New Zealand. In such cases, territorial solutions may not be feasible; instead, one should explore the option of personal autonomy.[14]

Personal autonomy has a great advantage over territorial autonomy: As mentioned, it usually applies only to people who opt to be members of the group for which it is established. Territorial autonomy, on the other hand, may apply to all the inhabitants of a certain region, thus including those who are not members of the group for whose benefit the regime is established and who may even resent it (for example, Finns who live in the Åland Islands or Italians who live in South Tyrol). Territorial autonomy has yet another disadvantage: Since people tend to move from one place to another, the composition of the population of a given region may change; the former majority in the region might become a minority and consequently the regime of autonomy may lose its raison d'être. This phenomenon may be particularly disturbing if the relocation that changes the composition of the population is encouraged by the central government.

In conclusion, territorial autonomy has the advantage that in addition to cultural matters, it can also apply to a wide range of social and economic affairs, whereas personal autonomy has usually been limited to matters of culture, language, charity, religion, and education. However, the latter has a great advantage over territorial autonomy because it can apply to all the members of an ethnic group in a country, regardless of where they live. Perhaps the scope of personal autonomy could be extended to other spheres, beyond the above-mentioned ones; however, only powers that are not closely related to territory could be considered, such as health policy, welfare matters, personal status, protection of minors, the media, sports, and tourism.

# 5

# AUTONOMY AND SOVEREIGNTY

The relationship between autonomy and sovereignty is important not least because of the conflicting ambitions of the central government and the regional group. On the one hand, the central government usually wishes to prevent the regional entity from acquiring sovereignty, fearing that this will lead to full independence and secession. On the other hand, the regional group strives for sovereignty either because of a hidden (or not-so-hidden) wish to eventually gain full independence or to assert its distinct national identity.

Examining the relationship or interaction between autonomy and sovereignty requires understanding what the latter means. It was hard enough to define the concept of autonomy; to characterize sovereignty may prove to be an even harder task. Not only has the concept of sovereignty been subject to many interpretations, but also it has been the object of much criticism. In fact, it is one of the most controversial notions in constitutional law and international law, as well as in political science and international relations. It has been linked to the idea of indivisible, absolute political authority and has been considered one of the main attributes of statehood. In some cases it has been used, or rather abused, to justify totalitarianism and expansionist regimes or to glorify the state. In the words of Louis Henkin, "sovereignty has . . . grown a mythology of state grandeur and aggrandizement that misconceives the concept and clouds what is authentic and worthy in it, a mythology that is often empty and sometimes destructive of human values."[1]

Etymologically, the term "sovereignty" derives from the Latin word *supra* and has been used over time to denote various forms of superiority.

During the late Middle Ages, territorial rulers used the concept of sovereignty for two purposes. Externally, rulers invoked sovereignty to justify their aspirations for freedom from the influence of the emperor and the pope; internally, sovereignty was used to strengthen the control of the rulers or monarchs over autonomous vassals and to consolidate their exclusive territorial jurisdiction, in contrast to overlapping medieval personal jurisdictions.[2]

The first author to develop a comprehensive theory of sovereignty was Jean Bodin, who maintained in his *Six livres de la République* of 1576 that sovereignty represented "la puissance absolue et perpétuelle d'une République" (the absolute and perpetual power of a republic). The term "absolute" meant that the ruler had the totality of legislative power, as well as the power to change or abrogate the laws. In the exercise of these powers, the ruler was not legally responsible to any higher authority. Bodin conceded, however, that the sovereign was subject to the laws of God and nature, as well as to certain human laws common to all peoples. Similar limitations on sovereignty were also recognized by some of the classic authors of international law, like Hugo Grotius and Emeric de Vattel.

Thus enunciated, the concept of sovereignty had a considerable impact on the rise of the state system in early modern Europe. With the 1648 Peace of Westphalia, which ended the Thirty Years' War, a process started that substituted the independence of sovereign states for the unity of the Christian empire led by the Holy Roman Emperor and the pope. At the same time, the idea of sovereignty continued to develop. In 1651, Thomas Hobbes advanced his theory of sovereignty in *Leviathan*. In Hobbes's opinion, the war of all against all (*bellum omnium contra omnes*) in the "state of nature" of a society could be overcome only if all members conferred all their powers upon one man or an assembly, whose will would then replace their own. The body thus established would be a "great Leviathan," the sovereign, and all others would be its subjects. The Leviathan would have the power to decide what is good and evil and would not be bound by any superior law.

With Hobbes's theory, sovereignty shed its previous limitations and became an absolute concept, an idea extended by Baruch (Benedictus) Spinoza and Georg W. F. Hegel in the seventeenth and eighteenth centuries. This absolute conception of sovereignty was slowly translated into practice and occasionally led to the use of the notion of sovereignty to support totalitarianism and expansionism. The logic was that if the state had absolute power to command and was under no obligation whatsoever to obey any other authority, it had no duty to respect the rights of its citizens nor those of other states.

In spite of these developments, states did not publicly claim to have complete freedom of action and continued to pay lip service to the principles of international law. The absolute concept of sovereignty may have reached its peak in the nineteenth century, with the recognition of the *liberté de guerre,* the complete freedom of states to resort to war. In contrast, in the twentieth century, the notion of sovereignty has been considerably limited, both in theory and in practice, as we discuss below.

Experts in political theory, international relations, constitutional law, and international law have proposed numerous definitions of the notion of sovereignty, each emphasizing a certain aspect of the concept. The study of many of these definitions has led this author to an eclectic description of sovereignty. A clear distinction must be made between the internal and the external aspects of sovereignty. The former denotes the highest original, as opposed to derived, power within a territorial jurisdiction. This power is not subject to the executive, legislative, or judicial jurisdiction of a foreign power or any foreign law other than public international law. The external aspect of sovereignty underlines the independence and equality of all states. It emphasizes that the state is an immediate and full subject of international law, that it is not under the control of any other state,[3] and that it is, in fact, able and free to exercise a fair amount of state power, subject only to the limits of international law.

While there are no clear criteria for determining what constitutes a fair amount of state power, it may typically be assumed to include territorial jurisdiction within the borders of the state, personal jurisdiction over its citizens, the power to have a foreign policy and diplomatic relations, the right to be a member of international organizations, and the right to use force within the confines permitted by international law. However, it is a relative notion that may change with circumstances, in particular with changes in the international system and the intensity or diversity of international cooperation.

The notion of state sovereignty has led to the development of certain significant concepts: for example, the principle of "sovereign equality" of all states; the right of the state to be free from intervention in its internal and external affairs; the exclusiveness of the state's power over all persons and all activities in its territory; the presumption in favor of a state's competence; the absence of an obligation to submit disputes to third-party adjudication; the right to use force; and the positivist theory of the law of nations, under which the sole source of the validity of the rules of international law is the power and will of the states.

In the light of the preceding analysis of sovereignty, autonomy and sovereignty have very little in common, if anything at all. However, as is shown below, certain theories and modern developments lend support to the view that the distance between the two notions has been considerably reduced.

The rise of democracy and federalism has brought about a loosening of the notion of sovereignty, in particular when determining who is sovereign within the state. Whereas in the remote past the monarch was considered to be the sovereign, the American Declaration of Independence of 1776 favored popular sovereignty. The French constitution of 1791 declared that sovereignty belonged to the nation, while John Austin, under the influence of the British system, was of the opinion that sovereignty was vested in a nation's parliament. The complex federal structure of the United States made it difficult to designate a sole repository of sovereignty, which led to the idea of the dual sovereignty of the Union and the component states.[4] Assuming that the people of the United States are vested with sovereignty, it is exercised on their behalf on the basis of a functional division of powers between the center and the states.[5] Moreover, the United States has recognized, albeit to a very limited extent, the tribal sovereignty of native peoples ("domestic dependent nations")[6] as existing in parallel with state or Union sovereignty.

Although some earlier scholars were of the opinion that sovereignty is indivisible, sovereignty has, in fact, been divided in a number of historical and contemporary instances. Condominia, in which two or more states jointly exercise sovereignty over a territory, represent one group of such cases. The Sudan, which was under an Anglo-Egyptian condominium between 1898 and 1955, and Andorra, which was under the condominium of France and Spain from 1278 until 1993, are two examples. Some instances of lease also involved a division of sovereignty, which is the case with certain territories, such as Hong Kong and Port Arthur, leased by China. There may also be situations where one state exercises sovereignty that by law belongs to another state, like the zone around the Panama Canal, which was under U.S. rule from 1903 until recently. Similarly, Egypt was under a British protectorate from 1914 until 1922 while formally under Ottoman sovereignty.

In the eighteenth and nineteenth centuries, the expression "half-sovereign" states was used to describe entities, such as protectorates, that were dependent upon other states. Today, numerous conceptions of qualified sovereignty and of a variety of notions related to sovereignty have acknowledged its flexible nature. Residual or de jure sovereignty denotes a right to sovereignty that may be subject to certain limitations, while de facto sovereignty refers to the actual exercise of power over a territory. Others distinguish between *territoriale Souveränität* (legitimate title to an area) and *Gebietshoheit* (physical control).[7] In Quebec's political parlance, the expressions *souveraineté-association*[8] and *souveraineté partagée*[9] have been used. The practical differences between developed and developing states have led one scholar to draw a distinction between "negative sovereignty," the passive freedom from outside influence, and "positive sovereignty," the ability to act and collaborate domestically and internationally.[10] According to other scholars, sovereignty may be in abeyance.[11]

Of particular interest is the notion of spiritual sovereignty—an attribute of the Holy See under the 1929 Laterano Treaty between the pope and Italy: "Italy recognizes the sovereignty of the Holy See in the international domain as an attribute inherent in its nature, in accordance with its tradition and with the requirements of its mission in this world." This spiritual sovereignty was recognized in addition to, and independently of, the pope's "sovereign jurisdiction over the Vatican."[12]

One should also mention "functional sovereignty." This is a notion based on recent developments in the law of the sea. The rights of littoral states on their continental shelf, or continental margin—the soil and subsoil of the seas adjacent to the coast but beyond the territorial sea—have been defined as "sovereign rights for the purpose of exploring it and exploiting its natural resources." In addition, all coastal states are entitled to a 200-mile exclusive economic zone in which they enjoy "sovereign rights for the purpose of exploring and exploiting, conserving and managing the natural resources."[13]

Finally, the theory of pluralistic sovereignty developed by Leon Duguit, H. Hugo Krabbe, and Harold J. Laski should be mentioned. This concept is intended to express the fact that various political, economic, social, and religious groups dominate the government of each state. In a famous 1915 lecture, Harold Laski rejected the notion of state sovereignty: In his opinion, the individual belongs to various associations, and the state has preeminence only insofar as this has been approved by consent based on moral value.[14]

These developments seem to confirm that sovereignty is not indivisible, but that two or more authorities may have either limited or relative, differential or functional sovereignty over certain areas, groups, or resources.

The demise of the idea that the state has full, comprehensive, and exclusive sovereignty is warranted by developments of the international system. Today's financial markets are globally interconnected by modern communication systems. People, ideas, and criminals move across borders in great numbers, while pollution and ballistic missiles reduce the relevance of those borders. The permeability of borders necessarily reduces the effectiveness and relevance of territorial sovereignty, while free trade agreements and common markets work to render ideas of a state's self-contained economic system obsolete.

Developments in international law have reinforced these practical limitations on sovereignty. States are today assuming more and more international obligations and are participating in a large number of international organizations, both of which may involve a considerable limitation of the state's freedom of action. Indeed, some nations (mainly Western European ones, such as The Netherlands and Germany) have included in their constitutions express provisions permitting the limitation of their sovereign powers if required for international cooperation.[15] It is generally recognized that obligations and commitments under international law do not infringe upon a state's sovereignty unless they place the state under the control of another state.[16] Nevertheless, as explained above, if the limitations on freedom of action imposed by international law reach certain qualitative and quantitative levels, a restriction or division of sovereignty may in fact be involved.

The severe limitation on the right to wage war constitutes a considerable restriction on one of the classic attributes of sovereignty. In a gradual process that started at the beginning of the twentieth century, the international community has restricted the permissible use of force in international relations to cases of individual and collective self-defense and of collective security (namely, action by the UN Security Council in response to a threat to the peace, a breach of the peace, or an act of aggression).

Another traditional implication of sovereignty, the prohibition against intervening in matters within the domestic jurisdiction of another state, has also been questioned in recent times. The development of a right of self-determination, of international protection of human rights, and of humanitarian law has challenged the core of state sovereignty, namely, the exclusive right of the state to govern its citizens according to its own discretion.

To conclude, the concept of sovereignty—in its classic meaning of total and indivisible state power—has been eroded by modern technical and economic developments, as well as by certain principles included in modern constitutional and international law. As a result of innovations in the sphere of communications and transportation, state boundaries are no longer impermeable, and all national economic systems have become interdependent. Various new rules—in particular those concerning human rights, self-determination, and the prohibition of the use of force—have severely undermined some of the basic ideas related to sovereignty. Participation in international organizations that have wide powers, particularly in the supranational European Union,[17] has gradually reduced the substantive amount of powers that are part and parcel of sovereignty. As Horst Dreier has put it, doubts are growing concerning the viability, extent, and usefulness of the concept of sovereignty in the twentieth century; he spoke of "a loosening of monolithic sovereignty."[18] Similarly, according to Luzius Wildhaber, "[s]overeignty must be mitigated by the exigencies of interdependence." This can be done, since "sovereignty is a relative notion, variable in the course of times, adaptable to new situations and exigencies."[19]

The ethnic revival presents yet another severe challenge to the old notion of sovereignty. Because several thousand peoples or ethnic communities exist in the world,[20] but the planet is too small to provide each of them full sovereignty over a piece of land, compromises must be found to satisfy, at least partially, the aspirations of these various groups. As the above analysis has shown, the term sovereignty can be used in a flexible manner. It is suggested that in a case of diffusion of power, the central government and the regional or autonomous authorities could each be the lawful bearer of a share of sovereignty, without necessarily leading to the disappearance or dismemberment of the state.

# 6

# TERRITORIAL AUTONOMY AND OTHER ARRANGEMENTS FOR DIFFUSION OF POWER

In order to understand the concept of autonomy better, it may be useful to compare it with other arrangements for the diffusion of authority. Arrangements for diffusion are based on a variety of political and constitutional methods or institutions.[1] These may be conveniently categorized into five main types: federal systems, decentralization, self-government, associate statehood, and self-administration.

We shall not consider the term "devolution"; this term, which is generally used in the context of the aspiration of certain Scots and Welsh to autonomy, denotes the mere act of transferring powers and does not indicate the content or nature of those powers. Nor is there a need to examine the concept of confederation (a loose association of independent states). The difference between autonomy and confederation is clear, and the two concepts are not likely to be confused.

Some scholars and politicians use the term "autonomy" or "autonomous" as a generic term for all subnational entities, even those that do not conform with the stricter characterization of the concept described above. Similarly, the term decentralization is sometimes used to describe all shades of devolution or delegation of functions.[2] Although an attempt is made below to clarify the concepts, the differences and distinctions are not always sufficiently clear, and a certain term may have different meanings to different scholars and officials.

## AUTONOMY AND FEDERALISM

Some scholars, such as Daniel Elazar, distinguish between federal systems and the federal principle, between federations and federal arrangements. A federation is a clearly defined constitutional structure under which the state is divided into regions that assume different names in various countries, such as "state" in the United States, "province" in Canada, "Land" in Germany, and "canton" in Switzerland. The constitution usually allocates powers to both the central authorities and the regional ones. In cases where the entities that make up the federation existed before the latter and united in order to establish it, these entities are often in control of residual powers. The regions, as such, participate in the legislative function of the central authorities: Their representatives are members in an upper house, and the consent of the local parliaments is required to amend the federal constitution. Usually, there is a special tribunal for settling disputes among the various regions or between a region and the center. On the other hand, federalism with the meaning of mere federal arrangements "is a form of political organization which unites separate polities within an overarching political system so that all maintain their fundamental political integrity."[3]

A regime of autonomy may perhaps be regarded as a certain kind of "federal arrangement"; there are, however, several significant differences between autonomy and a "federal system" in the constitutional sense of the term. As already noted, autonomy can be established by a treaty, by a constitution, by a statute, or by a combination of these tools, whereas a federation is usually established by a constitution. In most cases, the autonomous entity, as such, does not participate in the activities of the central authorities,[4] whereas the cantons in a federation, as has already been mentioned, play an important role in the central authorities (membership in the upper house and participation in the process of amending the federal constitution). Autonomy is usually established in regions that have a particular ethnic character, whereas the federal structure applies to the entire territory of the country.

How should one categorize a state in which the autonomy (or diffusion of powers) applies to the whole territory (as is usually the case in federations), yet in which the component entities do not participate in the activities of the central authorities (as happens in regimes of autonomy)? Some authors would consider these as a separate category—*Etats autonomiques* (autonomist states).[5]

In the case of autonomy, no special tribunal is established to deal with disputes between the autonomous entity and the central government, although a system for settling disputes may be set up. Moreover, federalism is always based on a territorial and functional division of powers, whereas autonomy can also assume a personal nature.

Sometimes federalism and autonomy have been combined. Thus, the Soviet Union and the former Yugoslavia were at least formally federations, and they also included autonomous entities (the autonomous republics, *oblasti,* and *okruga* in the Soviet Union,[6] and the provinces of Kosovo[7] and Vojvodina[8] in the former Yugoslavia). In those cases, the autonomous areas were not full-fledged federated units. However, one could also think of a situation where a component entity of the federation would wish to enjoy additional rights on the basis of autonomy, namely, powers not granted to the other federated entities. Perhaps this is more or less what the Canadian province of Quebec has aspired to: recognition as a "distinct society" and more powers. At the time of this writing (March 1996) no solution has yet been found, and many Quebecois still strive for independence.[9]

Despite the considerable differences between autonomy and federalism, it appears that there is some similarity between their objectives, and therefore it may be useful to draw analogies between them in various areas.

## AUTONOMY AND DECENTRALIZATION

As noted, some authors use the word decentralization as a general term for all types of devolution of power from the center to the periphery.[10] However, in a narrower sense, decentralization implies a limited delegation of powers, subject to the control and overriding responsibility of the center. There are various degrees of decentralization, depending upon the scope of the delegated powers, the extent of participation of locally elected officials, and the degree of supervision.

Autonomy differs from decentralization mainly in the following matters: Whereas decentralization involves solely a delegation of powers, autonomy assumes a transfer of powers. Decentralization may include limited participation of locally elected persons in the regional authorities, whereas in the case of autonomy the basic assumption is that all the transferred functions are exercised by the locally elected representatives. The central government may revoke the decentralization unilaterally, whereas in certain cases the abrogation or amendment of autonomy is in principle subject to the consent of both the central authorities and the autonomous entity. Whereas under a regime of decentralization the central government is fully empowered to control, supervise, and revise the acts of the decentralized authorities, it may interfere with acts of an autonomous entity only in extreme cases (for example, when the latter has exceeded its powers or has endangered the security of the state).

It should be noted that various authors use the expressions noncentralization and deconcentration.[11] For the purpose of the present study, however, there is no need to examine these notions.

## AUTONOMY AND SELF-GOVERNMENT

It appears that the concept of self-government or self-rule closely resembles autonomy.[12] It is therefore not surprising that during the various stages of the search for a solution to the problem involving the Palestinian Arabs, one term was used in some documents and another term in others. Thus, the "Framework for Peace in the Middle East," agreed upon by Egypt and Israel at Camp David in 1978, refers to "full autonomy," whereas the 1989 peace initiative of the government of Israel refers to "self-rule"; the term used in the negotiations that have taken place between Israel and the Palestinians in the wake of the 1991 Madrid Conference and in various recent agreements is "self-government."

It is generally accepted that under self-government a territorial community manages its own internal affairs by itself, with no external intervention.

The meaning of the term "self-government" has been discussed by the United Nations in the context of Chapter XI of the UN Charter, the Declaration Regarding Non-Self-Governing Territories. Under Article 73 of the charter, member states administering "territories whose peoples have not yet attained a full measure of self-government" have, inter alia, a duty "to develop self-government" and "to transmit regularly to the Secretary-General . . . statistical and other information of a technical nature relating to economic, social, and educational conditions in the territories."[13] The question arose under what circumstances a territory ceases to be "non-self-governing," thus releasing the administering powers from the duty of submitting information.[14] The administering powers favored a broad interpretation of the term, in order to be freed from the obligation to report as early as possible, while other member states preferred a narrow interpretation, so that only upon reaching independence would a territory be considered as possessing self-government. The General Assembly adopted lists of factors to serve as guidelines when determining whether a certain territory has achieved self-government.[15]

It is doubtful whether the guidelines suggested by the UN General Assembly resolutions can guide us in our attempt to interpret the term self-government in general. It is more likely that they are relevant only to the interpretation of Chapter XI of the charter for three reasons: (1) the question discussed by the General Assembly was not what constitutes "self-government" but rather what is "a full measure of self-government"; (2) the deliberations were closely related to the idea of self-determination; and (3), the aim was to encourage decolonization. Consequently, the tests recommended by the General Assembly were very strict, indeed too strict to serve as general criteria.

Nevertheless, certain elements of self-government, which were suggested by a subcommittee and approved by the General Assembly in 1952, may perhaps provide some inspiration:

1. *Territorial government:* Freedom from control or interference by the government of another State in respect of the internal government (legislature, executive, judiciary) and administration of the territory.
2. *Participation of the population:* Effective participation of the population in the government of the territory by means of an adequate electoral and representative system.
3. *Economic and social jurisdiction:* Complete autonomy in respect of economic and social affairs.[16]

A comparative study of self-government and autonomy shows a great resemblance, so much so that Louis B. Sohn compares self-government to autonomy and considers a "full measure of self-government" to be equivalent to "full autonomy."[17] Yoram Dinstein has also expressed the opinion that "autonomy . . . denotes self-government."[18]

Despite the great similarity between autonomy and self-government, one may point out that there are several differences between the two concepts. It appears that the term self-government implies a considerable degree of self-rule, whereas autonomy is a flexible concept, its substance ranging from limited powers to very broad ones. In addition, self-government usually applies to a specific region, whereas autonomy can be personal.

At first sight it may seem that self-government amounts to autonomy with broad powers. However, according to some experts, autonomy is a much broader concept than self-government. At the above-mentioned conference (in Greenland, September 1991), Augusto Willemsen Diaz, an expert on the subject of autonomy of indigenous populations, expressed the view that, at least in the Spanish language, the term autonomy has a much broader meaning than self-government. To emphasize this point, he used a picturesque metaphor: If autonomy were a house, then self-government would be one room in that house.[19]

### AUTONOMY AND ASSOCIATE STATEHOOD

As has been observed, one means for implementing self-determination is the establishment of a relationship of association.[20] According to W. Michael Reisman, "A relationship of association in contemporary international law is characterized by recognition of the significant sub-ordination of and delegation of competence by one of the parties (the associate) to the other (the principal) but maintenance of the continuing international status of statehood of each component."[21] According to Menachem Mautner, it is a functional qualification of a state's authority, resulting from "an authorization to another State to administer some of its functions."[22] The main examples of associate statehood are the Cook Islands and Niue, which are associated with New Zealand, and several islands associated with the United States: Puerto Rico, the Marshall Islands, the Federated States of Micronesia, and the Palau Islands.[23] There are, however, great differences among the various cases.

An associate status is established with the consent of both the principal and associate. The associate is interested in the relationship in order to enhance its security and its economic viability. It retains full internal self-government regulated by its own constitution, which in most cases is approved by both the principal and the associate. But certain matters agreed upon by the two parties are dealt with by the principal, mainly matters of defense and, to a certain degree, foreign affairs. There are various nuances with regard to foreign affairs: In some cases they are fully within the responsibility of the principal; according to other arrangements, the principal has to consult with the associate when dealing with the foreign relations of the latter; under other agreements, matters of foreign relations are divided between the two parties. Some associate states are even members of the United Nations (for example, the Marshall Islands and the Federated States of Micronesia since 1990, and Palau since 1994). In principle, any two or more states could agree on an association; in practice, however, such arrangements have so far been made only between entities that had been linked in the past by a colonial relationship or a trusteeship.

As mentioned, the United Nations has recognized an association as a valid act of self-determination, but only if certain conditions are fulfilled.[24] It is believed that associated status may be a helpful solution to the many small territories and entities that strive for self-determination but cannot afford independence.

It follows from this short survey that associated statehood can be described as autonomy with very broad powers.

## AUTONOMY AND SELF-ADMINISTRATION

Since 1991 the Principality of Liechtenstein has been initiating both a debate in the UN General Assembly[25] and research[26] on the idea that "self-administration" could be a valid means of self-determination in many circumstances. It was emphasized that there was no intention to restrict the recognized right of self-determination, but only to propose an additional modality for its realization. This initiative led to the submission to the United Nations, in April 1994, of a Draft Convention on Self-Determination through Self-Administration.[27] The beneficiaries of this right would be "communities"—"the members of a distinct group which inhabits a limited area within a State and possesses a sufficient degree of organization as such a group for the effective application of the relevant provisions of this Convention."[28] The text outlines three different levels of self-administration, as may be appropriate for the stage of political and administrative development attained by a "community." While the more advanced levels are optional,[29] the initial one[30] would be mandatory for all contracting parties.

Once it is established that such a community exists, the state would have to grant its members the right to enjoy their own culture, to practice their religion, and to use their own language. In addition, the members would have a right to take part in the conduct of public affairs and to participate in the elections for central, regional, and local institutions of the state. Moreover, the community would be allowed to establish an appropriate elected organization to represent the community's interests in public affairs. The group should also be allowed to participate in the various levels of governmental organs concerned primarily with matters affecting the community's interests and to be involved in decisions directly affecting the community, including the administration of relevant state funds. The draft also forbids any discrimination against the community, and it permits the state and the community to agree on additional rights for the latter.[31] It seems that this level of self-administration involves little more than the right to full equality, participation in the political arena, and administrative autonomy.

As mentioned, the above arrangement would be mandatory for those states that become parties to the convention. The two additional levels would be optional and would depend on the wish of the state. The latter may declare that a "community" has "over a reasonable period acquired satisfactory experience" in acting under the regime described above. As a result, the community would have additional rights: the right to administer state funds; to have its own police force; to "nominate judges for the lower courts sitting in the community's area and dealing with matters directly affecting the community's interests"; and to administer schools in the area for the community's children. The arrangements should also include a financial compensation plan. Again, as in the case of basic self-administration, the state and the community may agree on additional rights.[32]

The third, most advanced, level of self-administration also depends on the state's readiness to declare that the community has "over a reasonable period acquired satisfactory experience in fulfilling its role" at the former stage. Such a declaration would endow the community with the authority to elect a representative legislature with powers to legislate for the community and its members, to raise taxes, and to "assume responsibility for the administration of all State functions within the community's area, with the exception of matters of foreign affairs or defence which shall remain the responsibility of the State."[33] This stage virtually amounts to full internal self-government.

In all three stages, the community has to act within the limits of the constitution and laws of the state. In each case, the details of the arrangement should be established by an agreement between the state and the community. A community that has "over a reasonable period acquired satisfactory experience in fulfilling its role" and wishes "to establish itself as a sovereign and independent State" should first discuss the matter with the state.[34] The draft convention enumerates certain relevant matters to be taken into consideration in such an event.

Although the three regimes of self-administration are intended to be of a permanent nature, the state's consent may be withdrawn if there has been a fundamental change of circumstances essential to the making of the declaration.[35] Moreover, in time of public emergency threatening the life of the nation, a derogation from specified provisions would be permitted.[36]

The draft convention also foresees the establishment of a machinery of implementation, including a foundation managed by a board, a secretary, a court, and perhaps an advisory council.[37]

Although at first glance the proposal seems to imply that a community cannot reach a higher level of self-administration unless it has first gone through the lower stages, in fact it can practically acquire larger powers inherent in a higher level because, as mentioned, at each level the state and the community may agree on the latter acquiring additional responsibilities.

The draft is targeted for a "distinct group which inhabits a limited area." It tries to focus the powers of the community on its own members. However, it seems that the rights of those inhabitants of that area who are not members of the specific community need further elaboration, especially when the third level of self-administration is reached.

Although it uses the term self-administration, this interesting document practically describes autonomy. In fact, during the earlier deliberations at the UN General Assembly, the representatives of the Principality of Liechtenstein used the term autonomy.[38] The first level of self-administration corresponds to administrative autonomy, while the third level involves territorial political autonomy of a high degree.

To conclude, the analysis of the various arrangements for diffusion of power has shown that neither the concepts themselves nor the differences among them are quite clear. Hence, one has to infer from the context what was a particular author's conception of a concept. For the purposes of our study, certain interpretations have been adopted, although not all of them are universally accepted. The examination has shown that autonomy has much in common with some of the other

# PART III

# AUTONOMY AT WORK

*Despite certain common features discussed earlier, each case of autonomy has its own characteristics. The differences among the cases are varied: the nature of the act that established the autonomy, the geographical distance between the mother state and the autonomous region, the nature of the regime (that is, whether it is a territorial or a personal autonomy), the reasons for its establishment, the scope of the powers of the autonomous authorities, and more.*

*An attempt is made here to examine some of the best-known instances of autonomy and to outline their background and their special features.[1] These cases have been chosen to represent the historical record and the diversity of autonomous regimes, as well as to illustrate those factors that seem instrumental in determining the eventual success or failure of a regime. Some cases merit only brief discussion since they are linked to unique historical circumstances and therefore cannot contribute to general conclusions. We focus on cases that reveal those elements most likely to produce a workable regime.*

*Each case is described within the time frame when autonomy was first established; however, once a case is introduced, all later developments will be discussed in the same context.*

# 7

## SOME EARLIER CASES

### A. THE TRADITIONAL MINISTATES IN EUROPE

Europeans who look for early cases of autonomy will naturally think about the ministates, as well as about several British dependencies.

Each of the ministates is discussed separately here because of the considerable differences in their political status.

### Andorra

Andorra is a small territory in the Pyrenees between France and Spain, with a population of about 61,000.[2] The official language in the region is Catalan. Under a 1278 *pareage* (a kind of arbitration), Andorra came under the joint control of two "co-princes," the bishop of Urgel (in Spain) and the count of Foix (France). The rights of the latter were eventually vested in the president of France.

At the time, Andorra was a unique phenomenon. Although legislative power was officially vested in the two co-princes, a General Council of the Valleys was constituted in 1866. Its twenty-eight members were locally elected by native-born Andorrans. The council could adopt decrees which, in principle, required the approval of the representatives of the co-princes, but, in fact, the council acquired some degree of autonomy. The territory has had its own flag and anthem.

Until 1993, Andorra was not a subject of international law; France undertook the diplomatic and consular protection of Andorrans abroad, and the French co-prince exercised treaty-making power. Andorra of those times was described as "an entity *sui generis*,"[3] as "une survivance féodale anachronique dans le monde contemporain" [an anachronistic feudal relic in the contemporary world],[4] or as an autonomous coprincipality under the suzerainty of the president of France and the Spanish bishop of Urgel, with a "peculiar autonomy [that] is a legacy of feudal conditions."[5]

However, Andorra has undergone far-reaching constitutional changes. Since 1982, the General Council has been authorized to appoint a six-member Executive Council. But the greatest change was caused by the adoption of a constitution in 1993; the constitution was approved by the General Council, by a referendum, and by the co-princes. Andorra became a sovereign, democratic state with full international personality and the capacity to conclude its own treaties. If Andorra does not itself appoint a diplomatic representative to a certain country, it may ask either France or Spain to represent it. In 1993 Andorra was admitted to the United Nations by acclamation.

The only peculiar phenomenon that still lingers in Andorra is the formal maintenance of the institution of the co-princes, who as head of state have mainly symbolic roles and some functions in the sphere of the conclusion of treaties.[6]

### Liechtenstein

Liechtenstein has a quite different status from that of Andorra. This small principality is located between Switzerland and Austria. It has been independent since 1719, except for a short period of French domination in the early nineteenth century.[7] Until World War I, Liechtenstein was associated with Austria, but since 1919 it has been in a close relationship with Switzerland.

The principality has a parliament (the Landtag) composed of twenty-five members, and a five-member government, elected by the Landtag and confirmed by the sovereign, as well as its own court system. It also has a flag and a national anthem.

Liechtenstein's application for membership in the League of Nations was rejected in 1920 due to its small size, but in 1990 it was admitted to the United Nations. It is also a member of the Council of Europe and takes part in the OSCE process. In December 1992 it decided, by referendum, to join the European Economic Area, even though Switzerland had voted against joining.

Although Liechtenstein has transferred a considerable part of its powers to Switzerland, it is considered by its neighbors and by the international community to be a state,[8] and therefore it can probably be defined as an associate state.[9]

### Monaco

The status and history of Monaco are different.[10] This principality situated on the coast of the Mediterranean is almost completely surrounded by French territory. It is a hereditary constitutional monarchy, which has been ruled by the House of Garibaldi since 1297, with the exception of the period of the French Revolution. Monaco was successively a protectorate under Spain, France, and Sardinia. In 1861, a treaty with France reduced the principality's size, and later agreements with France considerably reduced its powers and freedom of action.

Monaco has a national council—the Conseil National—with eighteen members elected by universal suffrage, which exercises legislative power together with the prince—a hereditary ruler. Executive power is vested in the prince and is exercised jointly by the four-member Council of Government headed by a minister of state—a French civil servant chosen by the prince from a list of candidates submitted to him by France. The principality has its own flag. The prince represents the principality in its relations with foreign powers; he also signs and ratifies treaties. Monaco was admitted to membership in the United Nations in 1993, and it also participates in the OSCE process. It has consular relations with about forty-eight countries.

Is Monaco a sovereign state? Is it a "quasi-protectorate"?[11] Is it an autonomous entity? In view of our analysis of sovereignty (in chapter 5), it could perhaps be considered a sovereign state, but due to its limited powers and restricted discretion it might also be described as an autonomous principality. However, its admission to UN membership supports the view that it is an associate state.[12]

### San Marino

The last among the European traditional ministates to be discussed is San Marino, an enclave in Italy, located in the Apennines not far from the Adriatic Sea.[13] It evolved as a city-state in the early Middle Ages, and its independence was recognized by the pope in 1631. It is the sole survivor of the independent states that existed in Italy prior to the latter's unification in the nineteenth century; in the wake of that unification, an agreement was made (in 1862, later reviewed and amended) whereby San Marino accepted Italy's protection.

San Marino has been a republic since the thirteenth century, with legislative power vested in the Great and General Council (Consiglio Grande e Generale), an assembly of sixty members elected by universal suffrage. Executive power is vested in the Congress of State (Congresso di Stato), with ten members elected by the council. It has its own flag.

San Marino has consular relations with several countries and in others it is represented by Italy. It has been a member of the United Nations since 1992 and of the Council of Europe since 1988. It also participates in the OSCE process.

Again one may ask whether San Marino is a sovereign state[14] or an autonomous entity. From the above description, it could be best characterized as an associate state.

## B. UNITED KINGDOM CROWN DEPENDENCIES

The United Kingdom has granted many of its dependencies a certain extent of self-government, the modalities varying from case to case.[15] Here we briefly discuss two of them that have a considerable amount of internal self-government, namely, the Crown Dependencies: the Isle of Man (located in the Irish Sea between England and Northern Ireland) and the Channel Islands (located off the northwest coast of France). These regions are neither integral parts of the United Kingdom nor colonies.

### The Isle of Man

The Isle of Man came under the rule of the British Crown in the fourteenth century, but beginning in 1866 more and more control has been transferred to the local population.[16] The lieutenant-governor is the Crown's personal representative. The Crown also appoints the High Court judges and the attorney-general. The island has a legislature—Tynwald—composed of two branches: the Legislative Council and the House of Keys, sitting together as one body but voting separately on most questions. Although the UK Parliament retains the power to legislate, the local authorities have been exercising a considerable degree of self-government. The Isle of Man Act of 1958 gave Tynwald greater control over fiscal matters, and a 1961 act established an executive council.

According to a 1969 report, Parliament at Westminster has ultimate legislative supremacy and the Crown has responsibility for the defense and international relations of the island. However, "[t]he government and legislature of the Isle of Man are autonomous in respect of matters which do not transcend the frontiers of the Isle of Man . . . ; including (but not limited to) the levying, the collection and the control of insular revenues, finance, agriculture and fisheries, criminal law, harbours, mineral rights, police, social services, trade and professions. Legislation passed by the legislature of the Isle of Man . . . requires the Royal Assent in order to complete its enactment."[17]

It is interesting to note that the United Kingdom's practice of non-interference in the island's internal affairs has been interpreted by the islanders as a binding constitutional convention and by London as a nonbinding practice.[18] The Isle of Man has its own flag, and its official languages are English and Manx.

### The Channel Islands

The Channel Islands are situated 6.6 miles off the coast of France; they include the Bailiwick of Jersey and the Bailiwick of Guernsey.[19] They have been under British rule since William the Conqueror became king of England in 1066, although from time to time they have been occupied by enemies of the Crown. They have always had their own institutions, separate from those in London. Each bailiwick has a lieutenant-governor and other officers appointed by the Crown, as well as a legislative assembly. On local matters, the islands' legislatures adopt laws that are submitted to royal assent. The legal system is separate from the British one, and acts of Parliament in London apply to the islands only if expressly stated; such an extension of statutes is usually preceded by consultation with the islands' authorities, and in fact it does not involve statutes that deal with internal matters.[20]

A 1973 Royal Commission on the Constitution thought it was not "practicable to define an area of domestic affairs in which the Islands' autonomy should be complete," but that the United Kingdom would exercise power mainly in five areas: "i) defence, ii) matters of common concern to British people throughout the world, iii) the interests of the Islands, iv) the international responsibilities of the United Kingdom, and v) the domestic interests of the United Kingdom."[21]

Before concluding international agreements that may apply to the islands, "Her Majesty's Government will always endeavour to discuss the implications as fully as possible with the Insular Authorities."[22] Both the Channel Islands and the Isle of Man are only partly bound to apply the rules of the European Union.[23] The Channel Islands have their own flags, and their official languages are French and English. Apparently, these Crown Dependencies enjoy territorial autonomy.

## C. CASES OF AUTONOMY IN THE NINETEENTH CENTURY

Several interesting cases of autonomy occurred in the nineteenth century, but none of them still exists today. First, in the nineteenth and early twentieth centuries some of Britain's colonies acquired extensive powers of self-government and became dominions (Canada in 1857, Australia in 1901, New Zealand in 1907, and South Africa in 1910).[24] In the report of the 1926 Imperial Conference, they were described as "autonomous Communities within the British Empire."[25] According to Heinrich Dörge, these were the real forerunners of modern autonomy —"die höchst entwickelten Typen der autonomen Territorialverbände"[26] [the most developed kind of territorially autonomous entities]— and in Dörge's opinion President Wilson had them in mind when he recommended the establishment of autonomy for certain areas at the 1919 Peace Conference.[27]

Another state that granted autonomy in the nineteenth century was the Ottoman Empire. Various provinces enjoyed territorial autonomy, including Egypt, Bulgaria, Bosnia-Herzegovina, Walachia-Moldavia, Serbia, East Rumelia,[28] and Mount Lebanon. In addition, non-Muslim religious communities in the empire had extensive personal autonomy under the *millet* system.[29]

A third famous case in the nineteenth century was Finland within the Russian Empire. At the end of the war between Russia and Sweden, the latter ceded Finland to Russia, under the Peace of Fredrikshamn of 1809.[30] During its first eighty years under Russia's rule, the Finnish Grand Duchy enjoyed a large degree of autonomy:

> The sole prerogatives which the suzerainty of the Czar retained for itself consisted of the right to regulate the succession to the Grand-Ducal throne in accordance with the succession to the Imperial Crown, and in the direction of foreign policy. Finland was a constitutional State united to a State which had absolute government. This State had all the attributes of sovereignty, except as far as her external relations and the defence of the Empire were concerned:[31] a Constitution, legislation and regular government. The Diet voted

taxes. Without its assent the Czar could not cede any portion of Finnish territory.[32]

However, toward the end of the nineteenth century Alexander III (and after him, Nicholas II) decided to "Russify" Finland and to curtail the Finns' autonomy.

The various instances of autonomy in the nineteenth century led to the development of certain theories. Thus, Georg Jellinek spoke of the *Staatsfragmente:* "politische Gebilde, die zwar einer Staatsgewalt unterworfen sind, aber nicht gänzlich in diesem Staat aufgehen, die zwar nicht selbst Staaten sind, aber die Rudimente eines Staates darbieten. Es sind dies die *Staatsfragmente,* die weder völlig Staaten noch völlig Staatsabteilungen oder dem Staat unterworfene Kommunalverbände sind"[33] [political phenomena that, although subject to a certain state, nevertheless are not completely absorbed by it; although not states, they display the essentials of a state. They are state fragments that are neither fully states nor departments of a state, nor local communities subject to the state].

Robert Redslob, on the other hand, spoke of *abhängige Länder* (dependent countries), and this included every territory without original, nonderivative powers, whether an autonomous entity or a decentralized unit.[34]

# 8

# Autonomies Established after World War I

The nineteenth century saw the flourishing of the principle of nationalities, that is, the right of every nation to have its own state; and in the twentieth century this idea was transformed into the concept of self-determination, that is, the right of every people to decide its own political status (discussed in chapter 1). As a corollary, the awareness of the need for autonomy grew: In those cases where a people could not have its own state or freely choose its political status, compromises had to be found, and autonomy was one option. It is therefore natural that several autonomies were established in Europe after World War I. The main territorial ones were set up in the Åland Islands and in the Memel territory (Klaipeda). Autonomy had also been foreseen for Carpatho-Russia,[1] East Karelia,[2] East Galicia,[3] Imbros and Tenedos,[4] Silesia,[5] and Catalonia.[6] Moreover, the Soviet Union included some elements of autonomy in its constitutional system. Other countries granted personal autonomy to their minorities, for example, Lithuania, Latvia, and Estonia.[7] In addition, the following enjoyed a certain degree of personal autonomy: the Saxons and Szecklers in Transylvania (Romania);[8] the Walachs in Pindus (Greece);[9] the Muslims in Yugoslavia, Albania, and Greece;[10] and the non-Muslims in Turkey.[11]

## A. THE ÅLAND ISLANDS

Because the Åland Islands have had autonomy for more than seventy years and all those involved seem satisfied, it may be considered a successful case of autonomy, and it deserves a detailed discussion.

The Åland autonomous province of Finland consists of more than 6,500 islands and skerries, with a land area of 1,552 square kilometers (599 square miles) and a population of about 25,000.[12] The largest island is Fasta Åland (the Main Island), where 90 percent of the population lives. The islands are located in a strategically important area in the Baltic Sea between Sweden and Finland, at the entrance to the Gulf of Bothnia. This location also dominates the access to St. Petersburg, and is thus of great importance for the defense of three states: Sweden, Finland, and Russia. The inhabitants of the islands speak Swedish. Because of their strategic importance, the islands have been demilitarized. The linguistic difference between Finland and the islanders has led to the establishment of autonomy.

### Historical Development

When Finland was under Swedish rule, the Åland Islands were administered by the governor of Abo (Turku in Finnish), which is on the Finnish coast.[13] In 1809 Sweden lost both Finland and the islands to Russia.[14] The tsar fortified the islands heavily, but after the Crimean War a regime of demilitarization was established,[15] a regime which has since been reaffirmed.[16] When Finland became independent after World War I, the inhabitants of the Åland Islands wished to be incorporated into Sweden, to which Finland objected. The latter adopted a law on 6 May 1920 granting the islanders a wide measure of autonomy in order to reassure them.

Nevertheless, the problem was not solved, and in June 1920 Great Britain submitted it to the Council of the League of Nations. The council recognized Finland's sovereignty over the Åland Islands. However, upon the council's recommendation,[17] Finland and Sweden concluded an agreement intended to establish "further guarantees . . . for the protection of the Islanders."[18] Under the agreement, Finland undertook various commitments ("guarantees") concerning the language of instruction in schools, the limitation of the sale of land to persons not domiciled in the islands, the time needed for Finnish immigrants in the archipelago to acquire provincial franchise, the procedure for appointing the governor of the islands, financial matters, and a supervisory function for the Council of the League of Nations.

The matter of the nonfortification and neutralization of the Åland Islands was settled in a multilateral convention in 1921, as well as in later conventions.[19]

The provisions of the agreement on autonomy were approved by the Council of the League of Nations[20] and were incorporated into the Finnish legal system by the 1922 Åland Guarantee Act.[21] The autonomy act has been amended several times, with major amendments introduced in 1951 and in 1991.[22] The 1951 and 1991 versions do not include any international guarantee, whereas the 1921 agreement did allow the possibility of applying to the Council of the League of Nations, which Åland never did. It seems that the reason for the absence of an international supervisory mechanism after 1951 was the Soviet Union's strong objection.[23] However, the original provision still exists in the agreement of 1921 between Sweden and Finland, which, according to the opinion of the Secretariat of the United Nations, is still in force and may be activated by the United Nations.[24]

The following discussion of the regime of autonomy in the Åland Islands is based on the 1991 version,[25] with occasional reference made to earlier ones.[26]

### The Regime of Autonomy

The autonomy of the Åland Islands[27] is interesting not only because of the process of its establishment (just discussed), but also from various other points of view: the mechanism for introducing changes; the structure and composition of the provincial institutions; the division of powers between Finland and Åland; the substantive rules aimed at preserving the special character of the province; budgetary matters; the control exercised by the central government; the settlement of disputes; and the attitude of the foreign state to which the Ålands' population is culturally attached. These various characteristics will be briefly reviewed.

The introduction of changes into the regime requires an act of the Finnish Parliament adopted in accordance with the specific procedure for amending the constitution,[28] as well as the approval of the Åland Legislative Assembly by at least a two-thirds majority of votes cast (Section 69). Thus, collaboration or agreement between the central authorities and the province is indispensable.

The Åland Islands have a locally elected Provincial Legislative Assembly (Sections 3, 13). The assembly may, however, be dissolved by the president of Finland after consultation with the Speaker of the assembly (Section 15). The islands have also a provincial government appointed in accordance with an act of the Provincial Legislative Assembly (Sections 3, 16). The Finnish government is represented by the governor (Section 4), who is appointed by the president of Finland "after having agreed on the matter with the Speaker of the Legislative Assembly" (Section 52).

Another important institution is the Åland Delegation, a committee composed of five members. Åland and Finland each appoint two members, and the governor (or another person appointed by the president of Finland in agreement with the Speaker of the Åland Legislative Assembly) serves as chairman (Section 55). The Åland Delegation has the responsibility of seeking arrangements for fiscal adjustment between the central authorities and the province (Section 56). In addition, it offers its observations on laws adopted by the Provincial Legislative Assembly before their submission to the president of Finland for approval (Section 19). In certain spheres the Åland Delegation has also been authorized to settle disputes: controversies concerning the opening of new merchant shipping lanes and the allocation of land in Åland needed for state administration (Section 62). In general, the Delegation has to give its opinion upon a request from the central authorities or from the provincial ones (Section 56).

Although in principle Finland is in charge of the administration of justice (Section 35), the government of Åland may hear appeals against administrative decisions (Section 25). Moreover, Finland may establish in Åland an administrative court to which the Provincial Legislative Assembly may grant jurisdiction over administrative matters within the competence of Åland (Section 26).

Authority in matters of legislation and administration is divided between the center and the province. The division is not very clear,[29] but one may perhaps generalize and summarize that the local legislative assembly has powers in matters of communal administration: to a certain extent, maintenance of public order and security; building regulations and fire protection; protection of the environment; certain social services; education; certain aspects of health and medical services; road construction; expropriation; lease of land; water use; agriculture; hunting; fishing; certain economic activities; and certain matters of communication (Section 18).

In addition, Finland and Åland may agree to transfer to Åland some spheres of power that are within the ambit of the state: for example, the population registers, the trade and the shipping registers, employment pensions and other social insurances, and banking and credit services (Section 29). Furthermore, the state and the province may agree on a temporary transfer of administrative powers from the state to a provincial officer, or from the province to a state official (Section 32).

The state has the power to legislate on a large number of subjects, which may be summarized as follows: constitutional matters; certain basic human rights; foreign relations; family relations; commercial law; intellectual property; insurance; foreign trade; mineral finds, with some restrictions; nuclear energy (but establishing a nuclear power plant or stockpiling nuclear materials in Åland requires the consent of the government of Åland); labor law and criminal law, subject to certain powers of Åland; citizenship; firearms and ammunition; the armed forces; monetary matters; and other matters of private law (Section 27).

However, even in matters reserved for the state, Åland has a say: The provincial authorities may submit initiatives on matters within the legislative or administrative power of the state (Section 22). In addition, when the central authorities intend to enact a law that has special importance for Åland, the latter must be consulted; moreover, if the said law deals with ownership of real property or business property in Åland, the *consent* of the Provincial Legislative Assembly is required (Section 28). The duty of consultation also applies to administrative measures of special significance for Åland adopted by Finland (Section 33).

Although Finland is in charge of foreign affairs, the Åland Islands are represented in the Nordic Council and may participate in the work of the Nordic Council of Ministers, as well as in the committees of the Nordic Council.[30] Treaties that address matters included within the powers of the provincial legislature require transformation by the latter in order to become internally applicable in the islands (Section 59). Moreover, if the treaty contains a provision that is contrary to the 1991 act on autonomy, it will enter into force in Åland only after the adoption of an act in accordance with the cumbersome procedure for introducing changes into the act (Section 59).

In addition, Åland may propose to Finland to enter into negotiations on a treaty with a foreign state; it must be informed (not consulted) of negotiations on a treaty if the matter is subject to the competence of Åland; and "for a special reason" the government of Åland shall be permitted to participate in the negotiations (Section 58). It seems that special rules apply with regard to negotiations with a Nordic country.[31] The permission to use Åland's flag on vessels belonging to Åland (Section 18) is also related to matters of foreign affairs.

In view of its interesting, though limited, powers in matters of foreign affairs, it is unclear whether Åland has an international personality. Opinions differ on this matter.[32]

Of great interest is the provision on residual powers, a subject which engenders disagreement in many cases of autonomy: Matters of legislation that have not been expressly addressed by the act are to be assigned either to the central legislature or to the provincial one, according to the general principles derived from the division of other powers as dealt with expressly by the text (that is, by analogy).[33]

Another interesting feature of the Åland Islands autonomy is the obligation of consultation, which has been increased by the 1991 act. Several examples of the circumstances in which such a duty exists have been mentioned above.[34]

Some autonomous communities in other countries are in danger of losing their special character due to demographic changes, caused both by emigration and by immigration from other parts of the country. This danger has been eliminated in the Åland Islands by the far-reaching provisions concerning the language, provincial citizenship, and the severe restriction on the sale of land to outsiders. Of special importance to the inhabitants of the Åland Islands are the provisions concerning their language.[35] Whereas Finland has two "national languages"— Finnish and Swedish[36]—in the Åland Islands only Swedish is the official language (Section 36). Hence, the language of education in all schools maintained or subsidized by public funds must be Swedish unless otherwise provided by an act of the provincial legislature (Section 40); all local organs and officials of the state (that is, Finland), of the province, and of municipal administrations, as well as the Åland Delegation, must use Swedish (Section 36); even decisions of the Finnish Supreme Court relating to Åland have to be written in Swedish, as must all official correspondence between officials in Åland and in Finland (Sections 36 and 38); all state officials in Åland have to know Swedish (Section 42); graduates of schools in Åland have the right to be admitted to Swedish and bilingual state-maintained or subsidized educational institutions, irrespective of requirements of a knowledge of Finnish. On the other hand, there are certain concessions for non-Swedish speakers: a Finnish-speaking person may use that language when appearing in a court of law and with other *state* officials in Åland (Section 39);[37] upon his request, the courts and the representatives of the state in Åland will supply a translation into Finnish of their documents (Section 39).

The only exception to the "only Swedish" rule in public organs is the provision that a treaty referred to the Provincial Legislative Assembly for approval may be sent to Åland in the original language, "if the treaty by law is not to be published in Swedish" (Section 38).

In principle, only Finnish citizens who have resided uninterruptedly for five years in the islands and who have a satisfactory knowledge of Swedish may apply for Åland regional citizenship (Section 7). Only persons holding the regional citizenship may participate in communal elections and in elections for the Provincial Legislative Assembly (Section 9). However, the provincial legislature may, by an act adopted by a two-thirds majority, permit citizens of Finland and of other Nordic countries to participate in municipal elections (Section 67). Such persons may also be employed as officials of Åland or of a municipality, but only citizens of Finland may be employed in the police force (Section 24). The government of Åland may permit qualified people who are citizens of the Nordic countries to perform duties within the sphere of health care (Section 30[9]). Otherwise, most employment as well as trade and professional work may, in principle, be limited by a provincial act to Finnish citizens resident in Åland (Section 11).

The Ålanders are exempt from military service, but they have to serve in the civilian administration in lieu of military service (Section 12). Passports of people holding the Åland regional citizenship are to be marked with the word "Åland" (Section 30[2]).

As mentioned, another means of preserving the special character of the islands is the very strict rules concerning the acquisition of real estate in the Province of Åland: Only provincial citizens may acquire, possess, or lease land in the islands without the need for special permission from the provincial government (Section 10). The restriction, however, does not apply in case of inheritance (Section 63).

These strict rules on language, regional citizenship, and acquisition of land are intended to preserve the Swedish character of the islands. They may, however, not be compatible with the rules that apply in the European Union. Therefore, when Finland acceded to the Union, an express exemption of the Åland Islands from certain principles of the organization was stipulated. The exemption relates to the acquisition of real property, the provision of services, and the harmonization of indirect taxation.[38] A further question has been raised regarding whether the above rules restricting the use of the Finnish language in the Åland Islands are consistent with international human rights conventions.[39]

Budgetary questions used to be a bone of contention between Finland and Åland, since the allocation of resources from the center to the province required annual negotiations.[40] The 1991 act, however, established a general criterion for allocating the funds: 0.45 percent of the state income for the year (Sections 45, 46, 47). The sum thus received is called the "amount of equalization" (Section 45). The basis for equalization may be changed if the circumstances justify it, but the change requires an act of Finland, with the consent of the Provincial Legislative Assembly (Section 47). In addition, Åland may be granted an "extraordinary grant" (Section 48), a "tax retribution" (Section 49), "bond loans" (Section 50), and a "special subsidy" (Section 51). Åland may also impose and collect certain local taxes (Section 18[5]).

As in all other autonomies, the central government retains certain powers of supervision. The most important among them are the following: after consultation with the Speaker of the Åland legislative assembly, the president of Finland may dissolve that assembly and issue instructions for new elections (Section 15); all laws enacted by the Provincial Legislative Assembly require the approval of the president of Finland, but this approval may be denied only if, after having obtained an opinion from the Supreme Court, the president considers that the local legislature exceeded its powers or the security (internal or external) of the state is involved (Section 19);[41] the financial arrangements made from time to time by the Åland Delegation also require the president's approval (Section 56); an appeal as to the legality of a decision of the government of Åland may be brought before the Supreme Administrative Court of Finland (Section 25[2]); and a dispute of authority between provincial officials and state officials will be decided by the Supreme Court of Finland (Section 60).

Except for these two provisions limited to disputes about administrative powers, the act does not include special provisions for settling disputes between Finland and Åland. Perhaps no need for such a procedure was felt because of the proper functioning of the Åland Delegation; with its composition, it may be well suited for preventing or informally mediating disputes.

Perhaps typical of the relations between Finland and Åland is the provision that obliges Finnish state officials to respond to requests from Åland to assist provincial officials in the performance of duties relating to autonomy (Section 31). The residents of Åland participate in the elections for the president of Finland and its national parliament; that is, they take part in the political life of the state (Section 68). Both Finland and Åland are democratic communities.

Finally, Sweden's role in the success of the Åland autonomy should not be underestimated. After World War I the Ålanders wished to be reunited with Sweden. However, once the League of Nations had decided in favor of Finland, Sweden accepted this solution and collaborated in the establishment of the autonomy through the 1921 agreement. In 1945, when the wish for a reunion of Åland with Sweden was expressed again, Sweden immediately rejected the idea.[42] In other words, adherence to the autonomy solution by the state with which the local population has a strong affinity may have helped to make the regime a success.

## Conclusion

Although the population of the Åland Islands is fairly small, the case is important since it shows that a regime of autonomy can succeed even in a strategically sensitive area.

Some of the most interesting characteristics of this case concern the existence of an efficient organ of cooperation with a well-balanced membership, the increasing obligation of consultation, the clear though limited powers of supervision, the strict rules intended to preserve the special character of the islands, the unique arrangement concerning residual powers, the flexibility (some powers may be transferred later), and last, but not least, the supporting attitude of the culturally related foreign state.

## B. THE MEMEL-KLAIPEDA TERRITORY

Another autonomy established after World War I, but a less successful one, concerned the Memel Territory.[43] It did not survive World War II.

### Historical Background

The Memel area, with its famous port on the shores of the Baltic Sea, was part of Germany until World War I; under the 1919 Treaty of

Versailles, Germany renounced its rights to the area, the future of which was to be decided later. The territory consisted of some 1,700 square kilometers and had about 145,000 inhabitants. In 1922 the Conference of Ambassadors established a commission to draft a proposal on the future of the area. However, in January 1923 the newly established and recently recognized State of Lithuania invaded the Memel Territory, and thus the work of the commission became illusory. Under the pressure of the circumstances, the Conference of Ambassadors decided (on 16 February 1923) to grant Lithuania sovereignty over the territory, subject to certain conditions.[44]

Later (on 25 September 1923) the matter was submitted to the Council of the League of Nations, upon whose advice the Paris Convention Concerning the Territory of Memel and the Statute of the Memel Territory were signed on 8 May 1924 by Great Britain, France, Italy, Japan, and Lithuania.[45] The regime came to an end during World War II and was not reinstated after the war. The basic reason for establishing the autonomy was to grant self-rule to the mainly German-speaking population of the territory, which had been transferred to Lithuania without a referendum of the inhabitants.

### The Regime of Autonomy

The Paris Convention recognized Lithuania's sovereignty over Memel, subject to certain conditions: (1) the establishment of autonomy (Article 2); (2) certain rules with an international ingredient concerning the port of Memel (Article 3); and (3) matters of transit traffic (Article 3). Each of these subjects was dealt with in an annex to the convention. Another limitation on Lithuania's freedom of action resulted from Article 15 of the convention, which provided that "[r]ights of sovereignty over the Memel Territory or the exercise of such rights may not be transferred without the consent of the High Contracting Parties."

Annex 1 to the convention contains the text of the Statute of the Memel Territory.[46] Its first Article reiterates Article 2 of the convention, but it adds the need for democracy: "The Memel Territory shall constitute, under the sovereignty of Lithuania, a unit, organised on democratic principles, enjoying legislative, judicial, administrative and financial autonomy." The organs of government were to be the governor (Article 2 of the statute), the Chamber of Representatives or Seimelis (Article 10 of the statute), the Directorate (Article 17 of the statute), and an economic council (Article 14 of the statute).

The governor was appointed by the president of Lithuania (Article 2 of the statute). He had to promulgate laws adopted by the Chamber of Representatives within one month after their adoption, but he could exercise a veto if the law concerned a sphere not within the autonomy's jurisdiction or if it was incompatible with either Lithuania's constitution (except if the statute expressly permitted the derogation) or with its international obligations (Articles 6, 10, and 16 of the statute). The governor was authorized to use his veto power without having to consult a court of law. The Directorate (that is, the executive branch) consisted of five persons: the president of the Directorate was appointed by the governor (that is, the representative of Lithuania), but he also needed the confidence of the Chamber of Representatives of Memel. The four additional members were appointed by the president; the Directorate had to enjoy the confidence of the Chamber of Representatives (Article 17 of the statute). This system was intended to ensure that the executive would be acceptable to both Lithuania and the Memel legislature.

The Chamber of Representatives (Seimelis) was the legislature (Articles 10–13 of the statute), and it also determined the composition of the economic council, which was intended to advise the chamber on economic and fiscal legislation (Article 14 of the statute). The members of the chamber were elected in conformity with Lithuanian electoral law (Article 11 of the statute). The governor, "in agreement with the Directorate," could dissolve the chamber (Article 12 of the statute).

Memel's autonomy included the following areas: organization and administration of communes and districts; public worship; public education; public relief and health; social welfare and labor legislation; certain local railways; regulation of the sojourn of foreigners, in conformity with Lithuanian legislation; police power (to a certain extent); civil, criminal, agrarian, forestry, and commercial legislation (subject to Lithuanian legislation on credit and insurance institutions and the exchanges); the acquisition of rights of citizenship (in conformity with the rules laid down by the statute in Article 8); organization of the judicial system; direct and indirect taxes, with the exception of customs and excise duties, commodity taxes, and certain monopolies; the administration of public property belonging to the Memel Territory; regulation in Memel of timber-floating and navigation on rivers other than the Niemen and on canals, subject to agreement with the Lithuanian authorities in cases where such water courses were usable outside the Memel Territory for timber-floating; and registration of trading vessels in accordance with the laws of Lithuania. Moreover, the statute allowed the transfer of additional powers by later Lithuanian legislation (Article 5). A local police force was responsible for public order in the Memel Territory; however, the policing of the port, the frontier, customs, and the railway was under the authority of Lithuania (Article 20 of the statute). All matters not within Memel's jurisdiction were to be within the exclusive jurisdiction of Lithuania (Article 7 of the statute). Except where the statute provided otherwise, Memel's legislation had to conform with the Lithuanian constitution (Article 6 of the statute).

Both the convention and the statute dealt with matters of citizenship. Former German citizens living in the Memel Territory since 1920 or earlier were automatically granted the citizenship of Lithuania and Memel, unless they opted out; others (that is, persons born in the territory who had resided there for more than ten years, as well as persons who had been granted a permanent permit of residence by the Inter-Allied Administration) could opt for citizenship under certain conditions (Articles 8, 9, and 10 of the convention). Additional rules on the acquisition of citizenship were to be established by Memel legislation (Article 8 of the statute), and various later agreements, notices, and laws addressed this matter.[47]

The citizens of Memel had Lithuanian passports, with a note saying that they were citizens of Memel (Article 34 of the statute). They were exempted from military service until 1930, and they participated in elections for the Lithuanian Diet (Article 3 of the statute). The statute also provided for the protection of certain human rights (Articles 9 and 33).

The Memel judiciary was organized by local legislation (Article 22 of the statute), and the judges were appointed by the Directorate (Article 23 of the Statute). Sentences pronounced by the courts of both Lithuania and Memel were enforceable in the whole territory of Lithuania, including Memel; the same applied to warrants of arrest. The Supreme Court of Lithuania had jurisdiction over the Memel Territory, and a special section composed mainly of judges from Memel was established in order to hear cases concerning the territory (Article 24 of the statute). In 1935 Lithuania established a court with jurisdiction over cases concerning the question of the compatibility of acts of Memel with the statute.[48]

As mentioned, Memel was authorized to levy direct and indirect taxes in the territory, except for customs duties, excise duties, commodity taxes, and monopolies on alcohol and tobacco. A percentage of those taxes that it was not authorized to levy was returned by Lithuania in pursuance of negotiations that determined that percentage (Articles 5[12] and 35).

Memel was to apply the 1922 declaration of Lithuania concerning the protection of minorities (Article 11 of the convention and Article 26 of the statute). Lithuanian and German were equally recognized as official languages of the Memel Territory (Article 27 of the statute). Foreigners were accorded equal rights with regard to using the port and acquiring real property "for legitimate business purposes" (Article 12 of the convention).

The introduction of changes into the statute of autonomy required the agreement of the Memel authorities (by a three-fifths majority of the votes of all the members of the Chamber of Representatives) and, upon the request of a certain number of representatives or citizens, also of the population (a referendum with two-thirds in favor of the change). In addition, the approval of the Legislative Assembly of Lithuania given within one year from the date of the submission of the proposal was needed (Article 38 of the statute).

The League of Nations was to some extent authorized to supervise the implementation of the regime by Article 17 of the convention. This provision permitted members of the Council of the League of Nations to draw the attention of the council to any violation of the convention. However, the convention did not give Memel itself a right to apply to the council. It did address the settlement of disputes between Lithuania and the other signatories to the 1924 Memel Convention that were members of the Council of the League: Lithuania agreed in advance that upon a request of the other party, the dispute would be submitted to the Permanent Court of International Justice. Several complaints were lodged with the council, and one case was submitted to the court:[49] The president of the Directorate (Mr. Böttcher) had gone to Berlin. According to him, he traveled in a private capacity in matters related to his agricultural business; but Lithuania claimed that he went to negotiate an agreement between Memel and Germany—a matter which was not within Memel's powers. Thereupon the governor (appointed by Lithuania) dismissed the president of the Directorate. The signatories to the 1924 Convention of Paris disputed Lithuania's right to dismiss the president, since no such power had been expressly provided for in the convention or in the statute annexed to it. As mentioned, the president of the Directorate was appointed by the governor, but he also needed the confidence of the Memel Chamber of Representatives.

After the dismissal of the president, the governor appointed a new president (Mr. Simaitis) who, in turn, chose new additional members for the Directorate. This new Directorate, however, was not granted the confidence of the Chamber of Representatives; therefore the governor dissolved the chamber, with the approval of the Directorate that had never received the confidence vote (under Article 12 of the statute, the dissolution could be decided by the governor, but he needed the approval of the Directorate).

The court came to the following conclusions in this case: On the factual issue, the court found that the president had gone to Berlin to negotiate in the name of Memel for the admission of agricultural produce into Germany, an act that was *ultra vires* Article 5 of the statute, which had left the conduct of foreign relations to Lithuania (Article 7 of the statute);[50] therefore the governor was entitled to dismiss him.[51] The dismissal of the president of the Directorate did not by itself involve the termination of the appointment of the other members of the Directorate;[52] the appointment of the new Directorate headed by Mr. Simaitis was in order,[53] but since that Directorate had never received the vote of confidence from the Chamber of Representatives, it did not have the authority to agree to the chamber's dissolution.[54]

Most of the above conclusions were based on the specific documents related to the Memel case, and a detailed examination does not seem relevant to the present study. Some discussion seems merited, however, in respect of the general questions raised, in particular the reasoning of the court in reaching the conclusion that the dismissal of Mr. Boettcher was lawful. As mentioned, the statute provided for the president of the Directorate to be appointed by the governor, and stipulated that the president had to leave his office if he lost the confidence of the Chamber of Representatives. Despite the silence of the texts on a possible power of the governor to dismiss the president, the court concluded that such power existed in exceptional circumstances:

> The Governor must be regarded as entitled to watch the acts of the executive power in Memel in order to see that such acts do not exceed the limits of the competence of the local authorities as laid down in the Statute. . . . It follows that under the correct interpretation of the Memel Statute, the right of the Governor to dismiss the President of the Directorate is not excluded.

However, the dismissal of the president of the Directorate would be legitimate

> only in cases in which the acts complained of were serious acts calculated to prejudice the sovereign rights of Lithuania and violating the provisions of the Memel Statute, and when no other means are available.[55]

The court reached this conclusion by invoking Lithuania's sovereignty:

> [I]t is impossible to adduce the silence of the Statute in regard to any matter in order to restrict the sovereignty of Lithuania in favor of the autonomy of Memel, or to deny to the former the exercise of certain rights simply because they are not *expressly* provided for in the Statute of Memel. . . . The Court finds it impossible to believe that it was the intention of the Convention to leave Lithuania, the sovereign of the Memel Territory, with no remedy whatever if the executive authorities at Memel violated the Statute by acting in a manner beyond their powers.[56]

However, the court rejected Lithuania's claim to a general right of supervision over Memel:

> The Court does not consider that any right on the part of the Governor of supervision and control over the executive acts of the Memel authorities has been established over and above that expressed in an earlier part of this Judgment, namely, the right of the Governor to watch the acts of the executive power in Memel in order to see that these acts do not exceed the limits of the competence of the local authorities as laid down by the Statute, nor run counter to the stipulations of Article 6 of the Statute [that is, the obligation to conform with the constitution of Lithuania except where the statute provides otherwise] or to the international obligations of Lithuania.[57]

### A Comparison with the Åland Autonomy

In order to highlight certain variables typical for regimes of autonomy, as well as to clarify some of the choices that policymakers have to face, it may be interesting to compare the cases of Åland and Memel, two instances of autonomy established in the wake of World War I because of linguistic heterogeneity. The comparison considers the Åland regime as it developed in later years.

Both regimes were established by a combination of national legislation and international instruments, but in the case of Memel the international input was more substantial. In both cases, the introduction of changes required the consent of both the central authorities and the local ones. Memel had its own courts, but Åland's autonomy does not in principle include adjudication. Although there are differences in the powers transferred to the local legislature, the general scope does not seem to be very different. However, the question of residual powers has been given very different solutions: in Åland, under the 1951 and 1991 acts, these powers are to be allotted on the basis of the general principles resulting from the powers specifically mentioned; in Memel, residual powers belonged to the Lithuanian authorities.

Åland has several arrangements intended to ensure the preservation of its Swedish character (in matters of citizenship, acquisition of land, doing business in the islands, and language), whereas the parallel rules in Memel were merely intended to guarantee the rights of the inhabitants of German origin, not to preserve the German character of the area.

The control by the central authorities was somewhat similar: All local laws required approval or promulgation by the central authorities—in the case of Åland by the president of Finland, and for Memel by the governor. They could veto laws that were *ultra vires*; other reasons that could justify a veto were different in the two cases. Moreover, in the case of Åland the president of Finland has to consult the Supreme Court before using his veto power, while the governor of Memel acted at his own discretion. In both cases the central government could dissolve the local parliament: in Memel the consent of the local executive was needed, whereas in Åland the Speaker of the Provincial Legislative Assembly has to be consulted.

In both cases, an attempt was made to secure the involvement of both the central and the local authorities in the appointment and dissolution or dismissal of some of the local organs. Both agreements provided a way to appeal to the Council of the League of Nations in case of a complaint or a dispute. In Åland the local legislature itself could address the council through Finland (although in fact it has never done so); however, in Memel only members of the council had this right, and only signatories to the 1924 Paris Convention that also sat on the council could submit a case to the Permanent Court of International Justice.

Memel had no institution similar to the Åland Delegation, which is composed of representatives of both the central government and the local authorities and which deals with several delicate matters, including financial allocations. It is possible that this joint institution is able to prevent friction and disputes.

The most important difference between the two cases is the attitude of the country with which the ethnic group in whose favor the regime of autonomy was established had a strong affinity. Whereas Sweden collaborated with the League of Nations and Finland and has respected Finnish sovereignty over the Åland Islands, it seems that Memel's special regime was not encouraged and respected by Germany, in particular after the ascent of the Nazi party.

## C. Autonomy in the Soviet Union

### Introduction

So far, we have focused on small areas that enjoy or have enjoyed autonomy. In the Soviet Union, by contrast, autonomy was formally granted to large numbers of people in vast areas, but the content of this autonomy was minimal.

According to the 1989 census, the Soviet Union had a population of approximately 285 million, composed of 102 nations and ethnic groups, 22 of them major ones.[58] In order to accommodate the national aspirations of these various nations, the Soviet Union was formally molded in a complex structure: the state was organized as a federation sui generis, with union republics (SSR), autonomous republics (ASSR), autonomous regions (oblasti), and autonomous areas (okruga, first called national areas). The number of these units changed from time to time, but after 1977 there were fifteen union republics, twenty autonomous republics —sixteen of them within the Russian union republic (the Russian Soviet Federative Socialist Republic, RSFSR), one in Azerbaijan, two within Georgia, and one in Uzbekistan—eight autonomous regions (five within the Russian republic and one each in Azerbaijan, Georgia, and Tajikistan), and ten autonomous areas, all of them within the Russian republic (mostly in the north, bordering on the Arctic Ocean).

The Russian republic, to which most of the autonomous entities belonged, was formally structured as a federation, but the other union republics that included autonomous units were not.

Although the basic idea was that each territorial entity should correspond to a certain national group, this goal was achieved only to a very limited extent: In some entities various groups coexisted; sometimes the group for which the entity was established constituted only a minority in the area (for example, in 1979 the Bashkirs constituted only 24.3 percent of the population of the Bashkir autonomous republic, the Karelians were 11.1 percent of the population of Karelia, and the Jews were 5 percent of the population of the autonomous *oblast* of Birobijan); and in certain cases the majority of the ethnic group lived outside the special area (for instance, only 26 percent of the Tatars lived in the Tatar autonomous republic in 1979).[59]

The various categories of political units within the Soviet Union differed in the degree of powers or self-rule that they were granted (as discussed below). The Soviet Union and the union republics were considered "sovereign,"[60] while the autonomous republics, *oblasti,* and *okruga* had varying degrees of autonomy, decreasing in the above order. The criteria according to which one of these structures was assigned to each group related to the latter's characteristics. A distinction was made among *natsiya* (nation)[61] and *narodnost* (nationality, a small or less developed group), and later *natsionalnaya gruppa* (ethnic group).[62] A nation had to fulfill four criteria: All members had to share common economic conditions, have a common language, be territorially based, and have a common culture or national character.[63] In addition, a quantitative condition required that a nation number at least 80,000 to 100,000 people. All nations were to have either a union republic or an autonomous republic. Other groups with a lower degree of national development were given only an autonomous *oblast* or *okrug.*[64]

Some of the entities were shifted from one category to another. For instance, in 1940 the Karelian ASSR was changed into the Karelo-Finnish SSR, and in 1956 it was returned to its former status as the Karelian ASSR.[65] In other cases, autonomous provinces were "promoted" to autonomous republics (such as Udmurt, Mari, Yakut, and Tuva).[66] These changes were explained as resulting from the development of the specific groups or were undertaken as punitive measures. For example, the Crimean-Tatar and the Volga-German autonomous republics were abolished during and after the end of World War II to punish their populations for alleged lack of loyalty during the war.

To understand the essence of autonomy in the Soviet Union, we first analyze the ideological background, namely, the attitude of the founders of the USSR toward ethnic identity; a discussion follows of the status of the autonomous entities under the Soviet regime, as well as their later development in practice. We conclude with a look at the situation in Russia after the dismemberment of the Soviet Union.

### The Ideological Background

Tsarist Russia has been described as "essentially a supra-national, dynastic empire, though built round a national Muscovite state."[67] However, due to an aggressive Great Russian national sentiment that developed toward the end of the nineteenth century and because of fear of the awakening nationalism of the subject nations, the government repressed national agitation and encouraged Russification by threats and favors.

Marxism was originally opposed to all forms of nationalism, because its ideology was based on the workers' international.[68] But it soon became apparent that recognizing the rights of national groups would help the movement to gain the support of various subdued nations and to benefit from the latter's hostility toward their rulers. Thus, Marx at a certain stage emphasized the national setting of the class struggle, and Lenin favored national freedom and self-determination as a step toward the future proletarian revolution. In particular, Lenin underlined national equality as a reaction to past discrimination and oppression. It may be of interest to note that Lenin was fiercely opposed to *cultural* autonomy, because in his view it strengthened "bourgeois nationalism" and weakened "proletarian internationalism"; on the other hand, he did accept *territorial* autonomy.[69]

These ideas were further developed by Stalin, who wrote a famous essay on the subject in 1913, entitled "The National Question and Soviet Democracy."[70] According to this essay, the nation "has the right to arrange its life on the basis of autonomy. It has the right to enter into federal relations with other nations. It has the right to complete secession. Nations are sovereign, and all nations are equal."[71]

However, Stalin added various conditions to the exercise of these rights: Self-determination was declared to be subject to the dominating principle of socialist progress and could not justify the maintenance of petrified forms and reactionary institutions; the Communist Party would oppose any exercise of self-determination that did not represent a step toward communism. The idea was encapsulated in a famous motto—"national in form, socialist in content"—used by Stalin in 1925.[72] As Walter Connor has put it, the basic incompatibility between Marxism and nationalism "does not preclude Communists from appealing to nationalism in a prerevolutionary situation."[73]

## The Introduction of Autonomy and Its Modalities

To satisfy the request for self-determination of the various nations and nationalities incorporated into the USSR, Lenin reluctantly established a federal system, based on a 1922 Union Treaty and on a constitution approved in 1924. In this system—called "socialist federation" by the Soviet constitution[74] but "facade federalism"[75] and a "reluctant federation"[76] by others—most powers were allocated to the central government. The structure, which included union republics and various categories of autonomous areas, was described by Stalin as follows: "Soviet autonomy is not a rigid thing fixed once and for all time; it permits of the most varied forms and degrees of development. It passes from narrow administrative autonomy (the Volga Germans, the Chuvashes, and the Karelians) to a wider, political autonomy (the Bashkirs, the Volga Tatars, and the Kirghiz); from wide political autonomy to a still wider form of autonomy (the Ukraine and Turkestan); and finally from the Ukrainian type of autonomy to the supreme form of autonomy—contractual relations (Azerbaijan)."[77] (It seems that Stalin included the union republics in this description of autonomy.)

The various autonomous entities were represented in the Council of Nationalities of the Supreme Soviet, whose rights were formally equivalent to those of the Soviet of the Union,[78] but this was a "constitutional myth" since the Supreme Soviet (which was composed of these two chambers) had no real power.[79] Moreover, Stalin abolished the Presidium of the Council of Nationalities, which had attempted to seek means to represent the interests of the non-Russian peoples. The powers reserved for the autonomous entities were minimal.

Moving now to a more detailed analysis, a distinction may be made among the three categories of autonomous entities. *Okruga*[80] (autonomous areas) were first established in 1925 for smaller nationality groups in the northern part of the Russian republic. They were subordinate to the general administrative-territorial subdivisions of the republic. The 1936 constitution granted them representation (by one deputy) in the USSR Council of Nationalities.[81]

Each of the *oblasti* (autonomous regions) enumerated in both the Soviet and the republican constitutions,[82] sent five deputies to the Council of Nationalities.[83] These regions had administrative autonomy within a union republic, and the union republic had full control over them. The autonomy of the unit consisted of the following: The region's

Soviet was to recommend a law on the autonomous region, to be adopted by the Supreme Soviet of the union republic.[84] The law was to take account of the special ethnic features of the region and to address its administrative division. The administrative organs of an autonomous region were permitted to conduct their activities in the language of the group for whose benefit the autonomous region was established. While other regions did not have direct access to the central authorities, the autonomous region sent deputies to the Council of Nationalities of the Soviet Union.

A 1928 decree of the RSFSR gave the autonomous regions administrative powers in certain spheres.[85] Acts of the autonomous regions were subject to control and repeal by the authorities of the union republic.[86] It thus appears that the autonomous areas and the autonomous regions had very limited, purely administrative autonomy—if the expression is at all appropriate.

A symbolically somewhat more privileged status was enjoyed by the autonomous republics. Again, the list of these republics was established in the Soviet Union's constitution, as well as in the constitutions of the relevant union republics.[87] Each of them sent eleven deputies to the Council of Nationalities in Moscow,[88] and each was empowered to adopt its own constitution, which did not need the approval of the relevant union republic.[89] The constitution of the autonomous republic and its laws had to conform to the constitution and laws of both the Soviet Union and the relevant union republic, and they had to take into account the specific features of the autonomous republic.[90]

The autonomous republics had their own organs of government—legislature, executive, and judiciary. In addition, they participated in some of the organs of the union republic.[91] Moreover, the autonomous republics had been granted the right to initiate legislation in the Supreme Soviet of the union republics.[92] As already mentioned, representatives of the autonomous republics participated in the activities of the central government through their membership in the Council of Nationalities, which was one of the two chambers of the Supreme Soviet.[93]

An autonomous republic was constituted by the union republic to which it belonged, with the approval of the institutions of the USSR,[94] and its territory could not be modified without its consent.[95] Each was permitted to adopt its own flag and emblem and to determine its citizenship.[96]

In an autonomous republic, members of the ethnic group after which the republic was named were supposed to fulfill most of the governmental functions,[97] and the national language was used by the authorities and in schools. Linguistic rights were guaranteed by several provisions of the constitution of the USSR, such as "the possibility to use one's native language and the languages of other peoples of the USSR," the provision that judicial proceedings should be conducted "in the language of the majority of the population of the given locality," and the "possibility for instruction in school in one's native language."[98] Moreover, the provision granting equal rights to "[c]itizens of the USSR of different races and nationalities"[99] may also have implied a prohibition against discrimination on the basis of language. However, the promotion, especially from the mid-1930s, of Russian as at least a second language in order to enhance unity was resented as an attempt at Russification;[100] it appears that linguistic assimilation was strongly promoted in the various autonomous entities.[101]

The above somewhat rosy picture of the structural aspects of the autonomous republics loses much of its brightness when one looks at the division of powers among the three tiers (the central authorities, the union republics, and the autonomous republics). The Soviet constitution assigned most of the powers to the central government.[102] What was left was within the jurisdiction of the union republics.[103] Thus, when Section 82 provided that "[o]utside the limits of the rights of the USSR and the union republics, an autonomous republic independently resolves questions within its jurisdiction," one wonders what, if anything, was included in these "questions." It seems that the powers of the autonomous republics mainly involved the implementation of policies established by the central authorities.[104]

The limited scope of the powers of the autonomous republics was compounded by the strong and center-oriented influence of the Communist Party. In fact, in the Council of Nationalities of the USSR, the representatives of the minorities usually voted for the programs presented by the party.[105]

One may conclude that even formally the autonomous entities in the Soviet Union enjoyed only very limited autonomy of an administrative nature. The powers transferred to the local autonomous authorities were very limited and mainly in the sphere of administration; the relevant rules could be changed without the consent of those authorities; and the latter depended completely on the center for funding. It seems that this autonomy has mainly had symbolic value for the members of the relevant nationalities, and its application has practically been limited to matters of culture and language.

### The Development of Autonomy in Practice

Although Soviet autonomy has always been of a merely administrative and cultural nature, it was beneficial in the earlier days.[106] The various ethnic groups had their own administrative framework and could develop their culture and their language. Moreover, publication in the minorities' languages was encouraged. In certain cases the Soviet Union even supported the creation of a written language if a language existed only orally.

However, because autonomy and pluralism were fundamentally in conflict with Marxist-Leninist ideology, the above nationality policy was replaced by the mid-1930s by terror, population transfer, Russification,[107] and forced assimilation. Thus, the limited administrative autonomy that had existed became an almost-empty shell.

In the wake of *glasnost* and *perestroika*, the Soviet Union increased considerably the powers of the union republics, the autonomous republics, and other autonomous formations.[108] However, the dismemberment of the USSR in December 1991 ended that trend. All the former union republics have become independent and have been admitted to the United Nations. However, some of the former autonomous republics (for example, Chechnya) also strive for independence; so far, however, the former union republics in which the autonomous republics are located have objected to the latter's accession to independence.

To conclude, the considerable ethnic heterogeneity and certain tactical considerations prompted the Soviet regime to grant autonomy to various areas. It was a very limited autonomy of an administrative nature, which concerned mainly matters of language and culture. Since the 1930s, although autonomy formally continued to exist, it was actually drastically reduced. With *glasnost, perestroika*, democratization, and the dismemberment of the Soviet Union, ethnic consciousness has grown considerably, and many of the former "autonomous" units are claiming sovereignty, or at least increased autonomy.

### The Russian Federation and Its "Subjects"

Russia has tried to solve the problem of its heterogeneity by establishing a revised federal system, based mainly on a 1992 Treaty of Federation concluded with the various entities[109] and on a 1993 Constitution of the Russian Federation.[110] Under the new arrangements, the country has eighty-nine "subjects": republics (which have the attribute of "sovereign" in the treaty, but not in the constitution), *kraya* (territories), *oblasti* (regions), the cities of Moscow and St. Petersburg, an autonomous *oblast* (region), and autonomous *okruga* (areas).[111] The constitution emphasizes equality among all the subjects.[112] Indeed, all eighty-nine are represented equally in the federal legislature: Two representatives from each subject are members of the Council of Federation, which is one of the two chambers of the Federal Assembly (the parliament).[113] There are, nevertheless, certain differences with regard to powers and responsibilities. Moreover, some of the subjects (for instance, Tatarstan, Bashkortostan, and Udmurria) have concluded special agreements with the Russian Federation; these agreements have granted those subjects powers that are larger than those foreseen by the Treaty of Federation and by the federal constitution. The constitution, in fact, mentions the possibility that such additional agreements may be concluded,[114] but it provides that in case of contradiction, the Constitution of the Russian Federation should prevail.[115]

Although in principle all laws of the subjects should conform to the constitution and to those laws of the federation that deal with matters that are in the competence of the federation,[116] it seems that in practice not all local laws and regulations are in fact consistent with laws of the central authority.[117] The subjects are free to establish their "state power bodies," which must, however, conform to the "basic principles of the constitutional system of the Russian Federation."[118]

While Russian is the "state language" of the federation, the republics (but not all the subjects) may institute an additional state language, to be used alongside Russian in public affairs.[119] Moreover, all the "peoples" have the right to preserve their "native language."[120]

Under a special provision, the federation assumes the responsibility to guarantee the rights of "small indigenous peoples in accordance with the generally accepted principles and standards of international law and international treaties of the Russian Federation."[121]

The allocation of powers is based on a division into three categories. Certain powers are reserved for the federation,[122] such as defense, international relations of the federation, certain economic matters, law courts, criminal and civil legislation, and the legal regulation of intellectual property. A second group of powers is to be exercised jointly by the center and the subjects,[123] such as the protection of human rights and the rights of ethnic minorities, as well as issues concerning land, natural resources (including minerals), and education. In these spheres of joint jurisdiction, federal laws are to be adopted, and the subjects are free to act within the framework thus established.[124] The remaining powers—the third category—are within the jurisdiction of the subjects.[125] Interestingly, it seems that the subjects may also establish their own "international and external economic relations."[126]

The participation of the subjects is needed to amend the federal constitution.[127] They may also submit cases to the Constitutional Court concerning the conformity with the federal constitution of certain acts of the federal authorities and of the subjects, as well as disputes about jurisdiction.[128] The constitution has empowered the president of the federation to deal with disputes between organs of the federal government and organs of the subjects, as well as between subjects.[129]

At this writing (March 1996), it is not yet possible to evaluate this new Russian system. It is still an asymmetrical federalism[130]—Russia itself is not one of the subjects and there are great differences among the various subjects, mainly in the sphere of demography and economics. The actual implementation of the regime has involved a considerable devolution of power from the center to the subjects.[131] Moreover, due to the special agreements concluded by Russia with some entities, different areas are subject to different regimes.[132] Perhaps one could say that although formally a federal state, the Russian Federation is sui generis and may have some ingredients of autonomy.

### D. Personal Autonomies in Eastern Europe

As already mentioned, an attempt was made after World War I to draw the boundaries of states in accordance with the principle of self-determination. Where this was not achieved, minorities were granted protection against discrimination and involuntary assimilation.[133] Some of the relevant arrangements were made in the context of the postwar peace treaties, and others were based on bilateral agreements or on declarations made to the League of Nations; some granted a measure of control to the Council of the League of Nations, while others had no machinery for international supervision. Most of the instruments granted rights to members of the minority groups, but generally no autonomy was involved. A few countries, however, granted the minorities personal autonomy, allowing them to express their distinct identity.[134] These arrangements were usually based on internal legislation. Thus, Estonia, Latvia, and Lithuania had accepted the usual commitment toward the League of Nations,[135] but they also granted minorities the right to administer their cultural life through their own institutions.

### Estonia

In Estonia the 1920 constitution (Section 21) provided that "[t]he members of minority nationalities within the confines of Estonia may form corresponding autonomous institutions for the promotion of the interests of their national culture and welfare insofar as these do not run contrary to the interests of the state."[136] Moreover, "[i]n those parts where the majority of the inhabitants are not Estonian but local minority nationals, the business language in the local self-government institutions can be in the language of those minority nationals"[137] (Section 22). Linguistic rights were also ensured by special laws on public elementary schools (1920) and public intermediary schools (1922).[138]

The provisions of the constitution were expanded by the 1925 Statute on Cultural Self-Administration of the National Minorities of Estonia.[139] This law authorized all national minorities with at least three hundred members to establish associations of public law to protect and promote their national interests. Membership in a national group was established by a national register in which each citizen was free to enroll; the establishment of the autonomous association was optional. Once the minority applied for the establishment of the autonomous association (Section 16), the government asked the local authorities to prepare a provisional register of voters (Sections 17 and 18). The next step was to elect representatives to the Council for Cultural Affairs, which would be authorized to decide on the inauguration of a national "cultural self-administration," after which the government would declare it established (Section 27). In addition to the Council for Cultural Affairs, another central organ of the national minority was the Administration of Culture. Local organs for taking care of interests in matters of culture could also be formed (Section 5).

These bodies were authorized to organize, administer, and supervise public and private schools, as well as to fulfill other functions related to culture and to administer the institutions established for that purpose (Section 2). In order to fulfill their tasks, the organs of cultural self-administration were authorized to adopt binding regulations and to impose dues (Sections 3 and 6[b]). The state reserved to itself certain rights of supervision.[140] The government was empowered to decide on the establishment and on the termination of the cultural self-administration.

The autonomous organs were legal personalities of public law.[141] Both the German and the Jewish minorities applied in 1925 for the establishment of their autonomous institutions.[142]

In 1993 Estonia again introduced cultural autonomy for its minorities.

## *Latvia*

Latvia had intended to establish a similarly extensive regime of personal autonomy, but the relevant provision in the draft constitution (1922) was defeated. Thus, only schooling was submitted to autonomy, by virtue of the 1919 Law on the Education of National Minorities. The idea behind this law was that each nation had a right to educate its children in its mother tongue. This right was supplemented by the obligation incumbent upon the state and local authorities to establish the necessary schools in sufficient numbers (Sections 39 and 41). The system was directed by departments for minorities established in the Ministry of Education, and headed by a director of education. These departments were in charge of the administration of all internal school matters. The director was appointed by the government upon the recommendation of the minority (Section 8), and he represented the minority to the government. In addition, a Council of Schools had the power to decide on the opening and closing of schools, as well as on employment of officials (Sections 10–13). The financial burden was borne by the state or the local authority (Articles 2 and 41 of the general law on education).

States often prefer to grant rights to members of minority groups, and not to the group as such. However, in Latvia, the right to have its own schools was granted to the minority as a collective entity. The law speaks of the schools of the "national minority" and declares schooling to be "autonomous in its organization" (Section 1).[143]

The idea of personal autonomy was revived by Latvia in 1991.[144] The aim of the Law on the Unrestricted Development and Right to Cultural Autonomy of Latvia's Nationalities and Ethnic Groups adopted on 20 March 1991 was, according to its preamble, to guarantee all nationalities and ethnic groups in Latvia "the right to cultural autonomy and self-administration of their culture." It guarantees "equal human rights which correspond to international standards" to all the residents, regardless of their nationality (Paragraph 1), and "equal rights to work and wages" to all permanent residents (Paragraph 3). Every permanent resident has the right to freely indicate his or her nationality in official documents (Paragraph 2). While the government is responsible for preserving the national and cultural identity of Latvia's ancient indigenous nationality—the Livs (Paragraph 4)—members of other nationalities are free to observe their national traditions (Paragraph 8) and to establish associations and organizations (Paragraph 5) to further education, language, and culture. The government should financially support the development of these activities (Paragraph 10). National societies have the right to develop their own national educational institutions with their own resources (Paragraph 10).

Latvia permits the nationalities to maintain contact with other members of the group abroad (Paragraph 9) and to promote opportunities to receive higher education in their national language outside of Latvia (Paragraph 11). The national associations have the right of access to government mass media and may publish national periodicals and literature (Paragraph 13), as well as "undertake entrepreneurial activities in accordance with Republic of Latvia Law" (Paragraph 14). Moreover, representatives of all ethnic groups are to participate in the Supreme Council's Consultative Nationalities Council and, through its intermediary, to take part in drafting Latvia's laws (Paragraph 7). It is expressly mentioned that the national societies have to function in accordance with the laws of the state and to respect its "sovereignty and indivisibility" (Paragraph 6).

This law was considered of particular importance, because when Latvia regained its independence in 1991, nearly half of its inhabitants were members of ethnic minorities, mainly Russian. Unfortunately, in 1992 Latvia was reported to be trying to deny its inhabitants who were not of Latvian origin the right to Latvian citizenship. The situation has since considerably improved.

### Lithuania

Lithuania adopted far-reaching provisions on personal autonomy in its 1922–28 constitution. Larger national minorities could "autonomously administer the affairs of their national culture—public education, charity, mutual aid," and they had the concomitant right to "elect necessary bodies to conduct these affairs in the manner prescribed by law" and to impose dues upon their members. They could, moreover, call upon the national treasury for their share of the budget set aside for education and charity (Sections 73, 74).[145] The Jewish minority availed itself of these possibilities, and there was even a special ministry for Jewish affairs. However, the system soon fell apart (in 1924).[146]

In 1989, not long before the restoration of its independence, Lithuania adopted the Law on Ethnic Minorities,[147] which granted members of minority groups equality and guaranteed their right to develop their culture, education, and religion. Special emphasis was put on linguistic rights. The relevant provisions hardly amount to personal autonomy.

### Ukraine

A far-reaching personal autonomy existed in Ukraine in 1917–18, when it was independent.[148] The law of January 1918 provided that "[e]very nation which is not Ukrainian and lives on the soil of the Ukraine has within the territory of the Popular Republic of Ukraine the right to national-personal autonomy." This right was declared to be permanent and inalienable. The second section recognized the Russian, Jewish, and Polish peoples' right to national autonomy and established the conditions under which other nations living in Ukraine could enjoy national autonomy. All the citizens of the republic who belonged to a certain nation constituted a national association (Section 3); membership in the association was voluntary. The association was granted the right of administration, regulation, and imposition of dues. It was authorized to represent the nation and had a right to a proportional share of the income of the republic and of the local authorities.

The system was abolished when the Ukraine was occupied by the Red Army, because, as already mentioned,[149] Lenin was opposed to cultural autonomy.

# 9

# AUTONOMIES ESTABLISHED
# AFTER WORLD WAR II

## INTRODUCTION

In the period since World War II autonomy has been established or contemplated in a considerable number of cases. The main causes of this trend are (1) the development of claims for self-determination linked to decolonization; (2) recognition of the principle of self-determination; (3) the increase in ethnic (and religious or national) consciousness; and (4) a trend to recognize minority rights.

Well-known examples are the Faroe Islands, Puerto Rico, Greenland, Catalonia and the Basque Country, Corsica, the Palestinians, and the former trust territories that have become associate states (the Cook Islands, Niue, the Marshall Islands, the Federated States of Micronesia, and the Palau Islands).

It is interesting that both modernization[1] and decolonization have tended to increase ethnic tensions and the need for autonomy. While under foreign domination, the heterogeneity of the population of various colonies did not cause much friction; after independence, however, ethnic diversity became an important destabilizing factor.[2] This development may explain the establishment of autonomy in southern Sudan and in Mindanao, as well as the attempts to introduce autonomy for the Kurds in Iraq and the Tamils in Sri Lanka. Similarly, ethnic friction has considerably increased in the wake of the dismemberment of the former communist bloc, and solutions based on autonomy have been considered.

Although many of the above-mentioned developments may have been partly influenced by World War II, autonomy was established as a direct consequence of the outcome of that war only in a few cases: South Tyrol/Alto Adige, Eritrea, and the western part of Berlin.

Other plans for establishing autonomy have been intended to solve modern problems of economic heterogeneity in Hong Kong and Macao after their return to China.

Finally, the increasing recognition of the rights of indigenous populations has led certain nations to grant (or at least consider granting) autonomy to some indigenous groups. This trend explains the autonomy of Greenland and Nunavut (in Canada) and the efforts to grant autonomy to Yapti Tasba (in Nicaragua), the Cordilleras (in the Philippines), and the Samis (in northern Europe).

In this chapter we analyze seven cases. Those cases that offer the most in terms of general lessons are described in the most detail.

## A. South Tyrol/Alto Adige

The conflict between Austria and the German-speaking South Tyrolese, on the one hand, and Italy, on the other hand, has been settled by a regime of autonomy that was first established in 1948 and later reformed.[3] In 1992, after the completion of certain reforms, the modalities of this regime received the approval of a majority of each of the above three parties.[4]

### Historical Background

South Tyrol or Alto Adige, also called Bolzano or Bozen after one of its cities, is a relatively small area of about 7,400 square kilometers, less than 2.5 percent of the territory of Italy. Its population is less than half a million (0.75 percent of Italy's population), of whom 64 percent speak German, 30 percent Italian, and 4 percent Ladin (an ancient Rhaeto-Romanche language).[5] The area is located in northeast Italy, close to the Austrian border; both North Tyrol and East Tyrol are part of Austria.

South Tyrol had been almost uninterruptedly under Austrian rule for about 550 years. However, in the wake of World War I the area—together with neighboring Trento and certain other areas—was transferred to Italy by the Treaty of St. Germain,[6] in pursuance of a commitment given to Italy in 1915 by the Entente Powers in order to induce it to join the war on their side.[7] The population, which at that time was largely German-speaking with small Ladin-speaking and Italian-speaking minorities, was not consulted on the question of the transfer. Italy strove to annex South Tyrol mainly for strategic reasons, since the area is south of the Brenner pass in the Alps.

The fascist regime in Italy pursued a policy of assimilation in South Tyrol, a policy which included suppressing the German language and German names, replacing German officials with Italians, and promoting the immigration of Italians into the area (in particular, sending Italian workers to newly established industrial enterprises). This policy was supported by Hitler who, after the annexation of Austria, concluded with Mussolini in 1939 the "Options Agreement."[8] Under this agreement, the South Tyrolese were to opt either for Italy and assimilation or for moving to the German Reich. Although many opted for Germany, only some 70,000 actually left. The ratio of Italians in the population of South Tyrol had increased between the two world wars from about 3 percent to about 33 percent.

After the fall of Mussolini in July 1943, the Nazis took control of South Tyrol and the adjoining areas (Trento and Belluno). During the following period (until the surrender of Germany in 1945), tension between the German- and the Italian-speaking groups in South Tyrol grew considerably. Many members of the German-speaking group collaborated with the Nazis, while an Italian partisan movement developed.

After Germany's surrender, the area was returned to Italian sovereignty. Austria and the South Tyrolese demanded that it be returned to Austria, but Italy objected, not only for the above strategic reasons but also because of economic considerations: South Tyrol had become the source of hydroelectric power that is essential for the industries in northern Italy. The Allied Powers rejected Austria's demands, as well as the compromise solutions submitted by that country.

However, in a spirit of reconciliation, Karl Gruber, Austria's foreign minister, and Alcide de Gasperi, Italy's prime minister, signed an agreement in Paris on 5 September 1946 on the establishment of autonomy in South Tyrol. Coincidentally, both men were natives of the area. The agreement was incorporated into Annex IV of the 1947 Treaty of Peace between the Allied and Associated Powers and Italy.[9]

The text of the two first articles of that agreement reads as follows:

1. German-speaking inhabitants of the Bolzano Province and of the neighboring bilingual townships of the Trento Province will be assured a complete equality of rights with the Italian-speaking

inhabitants within the framework of special provisions to safeguard the ethnical character and the cultural and economic development of the German-speaking element.

In accordance with legislation already enacted or awaiting
enactment the said German-speaking citizens will be granted in
particular:

(a) elementary and secondary teaching in the mother-tongue;

(b) parification of the German and Italian languages in public
offices and official documents, as well as in bilingual topo-
graphical naming;

(c) the right to re-establish German family names which were Ital-
ianized in recent years;

(d) equality of rights as regards the entering upon public offices
with a view to reaching a more appropriate proportion of
employment between the two ethnical groups.

2. The populations of the above-mentioned zones will be granted the
exercise of autonomous legislative and executive regional power.
The frame within which the said provisions of autonomy will
apply, will be drafted in consultation also with local representative
German-speaking elements.

The Treaty of Peace itself, in Article 10, took note of the above
agreement. Soon after, an agreement was reached concerning the
return of most of those who had left or had lost their Italian citizenship
due to the 1939 Hitler-Mussolini agreement.[10]

In 1948 Italy's legislature adopted an autonomy statute, intended to
implement the 1946 Gruber–de Gasperi agreement.[11] However, the
South Tyrolese and Austrians were not satisfied with the regime established by this statute. Their dissatisfaction related mainly to the following matters: (1) they were of the opinion that the substantive provisions
of the statute fell short of the commitments undertaken by the Gruber–
de Gasperi agreement; (2) under the 1946 agreement the South
Tyrolese should have been consulted, and they claimed that no proper
consultation had taken place; and (3) due to the internal administrative
division of Italy, the German-language group in South Tyrol could
hardly benefit from the autonomy: The province of South Tyrol (or
Bolzano) with its German-speaking majority was linked to the more
populous province of Trento, which has a large Italian-speaking majority, to form the region of Trentino-Alto Adige. It was this region, with
its Italian-speaking majority, that was granted most of the autonomous

powers, while only very limited powers were granted to each of the two provinces that constitute the region.

Italy was of the opinion that it had fully complied with its obligations under the Gruber–de Gasperi agreement by enacting the 1948 statute, and therefore Italy considered that Austria had no *locus standi* in any additional negotiations.[12] Perhaps Italy was reluctant to grant a larger degree of autonomy for fear that autonomy would be a first step toward secession. This fear probably diminished in 1955, when Austria regained full independence within the frontiers it had in 1938—that is, without South Tyrol. These boundaries were guaranteed by the signatories of the Austrian State Treaty and, thus, a return of South Tyrol to Austria was excluded.

In 1956 the first acts of violence occurred, followed by a mass protest meeting in 1957. In 1960 and 1961 Austria submitted the dispute to the UN General Assembly, which urged "the two parties to resume negotiations with a view to finding a solution for all differences relating to the implementation of the Paris agreement of 5 September 1946."[13] Austria also initiated a debate in the Consultative Assembly of the Council of Europe (1959). In addition, it filed a complaint against Italy under the European Convention on Human Rights concerning the fairness of a certain murder trial of South Tyrolese youths, but the European Commission on Human Rights determined that the convention had not been violated.[14]

Throughout the 1960s more acts of violence occurred. Some of these acts were directed at the area's electricity installations, thus threatening to undermine the supply of energy to large parts of northern Italy.

In 1969, after long and arduous negotiations, Italy and the representatives of South Tyrol's mainly German largest party (the South Tyrolean People's Party—SVP) agreed on the "South Tyrol Package" (the "Südtirol-Paket," or "Pacchetto").[15] In parallel, Austria and Italy agreed on an operational calendar (*Operationskalender*),[16] which according to Christoph Schreuer is a "procedural gentlemen's agreement."[17] It consisted of a list of carefully balanced diplomatic steps to be undertaken by the two states, steps designed to lead to the implementation of the South Tyrol Package; to the acceptance of an enlarged jurisdiction of the International Court of Justice under the 1957 European Convention on the Settlement of Disputes; to declarations by the two governments that the dispute has been settled; and to the conclusion of a treaty of friendship and cooperation by Italy and Austria.

The package included 137 items, and its implementation required introducing major changes into the 1948 statute. As a result, in 1972 a New Autonomy Statute, which incorporated those provisions of the 1948 statute that were still valid, entered into force.[18] The autonomy statute has the status of a constitutional law. In addition, the implementation of other provisions of the South Tyrol Package required the adoption of certain ordinary laws and taking a number of administrative steps. In 1988 Italy enacted the last seven provisions necessary to implement the 137 requirements of the 1969 package, and in 1992 the process was completed.

### The Regime of Autonomy

When analyzing the autonomy regime of Alto Adige/South Tyrol, one has to remember that since World War II Italy has undergone a general process of regionalization.[19] Under its 1948 constitution, Italy established twenty regions "as autonomous territorial units,"[20] with five of them—two islands and three regions on the northern frontier—enjoying "[p]articular forms and conditions of autonomy, in accordance with special statutes":[21] Sicily, Sardinia, Trentino-Alto Adige, Friuli-Venetia Julia (surrounding Trieste), and the Valle d'Aosta.

Under the 1972 New Autonomy Statute the region of Trentino-Alto Adige and the two provinces of Trento and Bolzano (Bozen, or South Tyrol) continued to exist. The region retained certain limited powers,[22] while the provinces acquired additional expanded authority at the expense of both the region and the central government.

The powers of the region include the right to draw municipal boundaries and to establish and maintain land registrars; fire brigade services; health services and hospitals; chambers of commerce; public charitable institutions; and credit agencies. It can also expropriate land for purposes that are within the region's powers.

The institutions of the region include a legislative Regional Council (il Consiglio regionale, or Regionalrat) with seventy members; the presidency of the council alternates between a German- and an Italian-speaking council member. The council can be dissolved by the president of the republic in certain cases, such as violation of the constitution, grave violations of the law, and reasons of national security.[23]

The region has also a Regional Government (la Giunta regionale, or Regionalausschuss) and a president with executive powers.[24] When the national authorities deal with matters of communication and transport that are of particular interest to the region, the Regional Government must be consulted.[25] Moreover, the president of the Regional Government shall be present at meetings of the Council of Ministers of the Republic when questions concerning the region are under consideration.[26]

All laws of the region, like those of the provinces (discussed below), must be in accordance with the constitution and with the principles of Italy's legal system, its international obligations, and its national interests—which include the safeguarding of local linguistic minorities—as well as with the fundamental principles of the economic and social reforms of the republic.[27] In addition, when legislating on certain matters, the regional authorities must also conform to the principles set forth in the laws of the state.[28]

The laws of the region are submitted for approval to the representative of the central government in the region—the commissioner of the central government (il Commissario del Governo, or Regierungskommissar). The commissioner confirms the law unless of the opinion that it is in excess of the powers of the region or is contrary to the interests of either the state or one of the two relevant provinces.[29] The final decision is in the hands of the Constitutional Court of Italy, which also determines whether a law violates the equality of rights of citizens of the different language groups.[30]

All laws and regulations of the region (and of the provinces) must be published in Italian and in German; in case of doubt, the interpretation of the law has to follow the Italian version.[31] Similarly, national laws that concern the region shall also be published in German in the "Official Gazette" of the region.[32]

Of greater interest are the provisions of the 1972 New Autonomy Statute that deal with the powers of the provinces of Trento and South Tyrol/Alto Adige. Like the regional laws, the laws of the provinces must conform to the constitution, the basic principles of Italy's legal system, its international obligations, its national interests, and provisions related to socioeconomic reforms. Legislation in twenty-nine spheres is subject to the above restrictions, while legislation in eleven other spheres is also subordinate to national legislation.[33] Interestingly, the statute does not require provincial legislation to conform to laws of the region.

The powers of the provinces mainly concern economic activity, social matters, and culture. In the sphere of economics, these powers include, inter alia, town and country planning, public housing, the environment, water works, agriculture, fishing and hunting, tourism, communication, certain aspects of mining, transport of provincial interest, and trade. Of special importance in this sphere is the supervision of labor exchanges,[34] a matter that may have a considerable impact on emigration and immigration. Moreover, "[c]itizens resident in the Province of Bolzano have the right to take precedence in job placement in the territory of the Province itself, without discrimination on the basis of language group or length of residence."[35] Another power of decisive relevance for the policy of migration is the authority to deal with subsidized housing,[36] which, in turn, is related to the power to expropriate land for purposes within the powers of the province.[37]

Social matters within the jurisdiction of the province include health and public welfare, sports, and recreational activities.[38] In the sphere of culture, the province is inter alia in charge of toponyms (the establishment of place-names), with an obligation to bilingualism in Bozen; the protection of the historic, artistic, and national heritage; the preservation of local customs and traditions; and cultural institutions, including radio and television. Matters related to schools are only partly within the powers of the provinces.[39]

Foreign affairs are, in principle, exclusively within the competence of the central government. However, the Constitutional Court of Italy has held that "promotional activities" with foreign governments (for instance, for tourism) may be undertaken by the province.[40]

In certain important fields, South Tyrol has not been granted the autonomy it desired. Thus, overall responsibility for public order remains with the central government, although local city and rural police are within the jurisdiction of the province.[41] The regional and provincial authorities can request the intervention of the state police to assist in implementing regional and provincial enactments.[42] South Tyrol's autonomy in matters related to schools is only partial, since teachers are state employees.[43] Similarly, although the province has the authority to build schools,[44] it depends on the consent of Rome, which has to provide the teaching staff.

Of particular importance for the inhabitants of South Tyrol are the arrangements concerning languages. As mentioned, about two-thirds of the residents speak German, another 30 percent speak Italian, and about 4 percent speak Ladin. In analyzing matters related to language, a distinction must be made between language rights properly speaking—

namely, provisions aimed at preserving the language—and rights guaranteed to members of different language groups. As a measure to protect the various languages, the New Autonomy Statute states that "[i]n the Region the German language shall have equal standing with the Italian language which is the official language of the State. The Italian version is the authoritative one in legislative acts and in the cases for which this Statute provides for a dual language text."[45]

As is well known, people wishing to preserve their language must make sure that their children use it in school; hence the importance of the language in matters of schooling. Instruction is given in separate German, Italian, and Ladin schools. "In the Province of Bolzano/Bozen, instruction in the kindergartens, elementary and secondary schools is given in the Italian or German mother tongue of the pupils by instructors for whom that language is also their mother tongue."[46] Language instruction in the other main language of the province is obligatory. In the Ladin areas, the Ladin language is used in schools and the children must learn both German and Italian.[47] Children are registered in the respective schools upon the request of their father or a person acting for him.[48]

Another provision intended to preserve the language authorizes German-speaking citizens of the province to use their mother tongue in their dealings with the courts and the administration in the province, as well as with those having regional competence and with concessionaires of public services in the province. Moreover, the authorities have to respond in the language in which the citizen has addressed them.[49] Hence, all public officials, as well as judges, must have a good knowledge of both German and Italian.[50] In the army, however, only Italian is to be used,[51] and in certain matters (such as public acts) documents must be drafted in both languages.[52]

Turning now to rights guaranteed to members of different language groups, the statute requires that the composition of the main organs of administration in the province must reflect the numerical proportion of the language groups. This principle has been laid down with minor variations, in particular for the provincial government,[53] all local public bodies,[54] the Provincial Council for Education, and the Teachers Disciplinary Council.[55] The Autonomous Section for the Province of Bolzano of the Regional Administrative Court has to include judges from both the German- and Italian-language groups in equal numbers.[56] In some of the bodies where the language groups are represented, chairmanship or presidency has to alternate between them, as in the Provincial Council.[57] It is interesting that despite this division on the basis of language and the numerical superiority of the German-speaking group, the two groups often collaborate in a coalition.

Perhaps the most interesting provision intended to ensure the rights of the various language groups concerns the allocation of jobs in the public sector. The New Autonomy Statute provides that in South Tyrol most positions in offices of the civil service that become vacant should be filled on the basis of a proportional representation of the three language groups.[58] When filling judiciary vacancies, only the Italian and German groups are contemplated.[59] Certain careers are, however, exempt from the language group representation requirement: high-level positions in the civil administration of the interior, police personnel, and civilians in the defense ministry.[60] The principle of proportional participation has been upheld by the Italian Constitutional Court, which decided in 1988 that privatization of railways did not affect the applicability of the principle.[61] It may be a long time before the proportional representation of the various language groups in the civil service reflects their proportion in the population, but great progress has already been made.[62]

Implementing the principle has, however, encountered two difficulties. First, it appears that not many members of the German-speaking group wish to work in the civil service; others are probably discouraged by the need to take a language examination in Italian, as well as by the housing shortage in Bolzano (the capital of South Tyrol). They may prefer to work in the booming tourist industry. Another problem relates to the European Union's rules on the freedom of movement of workers: The Court of Justice of the European Union has established a restrictive definition of posts in the civil service that are excluded from the principle of freedom of movement and equality of treatment, thus drastically limiting the number of jobs available for implementing the principle of ethnic proportional representation in South Tyrol.[63]

A person's membership in one of the three language groups is established by a formal declaration that the individual makes at the time of the population census. This method, however, has not been without its difficulties. First, some members of the Italian community declared that they belonged to the German-speaking group, mainly for economic reasons, since the Italian-dominated industrial sector suffered from a considerable recession. Second, some people—particularly children of mixed marriages—did not wish to affiliate with any one of the groups. Others claimed that the obligation to give such a declaration violated the principle of equality of rights of all citizens without distinction, as laid down by the Italian constitution. In 1984 the Council of State declared that the law requiring the declaration of affiliation was illegal, because citizens could not declare themselves to be of another language or mixed language.

In 1991 a compromise was developed. It allowed two declarations, one for statistical purposes and one for preserving the system of ethnic proportionality.[64]

The institutions of the province include a legislative Provincial Council (il Consiglio provinciale, or Landtag) composed of those members of the Regional Council who were elected by the residents of the respective province.[65] This council can be dissolved by the president of Italy on grounds similar to those that justify the dissolution of the Regional Assembly discussed above (in particular, violation of the constitution, grave violations of the law, and reasons of national security).[66] In addition, the province has a Provincial Government (la Giunta provinciale, or Landesausschuss) elected by the Provincial Council. This government is composed of a president (Presidente, or Landeshauptmann), two vice presidents,[67] assessors, and substitute assessors elected from among the members of the Provincial Council. One of the vice presidents has to belong to the German-language group, the other one to the Italian group. The president of the government represents the province and shall be present at meetings of the Council of Ministers of Italy when questions concerning the province are under consideration.[68] For many years this office was held by Dr. Silvius Magnago. Like in the region, the national government is represented in South Tyrol by a commissioner of the central government (il Commissario del Governo, or Regierungskommissar).[69]

South Tyrol's autonomy does not include the administration of justice. However, the regime of autonomy has also had some impact on the judiciary. Thus, as already mentioned, the appointment of new judges has to follow the equality principle.[70] The Autonomous Section for the Province of Bolzano of the Regional Administrative Court is composed of an equal number of German-speaking and Italian-speaking judges.[71] This court has jurisdiction to hear claims against the administration for alleged discrimination on the basis of membership in a language group.[72] Moreover, "[a] Councilman belonging to the German language group of the Province . . . shall be a member of the sections of the Council of State having jurisdiction on appeals" against decisions of the above Autonomous Section for Bolzano.[73]

The New Autonomy Statute also includes detailed provisions on the financial resources of the region and the two provinces.[74] While the province itself has only limited powers to impose taxes, it is entitled to receive from the state a substantial part of certain taxes levied in the province, including 90 percent of property tax and income tax. The province also receives 1.61 percent of the sectoral government expenditures, as well as certain sums for farm modernization measures from the European Union's Common Agricultural Policy.[75]

The settlement of certain categories of disputes related to the autonomy has been entrusted to Italy's Constitutional Court, which has jurisdiction to review the constitutionality and conformity with the autonomy statute of laws enacted by the region and by the provinces. In particular, it has to ensure that none of these laws violates the principle of equality among the various language groups. Moreover, the court is also authorized to verify that laws and other measures of the republic do not violate the New Autonomy Statute or the rights of the German- or Ladin-language minorities within Italy.[76]

The introduction of changes into most of the provisions of the New Autonomy Statute has to follow the procedure established for constitutional amendments, and the consent of the local authorities is not needed. However, the Regional Council may take the initiative and propose an amendment.[77] The title dealing with financial matters and those provisions that concern the termination of the function of the president of the Regional and Provincial Councils may be amended by an ordinary law of the state at the joint request of the central government and the region or the two provinces, respectively.

Although South Tyrol/Alto Adige has no competence in the sphere of foreign affairs, the province has been involved in various transboundary regional organizations of the Alps, in particular in ARGE ALP (Arbeitsgemeinschaft Alpenländer). This group was established in 1972 and includes certain areas of Germany, Austria, Switzerland, and Italy (the provinces of South Tyrol and Trento, as well as the region of Lombardy).[78] It aims to further cooperation on matters of common concern, such as protecting the environment, planning roads and railways, and engaging in economic cooperation.

## Concluding Remarks

Although the autonomy in South Tyrol/Alto Adige is usually considered to be successful, it is not without problems. The difficulties related to the declaration of affiliation with a language group have already been discussed. In addition, the Italian-speaking minority has felt under-privileged, leading to two developments: an increase in the number of votes for the Italian fascist party (Movimento Sociale Italiano—MSI) in the 1984 elections and the emigration from the area of a number of Italian-speaking residents.

The South Tyrol "Pacchetto" or "Paket" and the implementing measures are among the most detailed autonomy arrangements. The drafters have tried to establish a relatively elaborate system of division of powers. It has certain peculiarities. First, this is a two-tiered structure, granting certain limited powers to the region and larger ones to the provinces. Second, while in most cases the instruments concerning the autonomy mainly address the rights of the group that is a minority in the state but a majority in the autonomous area, in the case of South Tyrol a serious attempt has been made to protect also the group that is the majority in the state but a considerable minority in the province.

Much emphasis is placed on language rights and on the rights of language groups. It appears, however, that the "language groups" actually represent groups that also differ in ethnic origin, culture, tradition, and way of life. Moreover, it seems that the emphasis on the rights of language groups is intended to preserve the status quo: The adherence to the proportionality principle in granting jobs in the public service and the preference granted to local residents at labor exchanges may perpetuate the linguistic division at its present ratio, as well as preserve the present character of the area (it may be interesting to compare this aspect with the case of the Åland Islands discussed above). This regime may, however, be at variance with certain notions of equality, non-discrimination, and freedom of movement of people within the European Union.

The South Tyrol autonomy relates to legislation and administration in specific areas and does not include adjudication. As in most other cases of autonomy, the legislative acts of the autonomous authorities require the approval by a representative of the central government. This approval may be withheld on certain grounds that have been quite broadly defined.

No joint organ of consultation or collaboration has been established, but the president of the respective autonomous entities may participate in the deliberations of the central government if questions concerning these entities are discussed. No international or joint mechanism for settling disputes has been established, and disputes related to the division of powers between the various authorities and to the protection of the rights of minority groups are addressed by the Constitutional Court of Italy. If a dispute arises between Austria and Italy, the matter is subject to the general mechanisms of dispute resolution that exist between the two states.

South Tyrol is one of the few cases of autonomy where the finances of the autonomous entity are mainly based on the transfer to it of a share of the state's income from the area itself, and no additional considerable subsidies are needed.

Achieving a compromise solution accepted by the majority of all those concerned—Italy, Austria, and the South Tyrolese—was certainly due to tolerance and goodwill on all sides. Perhaps the umbrella of the European Union, of which Italy was a long-time member and which Austria wished to join, may also have contributed to the process. Austria needed Italy's goodwill in order to be admitted to the Union. As for the German-speaking South Tyrolese, perhaps the prospect of cooperation between Italy and Austria within the Union contributed to reducing their misgivings and doubts. Another factor that may have influenced the parties is the tendency of the European Union to permit and encourage the involvement of subnational units in its activities.

## B. THE FAROE ISLANDS

Another regime of autonomy established soon after the end of World War II is the home rule in the Faroe Islands, a group of islands located in the North Atlantic Ocean between the Shetland Islands (north of Scotland) and Iceland.[79] Their population is about 45,500. The economy of the islands depends heavily on fishing and the fishing industry.

### Historical Background

The Faroes are part of the Danish Realm, but they have enjoyed limited self-government since 1852. During World War II, after Denmark's occupation by Germany, the islands were temporarily occupied by British forces, and in this period the desire for more self-government developed. After the war, a dispute between Denmark and the Faroe Islands on the future of the islands led to a unilateral declaration of independence followed by the dissolution of the local elected council by the king of Denmark. The negotiations that followed led to a Home Rule Act, which received the approval of the newly elected local council and was enacted by the Danish parliament in 1948.

## The Regime of Autonomy

The institutions of the autonomy include a legislature—Lagting—that consists of thirty-two directly elected local residents. It may be dissolved by the Lagmand, the Faroese prime minister. The Landsstyre (the government) is appointed by the legislature and is headed by the Lagmand. Denmark is represented in the islands by a high commissioner.

Faroese autonomy includes authority of legislation and administration, but Denmark retains adjudication. The Home Rule Act distinguishes among three groups of powers: matters that may be transferred to the jurisdiction of the islands; residual spheres that remain with Denmark (to "be handled as joint concerns," Section 6); and mere powers of administration in the areas within Danish responsibility, which may be transferred (Section 9).

The powers that may be entrusted to the autonomous authorities are enumerated in two lists. The first list includes subjects that may be transferred without further negotiations—mainly matters of economics and social and cultural affairs, including direct and indirect taxation, education, health, social welfare, labor relations, agriculture, fishing, and industry. The second list contains areas that may be transferred at a later stage, subject to agreement between the parties. These areas include the established church, police and prisons, natural and mineral resources, radio broadcasting, aviation, and import and export controls. Responsibility for radio broadcasting and import-export controls was assumed by the autonomous authorities in the 1970s; in 1992 an agreement was reached on natural resources. Each transfer of authority requires that the Faroes assume the expenses involved.

The main residual fields of jurisdiction that remain in the hands of Denmark include foreign affairs, defense, currency, the judiciary, health services, and primary schooling. In addition, Denmark is still in charge of other transferrable matters until they are actually transferred. However, Denmark has to consult the home government before submitting bills to the Danish parliament that include provisions relating exclusively to the Faroe Islands. Other Danish legislation that affects local Faroese matters has to be put before the home rule authorities for consideration before the legislation is enforced in the islands (Section 7). Spheres that are within Denmark's jurisdiction, but for which administrative authority has been transferred, include social security, hospital administration, and the educational system.

In principle, foreign relations are within Denmark's powers, yet the Faroese government has had considerable influence in this area, mainly in matters related to fishing and trade.[80] It has held this influence because the Faroe economy depends so heavily on the export of fish and fish products, while having to import almost all other necessities, including fuel and food. Thus, although Denmark has long been a member of the European Union, joining what was then known as the European Community (EC) in 1973, the Faroe Islands have remained outside;[81] they have instead concluded a trade agreement with the EC (1974), as well as with certain member states of the European Free Trade Association. These agreements were formally concluded by Denmark for the Faroes. The 1977 fishing agreement with the EC was signed by Denmark's deputy ambassador to the EC and by the head of the Faroese home government.

In 1977 the EC members, including Denmark, left the North East Atlantic Fisheries Convention, but Denmark did not end her membership as far as the Faroe Islands were concerned. In the North Atlantic Fisheries Organization, Denmark is not a member in its own name because the EC is a member, but Denmark did become a member as "Denmark in respect of the Faroe Islands." As these examples show, Denmark usually concludes treaties for the Faroe Islands, sometimes independently of its own participation or nonparticipation in the treaty. Only in rare cases have the home rule authorities themselves concluded an "agreed record" or an "administrative agreement." A fishing agreement with the Federal Republic of Germany was entitled "Kurzprotokoll" (short protocol).

When Denmark concludes a treaty with a considerable impact on the Faroe Islands, the home rule authorities are consulted and their representative often participates in the negotiations. If the Faroese government is opposed to the conclusion of the treaty, Denmark will usually make a statement excluding the islands from the application of the instrument. Not being a state, the Faroes cannot join international intergovernmental organizations. There are, however, special provisions concerning a limited participation in the activities of the Nordic Council and the Nordic Council of Ministers.[82]

The islands have their own flag (Section 12 of the Home Rule Act), which has been recognized since 1940 as a merchant marine flag.[83] The act recognizes as a Faroese citizen every person "who has Danish citizenship and is resident in the Faroe Islands" (Section 10). Their passports include both the words "Denmark" and "Faroyar."[84] The act stipulates that "Faroese is recognized as the main language, but Danish must be learned carefully and well, and Danish can be used in all official business on a par with Faroese" (Section 11).[85]

The Home Rule Act establishes an elaborate system for settling disputes: Four persons, two of them nominated by the central government and two by the home rule authorities, are to try to resolve the dispute. If they fail to reach agreement, the matter is to be decided by three judges of Denmark's Supreme Court. The system has never been used.

### Concluding Remarks

The autonomy of the Faroe Islands has been functioning for forty-eight years, and it served as a model for the home rule established in Greenland in 1979. Two factors may have contributed to this autonomy's success: First, the population has no affinity to a foreign country and hence outside interference is unlikely; second, there is no common border between Denmark and the islands (the "saltwater" effect).

The powers of the home rule authorities do not include adjudication. On the other hand, the Faroese authorities are given a say in the international relations of the islands. The islands depend heavily on Danish subsidies. The residents of the islands participate in the public life of Denmark. There is no special common organ. Laws enacted by the autonomous area do not require approval by any outside body.

### C. West Berlin until the Reunification of Germany

Of a completely different nature was the autonomy enjoyed by the western sectors of Berlin from the late 1940s until the reunification of Germany in 1990.[86]

### Historical Background

On 8 May 1945, at the end of World War II, Germany capitulated; on 5 June 1945 the Allied Powers declared that they had assumed supreme authority in Germany.[87] The arrangements for the occupation of Germany in general and of Berlin in particular had already been determined: the Protocol on Zones of Occupation in Germany and Administration of the "Greater Berlin" Area signed in September 1944 provided for Germany to be divided into three (later four) zones, with each of the occupying powers in charge of one zone. The protocol also established "a special Berlin area, which will be under joint occupation by the three [later four] Powers." This protocol further provided that "[a]n Inter-Allied Governing Authority (Komandatura) consisting of three Commandants, appointed by their respective Commanders-in-Chief, will be established to direct jointly the administration of the 'Greater Berlin' Area."[88]

Another agreement of November 1944 stated that the three (later four) commanders-in-chief would constitute the Control Council, with supervisory functions for the various zones of occupation and the responsibility "to direct the administration of 'Greater Berlin' through appropriate organs." The agreement reiterated the decision to establish the Komandatura (the Russian term), which—assisted by a technical staff—would supervise and control the activities of the local organs responsible for municipal services in Greater Berlin.[89] On 11 July 1945 the Allied Komandatura was constituted; a few weeks later the Control Council was established. In both organs decisions had to be passed unanimously. At the Yalta conference (February 1945) of the heads of government of the United States, the United Kingdom, and the Soviet Union, it was agreed, inter alia, that the headquarters of the Control Council should be in Berlin.[90]

At the end of the war, all sectors of Berlin were occupied by the Soviet Union, while the Western Allies were in control of large areas that, according to earlier agreements, were to come under Soviet occupation. This discrepancy was settled in July 1945, when Western troops entered Berlin and simultaneously withdrew from those parts of the Soviet zone of occupation they had earlier occupied. The Soviet Union had already established a central city administration in Berlin before the entry of the Western troops.

At the August 1945 Potsdam conference of the heads of government of the Allied Powers, Berlin was not dealt with separately. However, the decision to treat Germany as a single economic unit was relevant for Berlin.[91]

At the beginning, the Komandatura and the Control Council operated more or less satisfactorily, in spite of various disputes. In 1948, however, with the intensification of the Cold War, Berlin was the center of various severe crises: differences of opinion on who had authority to introduce a currency reform and, as a result, the introduction of two separate reforms in the two parts of the city; the end of collaboration on the municipal level, leading to the establishment of two separate municipalities; and the gravest one, the blockade of the Western sectors by the Soviet Union. Finally the Soviet Union quit the organs of joint administration—first the Control Council, later the Komandatura and its organs (except for the Air Safety Center and the joint control of the Spandau Allied Prison of major war criminals). By December 1948, however, the Western powers reconvened the Komandatura (now Kommandatura) and ensured its functioning without the Soviet Union.

In late 1949 the legal status of Germany and of Berlin underwent considerable changes. With the approval of the Western military governors, the Basic Law (Grundgesetz) for the Federal Republic of Germany (FRG) was adopted,[92] and in the same year the Law on the Constitution of the German Democratic Republic (GDR) was enacted.[93] The military governors of the Western powers were replaced by civilian high commissioners, and a Control Commission replaced the Soviet military administration.

West Berlin was represented in the council that drafted the Basic Law of the FRG by a delegation which, due to demands of the Western powers, was precluded from participating in the vote.[94] Provisions of the Basic Law that purported to give Berlin the status of a "Land" (a province and a member of the FRG) were vetoed by the Western powers, which stated that "while Berlin may not be accorded voting membership in the Bundestag or Bundesrat nor be governed by the Federation she may, nevertheless, designate a small number of representatives to attend the meetings of those legislative bodies."[95]

In practice, the Western powers permitted the development of close ties between West Berlin and the FRG. The Basic Law of the FRG was introduced in Berlin by a resolution of the City Assembly. It was again referred to in Berlin's 1950 constitution,[96] which granted the provisions of the Basic Law superiority over the Berlin constitution (subject to the power to override them by a two-thirds majority).

In the wake of the establishment of the FRG in 1949, the Western powers established a new occupation regime for Germany,[97] which did not, however, apply to Berlin. For the latter, a Statement of Principles Governing the Relationship between the Allied Kommandatura and

Greater Berlin was adopted by the Western commandants on 14 May 1949.[98] It granted a large measure of self-government to the Berlin local authorities, but expressly reserved to the Allied Kommandatura certain powers, as well as the right to resume other powers—"if they consider that to do so is essential to security or to preserve democratic government, or in pursuance of the international obligations of their Governments."[99] In the east, in the meantime (in 1949) Berlin was declared to be the capital of the GDR.[100] Two years later, the Congress of the United States unilaterally terminated the state of war between the United States and Germany.[101]

A considerable change occurred in 1955 when, in the wake of the revised 1954 Bonn/Paris Conventions,[102] the FRG was recognized as a fully sovereign state, although subject to certain reservations. In parallel, the occupation statute of Germany was revoked.[103] The above reservations concerned, inter alia, the preservation of the rights and responsibilities of the Western Allies over Berlin.[104] However, the West agreed to consult the FRG on the exercise of those rights with regard to Berlin.[105] Additional provisions included in an exchange of notes committed the FRG to grant extensive aid to Berlin, to represent the city as well as its inhabitants abroad, and to incorporate the city in suitable international treaties.[106] Thus, the occupation of Germany was terminated, but not of Berlin.

In the same year (1955) a treaty between the Soviet Union and the GDR recognized the sovereignty of the GDR but took into consideration "the obligations of the Soviet Union and the GDR under existing international agreements relating to Germany as a whole."[107]

Each of the two German governments claimed to be the sole representative of Germany. The Soviet Union objected to West Berlin's close ties with the FRG, while the Western powers protested against the transfer of certain powers related to Berlin to the GDR.

The 1955 change in the status of the FRG led to the introduction of minor changes in the occupation regime of West Berlin. On 5 May 1955 the Declaration on Berlin Governing Relations between the Allied (Western) Kommandatura and Berlin, Issued by the Three Western Commandants came into force (it is discussed below).[108] On the same day, the Western powers assigned responsibility for the occupation of Berlin to their ambassadors in the FRG.[109]

The Cold War again intensified in Berlin in 1958. At that time, the Soviet Union demanded that the whole of Berlin should be incorporated into the GDR and if this were not possible, then the Western sectors should become a demilitarized free city. These proposals met with strong opposition from the Western Allies. In the summer of 1960, the access routes to Berlin were again obstructed, and the movement of people between the Eastern and Western sectors was hampered. Berlin was completely divided in 1961 by the construction of the wall between its communist and Western parts.[110]

Tensions were relaxed in the early 1970s, with the conclusion of a number of agreements, including the 1971 Quadripartite Agreement on Berlin (discussed below).[111] Neither this agreement nor those that accompanied its conclusion established a new statute, but they clarified and regulated some of the disputed matters.

Berlin's tribulations at last came to an end in 1989–90, with the removal of the wall and the incorporation of the city as a Land into the FRG.[112] The Soviet Union and the three Western Allies terminated their rights and responsibilities relating to Berlin and to Germany as a whole.[113]

### The Regime of Autonomy

The Western sectors of Berlin enjoyed a large degree of autonomy from an early date: "Greater Berlin shall have, subject only to the limitations set out in this statement, full legislative and executive and judicial powers in accordance with the Temporary Constitution of 1946 or with any subsequent Constitution adopted by the City Assembly and approved by the Allied Kommandatura in accordance with the provisions of this statement."[114]

According to its 1950 constitution, West Berlin had an elected legislature named Abgeordnetenhaus (House of Representatives) that was composed of at least two hundred deputies and was headed by a president elected by the house.[115] The functions of government were entrusted to the Senat, composed of eighteen members at most, and headed by the acting mayor (Regierender Bürgermeister).[116] For many years, Willy Brandt served as mayor. The members of the Senat were elected by the House of Representatives.[117] In addition, Berlin had a judiciary.[118] West Berlin was divided into self-administering districts.[119]

Berlin's police force was subordinate to the Senat of the city, but the Western Allies had authority over it to the extent necessary to ensure the security of Berlin. Specific arrangements were made regarding liaison between the Berlin police and the Allies, as well as regarding the

Allies' control over the organization and functioning of the force. This special concern for the police was justified because of the grave danger engendered by the Cold War and the fact that Berlin's Western sectors were surrounded by hostile neighbors.[120]

As a result of the Cold War, Berlin had a complicated relationship with the FRG. Although the laws of the FRG did not apply to West Berlin, the latter's legislature was permitted to adopt laws similar to those of the Federal Republic.[121] However, the Allies insisted that the city was not a part of the FRG and was not governed by it.[122] The FRG was to be represented in Berlin only by a permanent liaison agency.[123]

In fact, the economies of West Berlin and the FRG were integrated, and the jurisdiction of all federal supreme courts except for the Federal Constitutional Court extended to Berlin.[124] Even in foreign affairs the FRG was authorized to act for Berlin, although in principle this sphere was within the responsibility of the Allied Powers. Thus, the FRG was permitted to perform consular services for the permanent residents of the Western sectors of Berlin, to extend the application of its international agreements to West Berlin on the condition that this extension was specified in each case (for example, Berlin was included in the FRG's membership in the European Community), and to represent the interests of the Western sectors in international organizations. Similarly, residents of West Berlin were allowed to join participants from the FRG in international exchanges and exhibitions. However, the consulate-general of the Soviet Union in the Western sectors of Berlin was accredited to the three Western powers.[125]

German residents of West Berlin held German citizenship.[126] Berlin was permitted to appoint a number of nonvoting representatives, elected by the local legislature, to participate in the meetings of the Bundestag and the Bundesrat in Bonn.[127] They had, however, full voting rights in the federal assembly that elects the federal president, as well as in committees of the two houses of parliament.[128] German citizens resident in Berlin could be candidates for all political offices in the FRG.[129]

The power to modify the provisions of the 1955 Declaration, which had redefined the division of powers between the Allied Powers and the Berlin authorities, was reserved exclusively to the Allied Kommandatura.[130] This division, as laid down in the 1955 Declaration,[131] followed an interesting pattern: Certain powers were reserved to the Allies; others would be exercised by the Allies only in case of emergency; a third category was entrusted in parallel to the Allies and the local authorities, on the condition that the latter comply with certain guidelines; and a fourth group of powers was fully within the jurisdiction of the local organs, subject to compatibility with the special status of Berlin. Acts of the local legislature did not need prior approval, but they could be subsequently invalidated by the Kommandatura.[132] In practice, repeal was usually avoided by prior consultation.[133]

The powers reserved to the Allied authorities included the following: "(a) Security, interests and immunities of the Allied Forces, including their representatives, dependents and non-German employees"—German employees of the Allied forces enjoyed only functional immunity from German courts; "(b) Disarmament and demilitarization, including related fields of scientific research, civil aviation, and prohibitions and restrictions on industry in relation to the foregoing"; "(c) Relations of Berlin with authorities abroad"—however, the Berlin authorities were permitted to make "suitable arrangements" in this sphere; "(d) Satisfaction of occupation costs"—after consultation with the appropriate German authorities; and "(e) Authority over the Berlin police to the extent necessary to ensure the security of Berlin."[134] Under a law adopted in 1950 by the Kommandatura, the appropriate sector commandant was authorized to "withdraw from a German Court any proceeding directly affecting any of the persons or matters within the purview of paragraph 2 [enumerating the powers reserved to the Allied authorities] of the Statement of Principles governing the relationship between the Allied Kommandatura and Greater Berlin."[135]

The powers that were to be exercised by the Allies only in time of emergency were not defined by their contents, but by their object: "The Allied authorities retain the right to take, if they deem it necessary, such measures as may be required to fulfill their international obligations, to ensure public order and to maintain the status and security of Berlin and its economy, trade and communications." These seem to be Cold War–related matters. The Allies were not limited in the choice of measures to deal with those situations.[136]

In other areas, the local authorities could act on the condition that they comply with the principles established by the 1955 conventions concluded by the Allies and the FRG and with Allied legislation in force in Berlin: "(a) restitution, reparations, decartelization, deconcentration, foreign interests in Berlin, claims against Berlin or its inhabitants, (b) displaced persons and the admission of refugees, [and] (c) control of the care and treatment in German prisons of persons charged before or sentenced by Allied courts." These areas were under concurrent jurisdiction of the local authorities and the Allies.[137]

Other spheres were within the jurisdiction of the local authorities, always subject to the right of repeal by the Kommandatura "in case of inconsistency with Allied legislation, or with other measures of the Allied authorities, or with the rights of the allied authorities."[138] The Berlin legislature was also authorized to repeal or amend legislation of the Allied authorities subject to the approval of the latter authorities.[139]

The special status of West Berlin and the division of powers between the Western Allies and the local authorities have been the subject of two interesting decisions of United States courts. The first was decided in 1979 by the U.S. Court for Berlin, and the second was the subject of an appeal decided in 1981 by the U.S. Court of Appeals for the District of Columbia.

The *Tiede and Ruske* case[140] dealt with hijacking: a Polish LOT civilian aircraft on a scheduled flight from Gdansk, Poland, to Schoenfeld Airport in East Berlin was diverted and forced to land at Tempelhof Airport in the U.S. sector of West Berlin. After consultation with British, French, and West German authorities, the United States decided to exercise its reserved responsibilities and to try the suspects in the U.S. Court for Berlin. That court had been foreseen by a 1955 law of the U.S. high commissioner,[141] but had never been actually convened. For the trial of Tiede and Ruske, the ambassador of the United States in the FRG[142] appointed a U.S. judge from the District of New Jersey (Herbert J. Stern) to sit as U.S. Judge for Berlin.

One of the main questions in dispute was whether the defendants were entitled to a trial by jury:

> This Court does not hold that jury trials must be afforded in occupation courts everywhere and under all circumstances; the Court holds only that if the United States convenes a United States Court in Berlin, under the present circumstances, and charges civilians with non-military offenses, the United States must provide the defendants with the same constitutional safeguards that it must provide to civilian defendants in any other United States court.[143]

In his decision, the judge reviewed the history and the development of the occupation of Berlin, with special reference to the exercise of judicial authority under the occupation. "The criminal jurisdiction of the Court is concurrent with that of the Berlin courts, except to the extent that the American sector Commandant withdraws jurisdiction from the German courts in a given case."[144] The judge mentioned that the defendants were German citizens, that is, friendly aliens, charged with nonmilitary offenses under German law. He also expressed the opinion that "[w]hat began as belligerent occupation of a vanquished enemy has turned into a 'protective occupation' of a friendly and allied people."[145]

The second case, *Rosemarie Dostal et al.,*[146] concerned an environmental complaint. The plaintiffs/appellants were seven persons residing in Berlin. They objected to the decision of the Berlin senator for construction and housing, who had determined that the construction of a housing project at Düppel Field for U.S. military dependents would not violate German zoning law. When the plaintiffs sought review of this decision in a German administrative court, the U.S. mission in Berlin objected to the jurisdiction. Thereupon the plaintiffs tried to bring the case to the U.S. Court for Berlin, convened earlier for the *Tiede and Ruske* case; but the U.S. ambassador notified the judge of that court that his jurisdiction did not include the *Dostal* case. The plaintiffs applied to the District of Columbia court, claiming that everyone has a constitutional right to litigate their grievances and that this right is protected against any executive branch action that frustrates this right.[147]

The Court of Appeal, however, found that

> the due process clause of the fifth amendment does not require U.S. officials to forgo normal and customary immunities [of military forces in friendly foreign countries], or to provide a judicial forum where individuals . . . may seek judicial redress, when such individuals are unable to allege impairment of liberty or property interests protected by the said clause.[148]

These two cases illustrate the complexity of the Berlin situation and the amazing consequences to which the division of powers could lead. In the *Tiede and Ruske* case, the decision to prosecute in the U.S. Court for Berlin was probably prompted by the Cold War. In the *Dostal* case, on the other hand, the denial of jurisdiction from both the local and the U.S. court was intended to assure the immunity of the rights of U.S. forces. In both cases, the discussion involved the human rights provisions of the Constitution of the United States.

## Concluding Remarks

West Berlin was a case of a special, perhaps unique, autonomy. Its origin was not in ethnic tension but in a regime of occupation complicated by the Cold War. The area was in dispute between two countries, the FRG and the GDR, and opinions differed considerably on its legal status.[149] The autonomy was granted by neither of these countries, but by the Western occupying powers, which had no territorial claims to the city. It was used to end in fact the regime of occupation, while formally leaving it in force. It also permitted Berlin to adapt its legal and administrative system to the one prevailing in the country that it wished to join.

Due to the dangers resulting from the Cold War and from Berlin's precarious geographical situation, the Western Allies had to reserve for themselves a considerable number of powers, as well as a de facto right to veto local legislation. The extent of the freedom of action of West Berlin grew with the improvement of relations between the Allies and the FRG—the country to which the Berliners had an ethnical, economic, and ideological affinity.

## D. ERITREA

The autonomy of Eritrea (1952–62) involved a case of annexation authorized by the international community on the condition that a regime of autonomy be established.[150] Moreover, the details of the regime were worked out in great detail by organs of the United Nations.

### Historical Background

Eritrea is located on the southwestern coast of the Red Sea. Its territory of 93,680 square kilometers is inhabited by a population of about 3.5 million people who belong to nine different ethnic groups.[151] Apparently, its central highlands had been the very cradle of Ethiopian civilization, and for a long time Eritrea was part of a decentralized Ethiopian kingdom. In the sixteenth century it came under Ottoman rule, and later the control of the territory was disputed among various countries (Ethiopia, the Ottomans, the Kingdom of Tigrai, Egypt, and Italy). In 1889 Menelik II of Ethiopia recognized Italian possessions on the Red Sea by the Treaty of Uccialli,[152] and in 1890 the Italian colony of Eritrea was established. The name was derived from the term *mare erythraeum*, the Roman name for the Red Sea—a term borrowed from Greek.

In 1935–36 Ethiopia too was occupied by Italy, but in the course of World War II the Italians were expelled from both Ethiopia and Eritrea. A British military administration was established in Eritrea in 1941; in Ethiopia Emperor Haile Selassie was reinstated.

Under the 1947 Treaty of Peace between the Allies and Italy, the latter renounced "all right and title" to her territorial possessions in Africa—including Eritrea—and their "final disposal" was to be decided upon by the four Allies.[153] Since, however, the Allies could not agree on a solution for Eritrea, the question was submitted to the UN General Assembly, in accordance with the provisions of the Treaty of Peace.[154]

The General Assembly discussed the matter in 1949 and 1950. Various solutions were proposed: outright annexation by Ethiopia; partitioning Eritrea and incorporating the predominantly Muslim western province into Sudan while annexing the rest to Ethiopia; establishing a trusteeship; and immediate independence. On 2 December 1950 the General Assembly adopted a resolution recommending that Eritrea should become an autonomous unit federated with Ethiopia under the sovereignty of the Ethiopian Crown.[155] The main provisions (Paragraphs 1–7) of this resolution were to constitute the "Federal Act," that is, the basic rules on the regime of autonomy. The future constitution of Eritrea had to comply with these rules.

In 1952 the British administration organized the first general elections, and the newly elected Eritrean Assembly approved a constitution prepared by the UN commissioner for Eritrea.[156] Soon after that, the constitution was formally approved by the commissioner and ratified by the emperor of Ethiopia. It entered into force upon ratification of the Federal Act by the emperor,[157] who also proclaimed the establishment of the federation. In September 1952 the British administration transferred its powers,[158] and in December of that year the UN General Assembly welcomed the establishment of the "Federation of Eritrea with Ethiopia under the sovereignty of the Ethiopian Crown."[159]

Soon, however, the regime faltered. In the late 1950s a strong independence movement developed in Eritrea, and in 1961 it turned into an armed revolution. At the same time Ethiopia, probably due to fear of the rising pan-Arabist fervor in the Middle East,[160] started to curtail Eritrea's autonomy: The powers of the *enderasse,* the emperor's representative in the area (who happened to be Haile Selassie's son-in-law), were considerably increased. Although his functions were originally intended to be mainly formal and ceremonial, he soon arrogated the power to appoint the local chief executive, who should have been elected by the local assembly. Moreover, the assembly was "guided" to adopt rules that severely reduced its independence. The new docile assembly gradually gave up parts of its autonomy (for example, the Eritrean flag and its criminal code), until on 14 November 1962 it voted under duress to abolish itself. On that same day Eritrea was fully annexed to Ethiopia by virtue of a resolution of the Ethiopian parliament and an imperial order.[161]

The communist regime that came into power in Ethiopia in 1974 did not reinstate autonomy in Eritrea. This regime was militarily defeated in 1991 by a coalition of Eritreans and several other groups. In 1993 the population of Eritrea voted in favor of independence.[162]

### The Regime of Autonomy

As mentioned, according to the Federal Act adopted by the UN General Assembly and ratified by the emperor, Eritrea was to be "an autonomous unit federated with Ethiopia under the sovereignty of the Ethiopian Crown."[163] Like most documents on autonomy, those concerning Eritrea (the Federal Act and the constitution)[164] included provisions on the division of power between the center and periphery, on the institutional arrangements, and on certain substantive provisions. The Federal Act listed the powers of the federal government (Ethiopia) as follows: "defence, foreign affairs, currency and finance, foreign and interstate commerce and external and interstate communications, including ports. The Federal Government shall have the power to maintain the integrity of the Federation, and shall have the right to impose uniform taxes throughout the Federation to meet the expenses of federal functions and services." On the other hand, "[t]he jurisdiction of the Eritrean Government shall extend to all matters not vested in the Federal Government, including the power to maintain the internal police, to levy taxes to meet the expenses of domestic functions and services, and to adopt its own budget." Moreover, the assessment and collection of the federal taxes in Eritrea were to be delegated to the Eritrean government. Eritrea was not to bear more than its just and equitable share of the federal expenses.[165]

The constitution specified more of the powers vested in Eritrea: "(a) The various branches of law (criminal law, civil law, commercial law, etc.); (b) The organization of public services; (c) Internal police; (d) Health; (e) Education; (f) Public assistance and social security;

(g) Protection of labour; (h) Exploitation of natural resources and regulation of industry, internal commerce, trades and professions; (i) Agriculture; (j) Internal communications; (k) The public utility services which are peculiar to Eritrea; [and] (l) the Eritrean budget and the establishment and collection of taxes designed to meet the expenses of Eritrean public functions and services."[166]

These lists call for a few remarks. First, a substantial number of powers were to be granted to Eritrea. Of particular interest is the fact that Eritrea was to have all the residual powers, even though sovereignty was attributed to Ethiopia. Key among the powers of Ethiopia was the authority "to maintain the integrity of the Federation," in other words, to prevent secession, with no indication of the means that Ethiopia was allowed to use for that purpose. The specific reference to ports as a power vested in Ethiopia derives from the importance of this sphere for Ethiopia: The ports of Assab and Massawa in Eritrea were Ethiopia's only outlet to the sea. No wonder that in his address after the ratification of the Federal Act the emperor expressly mentioned that "[t]hat association would give the Federation access to the sea."[167]

Eritrea's powers were to include "legislative, executive and judicial powers in the field of domestic affairs."[168] The laws adopted by the Eritrean Assembly did not require the approval of the central authorities; under the constitution, the representative of the emperor could only request that a certain law be reconsidered by the assembly if, in his opinion, it "encroaches upon Federal jurisdiction, or . . . it involves the international responsibility of the Federation." If such a request was made, the draft legislation had to obtain a two-thirds majority vote to be adopted.[169]

Eritrea had a unicameral legislative assembly of fifty to seventy members democratically elected by male citizens who had attained the age of twenty-one years.[170] The assembly voted on laws, as well as amendments to the constitution. These amendments, however, could not contradict the Federal Act; moreover, they required the approval of the emperor.[171]

The assembly also elected the chief executive and could submit questions to him, including a request for a debate on the government's policy.[172] However, once elected, the chief executive could not be removed by a vote of no-confidence. In budgetary matters, the assembly had large powers of decision and supervision.[173]

The executive and administrative functions were entrusted to the chief executive, elected by the local assembly by a two-thirds majority.

Only Eritrean citizens who had attained the age of thirty-five years were eligible for that office. The appointment did not require the approval of the Ethiopian authorities. The chief executive could appoint and dismiss secretaries of executive departments, without the approval of the assembly. In addition to his executive functions, he had the authority to issue temporary orders when the assembly was not in session, to be reviewed later by the assembly. The latter could also authorize the chief executive to restrict human rights temporarily in case of emergency.[174] Due to the chief executive's extensive powers, the regime has been described as a semipresidential system.[175]

Eritrea had its own judiciary, not subject to appeal to the Ethiopian courts.[176] The courts were to "apply the various systems of law in force in Eritrea," probably meaning the laws of the central Eritrean government and the customary or tribal laws of the various communities.[177] The Supreme Court was given jurisdiction over disputes concerning the constitutionality of laws and orders.[178]

The Federal Act did not mention the representation of the central Ethiopian government in Eritrea. The constitution, however, dealt with the subject. The emperor was to be represented by a person—the enderasse—who would have mainly ceremonial functions: He invested in office and took the oath of the chief executive and administered the oath of the secretaries of executive departments; he was authorized to deliver a speech at the opening and closing sessions of the assembly; and he had to promulgate laws adopted by the assembly. His main material power was the authority to request a reconsideration of laws that he thought encroached upon federal jurisdiction.[179] The appointment of the emperor's representative did not require approval by the Eritrean authorities. As already mentioned, it has been claimed that it was the unwarranted increase of the enderasse's powers and his abuse of these powers that eventually destroyed Eritrea's autonomy.

Eritrea was also to have an advisory council, a group of experts who would give advice and plan for economic and social progress. The Federal Act provided for the establishment of "[a]n Imperial Federal Council composed of equal numbers of Ethiopian and Eritrean representatives." The council was to "meet at least once a year and . . . advise upon the common affairs of the Federation."[180] A council that meets so rarely can hardly be considered a satisfactory joint organ.

A few substantive rules included in the Federal Act and in the constitution should be mentioned. Eritrea was to be based on the principles of democracy, the rule of law, and human rights.[181] Most residents of Eritrea acquired Ethiopian citizenship and, in addition, were to be Eritrean citizens in accordance with a law to be adopted.[182] Eritreans were to respect the federal flag and also to have their own flag, seal, and coat of arms.[183] The official languages were Tigrinya and Arabic, but the languages spoken by the various population groups were also to be permitted for use in dealing with the public authorities, as well as for religious and educational purposes.[184] Each group was subject to its own legislation governing personal status, legal capacity, family law, and the law of succession.[185] Eritreans were promised that they would participate in the public life of the federation.[186]

Ethiopia and Eritrea (the "Federation") constituted a single area for customs purposes. Revenue from customs duties for goods whose origin or destination was Eritrea was to be assigned to Eritrea.[187] Unfortunately, neither the Federal Act nor the constitution of Eritrea established proper machinery for settling disputes arising out of claims of encroachment upon Eritrea's powers by Ethiopia.[188]

### Concluding Remarks

Because the Federal Act spoke of "an autonomous unit federated with Ethiopia," one may ask whether the Ethiopia-Eritrea relationship was a case of federalism or of autonomy.[189] Despite the use of the terms "federation," "federated," and "Federal Act," the relationship can hardly be considered as federal in nature. No federal institutions were established, except for the Imperial Federal Council, which had only advisory functions and was to meet "at least" once a year.[190] Neither a federal legislature nor a federal executive distinct from those of Ethiopia was established. No upper house or federal organ for settling disputes existed. It thus appears that despite the use of the ambiguous "federal" expressions, Eritrea had the status of an autonomous area, not of a federated district.

The basic texts established an autonomy with large powers, encompassing legislation, administration, and adjudication in a great number of spheres, including residual powers. Of special interest are the arrangements respecting the great ethnic, linguistic, and religious heterogeneity of the country. The use of an unlimited number of languages was permitted "in dealing with the public authorities, as well as for religious or educational purposes and for all forms of expression of ideas."[191] Similarly, personal autonomy in matters of personal status was assured.[192] In addition, traditional land rights of the tribes and various population groups were protected against discrimination.[193]

The regime certainly had shortcomings. It lacked a mechanism to settle disputes. Moreover, while there was a limited means of preventing an excess of power by Eritrea, there was no remedy for such an excess by Ethiopia. In addition, the joint organ of consultation was not fit to address all the needs of coordination and cooperation.

It seems, however, that there were other reasons not related to the modalities of the autonomy itself that led to its failure. First, the difference of regime in the two partners probably undermined the arrangement: Ethiopia was an absolute monarchy and later a communist dictatorship, while Eritrea strove to be a democratic entity.[194] There were also political reasons not directly related to the two systems of government. The pan-Arab movement in the 1950s and 1960s may have encouraged the Eritreans to settle for nothing less than independence, while Ethiopia feared that such a secession not only would leave it without an outlet to the sea but also would encourage secession by other parts of Ethiopia. Probably, the basic condition for the success of any autonomy was missing: the joint wish for compromise and reconciliation. Because autonomy is, by its very nature, based on cooperation and coordination, it cannot succeed if the parties are unable to overcome their animosity.

### E. PUERTO RICO

In Puerto Rico the advantages and disadvantages of the regime of autonomy, which has been in force since 1952, are constantly a subject for public debate, arousing more discussion than in many other cases of autonomy.[195] By a decreasing majority, the electorate has expressed its continued preference for this system in several referenda, the most recent one held on 14 November 1993.[196]

#### Historical Background

The Commonwealth of Puerto Rico includes four small islands in the Caribbean: Puerto Rico, Vieques, Culebra, and Mona, with an area of about 3,435 square miles (8,959 square kilometers).[197] A large majority of the 3.6 million inhabitants reside on Puerto Rico, a very densely populated island.

Various cultural influences can be discerned among the population. There are traces of the local Taino Indian heritage and of the African heritage transmitted by the slaves (slavery was abolished in 1873). A much stronger influence has been the Spanish and Latin American culture. During the present century, the influence of the United States has also been felt. Most of the inhabitants of Puerto Rico are of the Catholic faith, and the predominant language is Spanish.

The area was claimed for Spain by Christopher Columbus, and it was under Spanish rule for about four hundred years. During various periods in the nineteenth century Puerto Rico enjoyed an autonomous or semiautonomous status, and in 1897 Spain granted the island a significant charter of self-rule.[198]

Very soon after the establishment of this self-rule, during the Spanish-American war, the island was conquered by the United States; by the 1898 Treaty of Peace of Paris[199] Spain ceded Puerto Rico to the United States. The military government, which ruled the country after the war, was replaced in 1900 by a civilian one established in pursuance of the Foraker Act (1900) adopted by the U.S. Congress.[200]

Under the regime established by this act, most power was concentrated in the hands of Americans appointed by the president of the United States. The act reserved to Congress the power to annul any locally adopted legislation and declared that all federal legislation—with the exception of laws concerning internal revenue and those considered by the U.S. Congress to be "locally inapplicable"—would be in force in Puerto Rico. In this early period the United States also tried to impose the English language on the local population. However, Puerto Rico was granted certain benefits in the economic sphere, which to some extent are still enjoyed to this day: free trade with the mainland (although at the start some nominal tariff was imposed), exemption from federal taxes, and the refund to Puerto Rico's treasury of sums collected by the United States as federal excise taxes on the importation from the island to the mainland of rum and tobacco. These benefits were granted to Puerto Rico to fight poverty on the island.

Soon after the adoption of the Foraker Act, the status of Puerto Rico was discussed by the U.S. Supreme Court in the famous *Insular* cases.[201] Under the Constitution of the United States,

[t]he Congress shall have Power to dispose of and make all needful Rules and Regulations respecting the Territory or other Property

belonging to the United States; and nothing in this Constitution shall be so construed as to Prejudice any Claims of the United States, or of any particular State.[202]

By virtue of this provision, which came to be known as the "territory clause," the courts recognized that Congress had much more extensive powers of control over territories than over states of the Union.[203] The courts, however, distinguished between two groups of "territories": (1) incorporated ones, to whose inhabitants the provisions of the U.S. constitution were fully applicable and which were destined to become states; and (2) unincorporated territories whose residents were to enjoy only certain fundamental individual rights and which were not destined to become states. As it was stated in one of the *Insular* cases, while the incorporated territory is treated "as to be in all respects a part of the United States," the unincorporated territory is not recognized "as an integral part of the United States."[204]

Under the *Insular* cases, Puerto Rico was considered to be an unincorporated territory. Hence, certain guarantees of the U.S. constitution did not apply to it, such as the right to citizenship, the right to trial by jury, and the right to indictment by a grand jury. This inferior status—"separate but unequal," in the words of one expert[205]—caused much frustration and resentment on the island.

On the other hand, if Puerto Rico had not been unincorporated, it could not have benefited from an exemption from federal taxes, because for a state of the Union to receive such treatment would have been contrary to the "uniformity clause" of the constitution under which "[t]he Congress shall have Power To lay and collect Taxes, Duties, Imposts and Excises . . . ; but all Duties, Imposts and Excises shall be uniform throughout the United States."[206] Since this provision was not considered a fundamental aspect of the constitution, it did not apply to Puerto Rico, an unincorporated territory.

In 1917 Congress passed the Jones Act,[207] which somewhat liberalized the regime in Puerto Rico in response to pressure from the population. This act included a bill of rights for the island; it granted U.S. citizenship to the residents;[208] and it increased the role of the local population in the designation of the various local organs of government.

The acquisition of U.S. citizenship was generally welcomed by the population, although there were also some who were not in favor of such a move. Despite the acquisition of citizenship, the Puerto Ricans were not granted the right to vote for Congress or for the president of the United States. They may only elect a Resident Commissioner, who represents the island in the U.S. House of Representatives without the right to vote. Moreover, Puerto Rico continued to be considered an "unincorporated" territory;[209] for Alaska, however, it was concluded that with the acquisition of citizenship, the territory had become incorporated.[210]

Puerto Rico was a very poor country when it was occupied by the United States. Until the early 1940s, it was mainly an agricultural society, growing sugar, tobacco, and coffee. In the early and mid-1920s there was significant economic progress, but in the late 1920s and the early 1930s the situation worsened again. The economic condition and the frustration over the status of an unincorporated territory led to an upsurge of nationalism, which was accompanied by acts of violence and of sabotage.

In 1947 the U.S. Congress enacted that henceforth the people of Puerto Rico should elect their governor.[211] Luis Muñoz Marín, who was elected in 1948, decided that improving the economy was a more urgent goal than dealing with the status of Puerto Rico. During his tenure Spanish was established as the language of instruction in local schools, but English was taught as a subject. Land reform was implemented and foreign investment and industrialization were encouraged. Between 1948 and 1967 the Puerto Rican economy progressed considerably.

Many Puerto Ricans continued to strive for greater autonomy, and their wish was fulfilled in the early 1950s: Congress passed Public Law 600,[212] recognizing the right to self-government of the people of Puerto Rico and the principle of government by consent. Congress described this law as a compact, which should be submitted to the Puerto Ricans for approval by a referendum.[213] In the wake of that approval, an elected Puerto Rican constitutional convention drafted a constitution. The only restrictions originally imposed by Congress were that a republican form of government should be established and that the constitution should include a bill of rights. The constitution had to be—and was—approved by both a local referendum and by the U.S. Congress. Upon the request of the latter, certain changes were made in the original text.[214] Those parts of the 1917 Jones Act that were not abrogated by Congress were included in the Puerto Rican Federal Relations Act.[215] The constitution that established the Commonwealth of Puerto

Rico was adopted in 1952 by a referendum,[216] despite acts of violence on both the island and the mainland.

This new regime received the blessing of the UN General Assembly.[217] In 1953 the latter expressed the opinion that "the Association of the Commonwealth of Puerto Rico with the United States of America has been established as a mutually agreed association" and that "the people of the Commonwealth of Puerto Rico have effectively exercised their right to self-determination." Moreover, the General Assembly recognized that

> the people of the Commonwealth of Puerto Rico have been invested with attributes of political sovereignty which clearly identify the status of self-government attained by the Puerto Rican people as that of an autonomous political entity.[218]

Hence, the United States was freed from the obligation to submit reports to the United Nations about Puerto Rico as a "non-self-governing territory" under Article 73e of the UN Charter.[219] Later, however, the UN Special Committee on Decolonization affirmed that the Declaration on Decolonization[220] did apply to Puerto Rico.[221] Probably these later resolutions were prompted by the Cold War, and the representatives of the United States strongly objected to those affirmations.[222]

Puerto Ricans have gone to the polls three times—in 1951, 1967, and 1993—to decide whether they should remain a commonwealth, become a state of the Union, or attain independence. Various presidents of the United States have declared prior to those referenda that they would respect the wishes of the people of Puerto Rico and would advise Congress accordingly.[223] So far, the citizens have voted to continue the status established in 1952, although with a decreasing majority.[224] Many have favored a "perfected" commonwealth—that is, one with certain improvements.[225]

### The Regime of Autonomy

The autonomy of Puerto Rico must be studied on the basis of the texts adopted in 1950–52 mentioned above and, of course, in view of various court cases and the economic and social conditions.

The powers of the commonwealth resemble those of a state of the Union: that is, Puerto Rico has jurisdiction over local matters, including large parts of criminal law and the administration of justice, civil law (including property, marriage, and divorce), various forms of licensing, matters of education, health, environmental protection, and social services. It also has the power to levy taxes and other fees. The federal government, on the other hand, has powers in Puerto Rico similar to those it exercises in the fifty states of the Union and the District of Columbia—namely, foreign affairs, defense, immigration, border control, interstate and foreign commerce, bankruptcy, monetary and currency policy, postal services, weights and measures, patents and copyright, customs control, and jurisdiction to deal with crimes against the United States. As stated above, in the states of the Union the federal government may also levy taxes for federal purposes on the condition that it does not discriminate among the states, but Puerto Rico has been exempted from this burden.

Although the division of powers between the federal government and the government of the commonwealth resembles the division between the federal authorities and the states of the Union, Puerto Rico's status is quite different from that of a state (as discussed below). The principles that are usually enumerated as the basic pillars in the U.S.-Puerto Rico relationship are common citizenship, common market, common currency, and common defense.

Laws adopted by the island's legislature do not require approval by Congress or the president, and they are not subject to presidential veto. Statutory laws of the United States that are "not locally inapplicable" will, subject to certain exceptions, be in force in Puerto Rico,[226] as in the other parts of the United States. It may be assumed that Congress will not legislate on a matter that is within the local authority of Puerto Rico. It seems possible, however, that an act of the U.S. Congress may override a local legislative act—a situation which Puerto Ricans resent. One of the famous cases in this sphere—*United States v. Quiñones*[227]—concerned the admissibility in evidence of consensually monitored telephone conversations: Wire tapping is absolutely prohibited under the Puerto Rican constitution, but it may be permissible in certain circumstances under a specific federal law. In this case, the court held that the provisions of the federal act prevailed over the Puerto Rican constitution. A similar conclusion would probably have been reached if the constitution of a state had been involved.

Sometimes the Supreme Court of the United States approaches matters related to Puerto Rico with the assumption that the powers and rights of the island and its inhabitants are similar to those of a state of the Union,[228] but in other instances it has approved federal acts that involved unequal treatment for the commonwealth. Thus, although a great number of unemployed and low-income Puerto Rican families receive considerable aid from Washington, they receive lower subsidies than residents of a state under various programs (such as medicaid, National Assistance Program, elementary and secondary education, Supplemental Security Income, food stamps, Aid to Families with Dependent Children, and Aid to the Elderly, the Blind, and the Handicapped). The courts have confirmed the legality of such unequal treatment.[229]

The governmental organs of Puerto Rico are quite similar to those of a state of the Union: Puerto Ricans elect their own governor without need for any confirmation by the central authorities.[230] Similarly, they vote for their bicameral legislature; the House of Representatives has fifty-one members and the Senate twenty-seven members.[231] The governor appoints the judges and cabinet secretaries with the advice and consent of the Senate.[232] He also approves or disapproves joint resolutions and bills passed by the legislative assembly.[233] None of the various appointments requires approval from Washington. All Puerto Rican public officials must take an oath to support the constitution of the United States as well as the laws and constitution of Puerto Rico.[234]

Although Puerto Rico has its own locally appointed judiciary, judgments of the island's supreme court may be appealed to the Supreme Court of the United States. The latter, however, has decided that it will not interfere in the interpretation of the local law adopted by the Puerto Rico Supreme Court unless that interpretation is "inescapably wrong" and the decision is "patently erroneous."[235]

In addition to Puerto Rico's own courts, the U.S. District Court for the District of Puerto Rico is located in San Juan; it has jurisdiction similar to that of federal courts in the states of the Union.[236]

The Puerto Rico Federal Relations Act has granted to the island "harbor areas and navigable streams and bodies of water and submerged land underlying the same in and around the Island of Puerto Rico and the adjacent islands and waters" not reserved by the United States for public purposes.[237]

The relevant texts also include several provisions concerning economic matters, similar to those applicable in the period before commonwealth status was granted:

- free trade between Puerto Rico and the mainland, with no tariffs;
- equal tariffs for imports into Puerto Rico and the mainland on all items, except coffee imported from abroad;
- exemption of Puerto Rico from federal internal revenue laws;
- the possessions tax credit (known as the "Section 936" exemption), which defers tax on income derived from Puerto Rico and other U.S. possessions until the income is received in the United States;
- no export duties levied on exports from Puerto Rico;
- excise taxes on goods transported from Puerto Rico to the United States and customs duties collected in Puerto Rico on foreign imports returned to the Puerto Rican treasury; and
- exemption from federal taxation of bonds issued by the government of Puerto Rico.[238]

Puerto Rico has two official languages: English and Spanish.[239] Since most of the inhabitants are more versed in Spanish, the role of Spanish has gradually increased. As already mentioned, since 1949 Spanish has been the teaching language in public schools and is used in the Puerto Rican courts. In the U.S. District Court English is still the required language,[240] but attempts are being made to introduce translations and to permit certain proceedings to be conducted in Spanish. A member of the legislative assembly has to be able to read and write in either Spanish or English.[241] The great majority of Puerto Ricans apparently wish to preserve the Spanish language and culture, while at the same time enjoying the "coexistence in Puerto Rico of the two great cultures of the American Hemisphere," as mentioned in the preamble to the constitution. Citizens of the United States who have resided in Puerto Rico for one year shall also be citizens of Puerto Rico.[242]

Puerto Ricans feel rather frustrated in the sphere of political participation. They may not vote for the U.S. Congress nor for the president of the United States. They may, however, participate in the vote to nominate presidential candidates of the political parties.[243] Their elected resident commissioner represents Puerto Rico in the House of Representatives in Washington, D.C., but without the right to vote. The commissioner may, however, participate actively in the work of various committees and subcommittees and may introduce legislation. There is no representation whatsoever of Puerto Rico in the U.S. Senate.

The lack of a meaningful political participation is even more frustrating because the people of Puerto Rico have had U.S. citizenship since 1917. They may freely travel to the mainland, and, once there, they have full political rights (that is, the right to vote and to run for office, like all other U.S. citizens).

An important area in which Washington and San Juan do not share the same opinion is international relations. There is no provision on that subject in the relevant documents. The island has a certain standing in some nongovernmental matters; for instance, it has its own Olympic team and its own candidates for the Miss Universe competition. In political matters, however, the United States restricts the island considerably. The State Department does not object to the opening of exclusively commercial, tourism, or trade promotion offices abroad, but no political, diplomatic, or consular functions are permissible.[244] Practically, it may be difficult to abide by this distinction, because nowadays political and economic matters are often interrelated. The United States does not permit Puerto Rico to conclude international agreements, as demonstrated by the 1986 refusal of the secretary of state to allow Puerto Rico to enter into a tax treaty with Japan.[245] It seems that with regard to the conclusion of international agreements, Puerto Rico has been restricted even more than the states of the Union: Although the latter are formally precluded from concluding agreements with other countries without the consent of Congress,[246] in fact they have sometimes been permitted to enter into agreements without such consent.[247] Moreover, other associated states—such as the Marshall Islands and the Federated States of Micronesia—are authorized to conclude at least certain categories of agreements. Foreign relations is certainly one area where Puerto Rico strives for changes in its commonwealth status.[248]

Puerto Rico has experienced considerable economic problems.[249] As noted above, in the years 1947–74 the economy made great progress because of certain policies: industrialization and attraction of private investments from the United States with the help of various arrangements: the exemption from federal income tax; the (former) exception from the application of the U.S. minimum wages; the common market with the United States; the possessions tax credit—the "Section 936" exemption;[250] and the Industrial Tax Exemption Act of 1948, by which Puerto Rico itself granted an exemption to manufacturers of certain items.[251] These various incentives attracted a considerable number of firms to the island, thus creating a number of new jobs. However, it seems that the advantage caused by foreign enterprises has diminished: Whereas in the past, labor-intensive industry was attracted (for example, manufacturers of textiles, leather, and clothing), at a later stage the industries were capital-intensive ones (such as petrochemicals, pharmaceuticals, and electronics). With relatively few employees, capital-intensive industries do not contribute much to relieving unemployment on the island.[252]

Puerto Rico's economy has deteriorated since the 1970s. Some of the above-mentioned incentives have undergone changes or have ceased to achieve the desired effect. In particular, the benefits under "Section 936" have been reduced, and the federal government has even considered abolishing this provision—a proposal to which Puerto Rico, of course, objects. Various other incentives have also gradually eroded: The general reduction of tariffs has reduced Puerto Rico's comparative advantage; the minimum wage on the island has been increased to the mainland standard; and federal environmental standards have increased local business expenses. The increase of petroleum prices in the early 1970s and the world recession in the 1980s have also aggravated Puerto Rico's economic situation. Reduction of taxes in the United States during the Reagan administration reduced Puerto Rico's attraction for mainland capital. Later the Caribbean Basin Initiative, which increased the number of countries with free access to the U.S. market, further weakened Puerto Rico's comparative advantage. As a result, the population has become more and more dependent on grants and assistance from the federal government.[253] It thus seems that although commonwealth status brought economic progress in its early years, this "miracle" did not last.

As with other cases studied in this volume, the procedure for changing the autonomy arrangements has to be examined. The constitution of Puerto Rico addresses the matter:

> No amendment to this Constitution shall alter the republican form of government established by it or abolish its Bill of Rights. Any amendment or revision of this Constitution shall be consistent with the resolution enacted by the Congress of the United States approving this Constitution, with the applicable provisions of the Constitution of the United States, with the Puerto Rican Federal Relations Act, and with Public Law 600, of the Eighty-first Congress, adopted in the nature of a compact.[254]

The second sentence of this provision was added to the constitution at the request of the United States.[255] This provision considerably restricts the powers of Puerto Rico to change its constitution: Any change that does not conform with the various documents mentioned in the text would require the assent of the U.S. Congress. In other words, a change in the commonwealth status has to be approved both by the central authorities in Washington and by those in San Juan. The text hints that the reason for limiting the freedom of action of the island in this sphere lies in the fact that the above arrangements were adopted as a compact, which implies the need for mutual consent for introducing changes. As mentioned, however, several U.S. presidents have declared that if Puerto Rico expresses the wish to change its status, the president will recommend that Congress agree to the change.[256]

Having studied various aspects of Puerto Rico's autonomy, one may now ask the more general questions about its status. Some pronouncements of the U.S. courts have emphasized the special status of Puerto Rico resulting from the compact relationship. Others have compared Congress's powers over the island to those it has over states of the Union: "Puerto Rico, like a state, is an autonomous political entity, sovereign over matters not ruled by the Constitution."[257] Other pronouncements have also used the term sovereign or sovereignty: "The Commonwealth of Puerto Rico is a body politic which has received, through a compact with the Congress of the United States, full sovereignty over its internal affairs."[258] Similarly, the Court of Appeals recognized Puerto Rico's "sovereign status and functional independence from Congressional control."[259]

Nevertheless, in other cases Puerto Rico has been treated as a mere "territory" for certain purposes.[260]

With such divergent pronouncements, one tends to agree with those authors who maintain that "its status is ambiguous,"[261] that a "complex and contradictory picture of Puerto Rico's status emerges from the perspectives of U.S. government agencies and particularly the Federal Congress."[262] This ambiguity is also apparent in Puerto Rico's name: in English, it is Commonwealth; in Spanish, Estado Libre Asociado (free associated state). When the Constitutional Convention of Puerto Rico dealt with the question of the name in 1952, it made the following declaration:

> Whereas, the word "commonwealth" in contemporary English usage means a politically organized community, that is to say, a state (using

the word in the generic sense) in which political power resides ultimately in the people, hence a free state, but one which is at the same
time linked to a broader political system in a federal or other type
of association and therefore does not have independent and separate
existence; . . .

Whereas, in the case of Puerto Rico the most appropriate translation of "commonwealth" into Spanish is the expression of "estado
libre asociado", which however should not be rendered "associated
free state" in English inasmuch as the word "state" in ordinary speech
in the United States means one of the States of the Union. . . .[263]

The term commonwealth is generally used in various contexts with
differing meanings. Thus, the Commonwealth of Nations is the term
used to denote the loose association between Britain and its former
colonies that are now fully independent. The Commonwealth of Independent States denotes the relationship among some of the states that
became independent when the Soviet Union broke up. On the other
hand, certain states of the Union of the United States are called com-
monwealths (for example, the Commonwealth of Virginia). The
Northern Marianas islands in the Pacific Ocean, formerly under U.S.
trusteeship, have become a "Commonwealth in Political Union with
the United States of America" by a "Covenant" of 1975. In this last case
the term commonwealth has a meaning somewhat similar to that used
to describe Puerto Rico.

It thus seems that in the context of

> insular political communities affiliated with the United States, the
> concept of a "commonwealth" anticipates a substantial amount of
> self-government (over internal matters) and some degree of auton-
> omy on the part of the entity so designated. The commonwealth
> derives its authority not only from the United States Congress, but
> also by the consent of the citizens of the entity. The commonwealth
> concept is a flexible one designed to allow both the entity and the
> United States to adjust the relationship as appropriate over time.[264]

The Spanish name, on the other hand, refers to associated statehood.[265] However, the drafters of the constitution did not use the exact
English translation in order to avoid the impression that Puerto Rico
was to be a state of the Union. A careful study of Puerto Rico led W.
Michael Reisman to the conclusion that Puerto Rico is an associated
state,[266] while Daniel Elazar considers it a "federacy."[267]

## Concluding Remarks

As in most other cases so far studied, the development of autonomy in Puerto Rico was influenced by the geographic, demographic, and economic situation of the area. The Puerto Ricans have a long-standing tradition of autonomy, which grew into commonwealth status, or associate statehood, in 1952. It is a case of considerable internal self-government accompanied by political inequality on the one hand, and economic preferences on the other hand.

Of special interest is the fact that Puerto Rico is an autonomous area linked to a federal state, a situation which invites a comparison between federalism and autonomy.[268] This characteristic has also led to some confusion in practice, because courts, legislators, and politicians have had some difficulty in distinguishing clearly between the two situations. Should Puerto Rico have fewer powers and rights than a state of the Union in the various fields, or more, or perhaps the same?

The wishes of the Puerto Ricans to preserve both their special culture and the economic benefits of this relationship with the United States while striving for political equality have played a crucial role in the debate about status: Those who strive for independence believe that independence is the way to preserve the national identity of Puerto Rico, and they would sacrifice the benefits involved in the relationship with the United States. Those who prefer statehood (that is, merging with the United States) wish to end the political inequality while keeping the benefits involved in the connection to the United States, even though statehood could mean giving up (at least to a certain extent) their Spanish heritage and the economic preferences. Those who favor continuing the commonwealth status think that this is the best way to preserve the national identity and the economic advantages. They would, however, try to eliminate the political inequality and increase the scope of the autonomy.

However, the alternatives open to the Puerto Ricans may perhaps be more encouraging. Statehood within the United States could probably be reconciled with a preservation of the Spanish heritage. Moreover, the economic disadvantage of losing the exemption from certain taxes[269] may be offset by increased welfare assistance from Washington, to which Puerto Rico would be entitled as a state of the Union.[270] On the other hand, commonwealth status does not have to involve political inequality. Since Puerto Ricans have U.S. citizenship, Congress could easily authorize them to participate in the vote for the federal institutions. Moreover, a more active role in international relations could also be reconciled with commonwealth status. The benefits of each option depend on the specifications attached to it.

The debate in Puerto Rico is sure to continue.

## F. GREENLAND/KALAALLIT NUNAAT

Greenland is the largest island in the world, with an area of 2,175,000 square kilometers, of which 83 percent is permanently under an ice cap 3 kilometers thick.[271] The population of around 55,000 (in 1993) is predominantly Inuit (Eskimo), and the rest (about 20 percent) are Danes. The main sources of livelihood are hunting, fishing, and sheep breeding. Since 1979 the Greenlanders have been enjoying autonomy ("home rule"). This case is particularly interesting because of its great success and because it concerns an indigenous population.

### Historical Background

Greenland has been linked to the Danish Crown since the fourteenth century; it was definitely colonized in the beginning of the eighteenth century, after the arrival of Hans Egede, a Danish missionary. Greenland was administered from Copenhagen, but in the second half of the nineteenth century organs of local government were established—first municipal councils and later also provincial ones.

During World War II, while Denmark was under German occupation, Greenland was under U.S. control and opened up to the surrounding world. After the war, the island was restored to Denmark, but it was felt that its status deserved to be changed. Thus, under the new 1953 Danish constitution, Greenland ceased to be a colony and became an integral part of the Danish Realm, with equal rights. This development and the satisfaction about it expressed by representatives of Greenland at the United Nations prompted the General Assembly to declare in 1954 that the island was no longer a non-self-governing territory for which the administering power had to submit reports to the organization.[272]

Although Greenland was a fully integrated part of the realm, the constitution and several laws of Denmark provided special rules for the island (for instance, the 1954 Greenland Criminal Code), adapted to its conditions and circumstances.[273] The formal integration was followed by an ambitious development program intended to bring Greenland to a standard of living equal to that of mainland Denmark.

In the 1960s and 1970s the Greenlanders developed a wish for more influence upon the future of the island. This trend evolved from tension between Denmark and Greenland caused by social uneasiness that grew as a result of the rapid development and modernization. In addition, Greenland was dissatisfied with having to become a part of the European Community because of Denmark's admission in 1973, and with the granting of some concessions for the exploitation of minerals not far from the island's coast.

After a request by the Greenland Provincial Council, a committee and later a joint commission were established. The latter's conclusions prompted the Danish parliament—the Folketing—to adopt in 1978 the Greenland Home Rule Act.[274] After its approval by a referendum held in Greenland, the act entered into force on 1 May 1979.

In a later (1982) referendum, the majority of the islanders voted in favor of withdrawal from the European Community.[275] Upon its withdrawal in 1985, Greenland became associated with the EC within the framework of the regime of Overseas Countries and Territories (OCT).[276]

### The Regime of Autonomy

The concept of Greenland's home rule is largely influenced by the model of the Faroe Islands, which were granted autonomy by Denmark in 1948 (see the discussion above).[277] However, the practical differences between the two cases—the economic situation, the level of education, communications, and climatic conditions—had to be taken into consideration.

The basic philosophy of the home rule arrangements has been defined by the Commission on Home Rule in Greenland as follows:

The Greenlanders are fighting not for national independence but for an identity of their own, or rather for better possibilities of strengthening and developing their identity through increased self-responsibility.[278]

This idea has found expression in Section 1(1) of the Home Rule Act:

Greenland is a distinct community within the Kingdom of Denmark. Within the framework of the unity of the Realm, the Greenland home rule authorities shall conduct Greenland affairs in accordance with the provisions laid down in this Act.

Three principles derive from this provision: (1) the unity of the realm is recognized; (2) so is the fact that Greenland is nevertheless a distinct community; and (3) home rule is established. The unity of the realm implies that sovereignty resides with the central authorities in Copenhagen, and hence certain powers inherent in sovereignty cannot be transferred to Greenland. This unity probably also implies an assumption of mutual solidarity.[279] The purely domestic nature of the home rule and the supremacy of Denmark are also reflected in the fact that the regime was established by a Danish act—although approved by the local population—with no international agreement and no involvement of any international institution.

A special feature of Greenland's home rule is the staged transfer of powers, which gives the island time to prepare for the additional burdens and responsibilities involved in each group of powers. In particular, the transfer was synchronized with the financial potential to assume the relevant responsibilities. The schedule to the Home Rule Act enumerates seventeen spheres in which powers may be transferred:

1. Organization of home rule in Greenland
2. Organization of local government
3. Direct and indirect taxes
4. The Established Church and dissentient religious communities
5. Fishing in the territory, hunting, agriculture and reindeer breeding
6. Conservation
7. Country planning
8. Legislation governing trade and competition, including legislation on restaurant and hotel business, regulations governing alcoholic beverages, and regulations governing closing hours of shops
9. Social welfare
10. Labour market affairs
11. Education and cultural affairs, including vocational education
12. Other matters relating to trade, including State-conducted fishing and production; support and development of economic activities
13. Health services
14. Rent legislation, rent support, and housing administration

15. Supply of goods
16. Internal transport of passengers and goods
17. Protection of the environment[280]

This is a typical list of economic, social, and cultural affairs.

The act distinguishes among several modalities for transferring powers. In spheres for which Greenland has the financial means to assume responsibility, powers are fully or partly transferred, either at the request of the home rule authorities[281] or at the initiative of Denmark after consultation with the home rule authorities.[282] In areas where Greenland assumes the financial burden, the local legislature has the power to adopt acts.[283]

In those spheres that require subsidies from Denmark, the transfer of powers requires a specific authorizing act of the Folketing for each sphere.[284] In this act, the national parliament also establishes a framework of basic principles to which Greenland has to conform.[285] The special authorizing acts should be preceded by negotiations between Greenland and Denmark, negotiations addressing the extent of the powers to be transferred, the timing of the transfer, and the size of the subsidy.[286] Rules enacted by the Greenland legislature on these matters are not called acts, but are designated "regulations," since the drafters of the Home Rule Act were of the opinion that the power of legislation also requires the assumption of fiscal responsibility.[287] By 1992, all the powers enumerated in the Home Rule Act had been transferred,[288] some with subsidies and others without.

The Home Rule Act does not preclude the transfer of additional powers not mentioned in the act. However, such a transfer requires prior agreement between Denmark and Greenland and has to be effected by an act of the Danish Folketing.[289] In determining in which fields jurisdiction should be transferred, "regard shall be had to the unity of the Realm and to the desirability of the home rule authorities' receiving an extensive role in matters which particularly affect Greenland interests."[290] In this category of powers to be transferred, the same distinction as mentioned above is made between a transfer with financial responsibility and a transfer requiring subsidies.

The act provides that the home rule authorities have legislative and executive power in the various areas in which powers were transferred, as well as financial responsibility (with or without subsidies).[291] Moreover, the laws enacted by the Greenland legislature in those spheres do not require approval by any Danish authority. However, the power of adjudication and enforcement is not included in the transfer. Although this power is reserved for Denmark, the courts system in Greenland is very different from the one that exists in Denmark, and it is mainly based on lay judges.[292]

In order to prevent undue influence by Copenhagen on Nuuk in the administration of powers transferred with subsidies, these subsidies are made in the form of a block grant that the home rule authorities may largely use without interference by state authorities.[293] The sum of the subsidy is established for a three-year period and has to be renegotiated periodically.

The act does not enumerate the powers that may not be transferred, except for foreign relations. However, the Commission on Home Rule in Greenland, in the summary of its report, mentioned the following as not transferable: "Constitutional matters, foreign affairs, central government finance, and defence."[294] The chairman of the commission, Professor Isi Foighel, gave a more detailed list in one of his articles:

> Constitutional law (including the highest branches of government, the right to vote at parliamentary elections as well as eligibility, the administration of justice, constitutional rights), external relations (including the treaty-making power), national finances (including the Central Bank and its functions), financial-, monetary-, and currency policy, defence policy, criminal proceedings and imprisonment, as well as fundamental principles regarding the law of persons, family law, inheritance law, and the law of contracts.[295]

The relationship between Denmark and Greenland involves the reciprocal consideration of each other's interests and joint consultation. Thus, when the home rule authorities consider measures "which would be of substantial importance for the foreign relations of the Realm, including participation by the Realm in international cooperation," these measures must be discussed with the central authorities before any decision is made.[296] On the other hand, the central authorities have to refer to the home rule authorities for their comment all legislative bills that include provisions that exclusively concern Greenland; this referral must take place before the bills are introduced into the Folketing.[297] A similar rule has been introduced for draft administrative orders.[298] Statutes and administrative orders that are of particular importance for Greenland, but do not concern the island exclusively, must be submitted to the home rule authorities before being put into force in Greenland (not necessarily prior to their adoption).[299] In general, the home rule authorities decide which statutes and orders are of particular importance for Greenland.[300] In fact, an increasing number of legislative bills and administrative orders are referred to the home rule authorities for their comments.[301]

This system of consultation and cooperation is particularly evident in the sphere of foreign relations. On the one hand, it was expressly stipulated that foreign relations are within the jurisdiction of the central authorities.[302] Moreover, the home rule authorities are subject to Denmark's international obligations—whether stemming from treaties or other sources—and powers delegated by Denmark to international authorities prevail over the powers of the home rule authorities[303] (probably a hint to the transfer of powers to the European Community). In addition, as just mentioned, Greenland must consult the central authorities before adopting measures "which would be of substantial importance for the foreign relations of the Realm."[304]

On the other hand, "treaties which require the assent of the Folketing and which particularly affect Greenland interests shall be referred to the home rule authorities for their comments before they are concluded."[305] This consultative procedure applies whether or not the treaty concerns a transferred field. Until such consultation has taken place, a reservation is usually made with regard to Greenland's participation in the treaty.[306]

Several means allow Greenland to take an active, though limited, part in foreign affairs. The islanders may demand that Danish diplomatic missions in countries in which Greenland has special commercial interests employ officers to look after those special interests.[307] The central authorities may authorize the home rule authorities to take part in international negotiations of particular importance for Greenland's commercial life,[308] and they even may authorize the islanders to negotiate directly, with the cooperation of the Danish Foreign Service.[309] For instance, representatives of Greenland often negotiate fisheries agreements with countries such as Russia and Canada.[310]

Greenland's de facto autonomy in the sphere of foreign relations was evident when the island was permitted to leave the European Community.[311] In recent years, Denmark has also included Greenlandic members in various delegations abroad (such as at the UN General Assembly).[312] The Danish delegation to the Nordic Council includes two Greenlandic members appointed by the legislative assembly in Nuuk, and the Greenland executive is an active participant in the work of the Nordic Council of Ministers, primarily in the areas of culture, education, and fishing.[313]

Denmark's special concern for Greenland's interests in the sphere of foreign relations was illustrated in the 1993 case concerning *Maritime Delimitation in the Area between Greenland and Jan Mayen (Denmark v. Norway)*,[314] decided by the International Court of Justice in The Hague. In this case Denmark protected Greenland's interests in the delimitation of the fishery zone and continental shelf area between Jan Mayen, which belongs to Norway, and Greenland.

Greenland has its own flag and its own language: "Greenlandic shall be the principal language,"[315] because the language "is an integral part of the way in which we conceive our own identity."[316] However, "Danish must be thoroughly taught,"[317] and "either language may be used for official purposes."[318] More recently, the study of English has also been introduced.

Of special interest to the Greenlanders have been the arrangements established in the sphere of natural resources, in particular minerals. The importance of the subject stems both from the possible financial gain involved and from the environmental consequences. The Home Rule Act has laid down three principles:[319]

- The resident population of Greenland has fundamental rights in respect to Greenland's natural resources.
- The exploration and exploitation of nonliving resources require agreement between Denmark and Greenland's executive (that is, a reciprocal right of veto has been introduced).
- Any member of Greenland's executive branch may submit an agreement that is under consideration to the island's legislative assembly, which may prevent the executive from consenting to that agreement.

The division of revenue was laid down in the Danish Act of Mineral Resources in Greenland of 1978, with later amendments of 1988: The revenue should first be used to compensate Denmark for previous transfers of subsidies. Additional sums should be divided equally between Greenland and Denmark, and sums in excess of DKr 500 million require additional negotiations.[320]

It is interesting to note that the parties have established a joint committee on mineral resources in Greenland to advise both the Danish and the Greenlandic executives. The committee is composed of an equal number of Danish and Greenlandic members.[321] In 1991 a new Act on Mineral Resources in Greenland was enacted. It articulates common policy for exploring and exploiting mineral resources and was endorsed by both the Greenland executive and the Danish government.[322]

When examining the institutional structure of the authorities, one finds that the Home Rule Act provides that "the . . . home rule authorities shall consist of an assembly elected in Greenland, to be called the Landsting, and an administration headed by a Landsstyre (Executive)."[323] The act lays down certain basic rules for the Landsting, namely, that it has to "be elected for a four-year term in general, direct and secret elections."[324] The Landsting itself has been authorized to legislate on detailed rules on the elections and to make its own standing orders.[325] The assembly has twenty-seven members, and it is in session twice a year for one month.[326] As mentioned, the laws enacted by the Landsting do not require approval from Copenhagen. The executive—the Landsstyre—is elected by the assembly,[327] and its members do not need confirmation by the central government. Similarly, the representative of Denmark in Greenland—the Rigsombudsman (commissioner)—does not need the approval of the home rule authorities. He may be invited to take part in the debates at the Landsting or the Landsstyre, and he has to be informed by home rule authorities of acts and regulations adopted by the Landsting.[328]

The Home Rule Act includes a provision for settling disputes that is identical to the one adopted for the Faroe Islands:[329] A special board should be established, consisting of two members to be appointed by the government of Denmark and two by the home rule authorities. In addition it should include three judges of the Danish Supreme Court to be appointed by the president of the court, who would also nominate one of those judges as chairman. Conflicts should first be handled by the representatives of the two parties, that is, by negotiations, but if no agreement is reached, the question should be decided by the three judges.[330] It is perhaps surprising that the final word has been given to an organ composed exclusively of Danish individuals. The matter is, however, of only theoretical importance since the mechanism has not yet been used, probably because disagreements are solved before they reach the stage of disputes.

Another matter of theoretical interest is whether or not Denmark may unilaterally repeal or amend the regime of home rule, without the consent of Greenland. Opinions on this matter are divided. According to some experts, due to the unity of the realm and to Danish sovereignty, "the Home Rule Government . . . is not . . . constitutionally protected against repeal of the Home Rule Act as such."[331] Others have expressed a somewhat different opinion:

> From the way that Home Rule has been established, that is:
>
> — prepared in a commission with a political composition,
> — the fact that the Greenland population approved by referendum the entering into force of the Home Rule Act,
> — the special and unusual preamble to the Home Rule Act, stating the special constitutional position of Greenland within the Realm,
>
> it follows that the Home Rule Act politically and morally is regarded as an agreement, that should not be changed by the Danish Parliament without the consent of Home Rule authorities, even if a unilateral change by Danish Parliament Act in theory might be regarded a possibility.[332]

The relevant provision of the just-mentioned preamble to the Home Rule Act says the following:

> Recognizing the exceptional position which Greenland occupies within the Realm nationally, culturally and geographically, the Folketing has in conformity with the decision of the Greenland Provincial Council passed . . . the following Act about the constitutional position of Greenland within the Realm.

This question, however, seems to be only theoretical as both Denmark and Greenland appear to be satisfied with their relationship.

### Concluding Remarks

As mentioned above, Greenland stands out as a successful case of autonomy, and it concerns an indigenous population. However, it is not a typical case of aboriginal autonomy because of several factors: the large concentration of members of the indigenous group so that they constitute a considerable majority, the well-defined geographical area, and the great distance from the mother country. Some experts are of the opinion that these same factors have also contributed to the success of the regime.[333] There are other helpful circumstances as well: the traditional Danish respect for human rights; the Danish tendency to grant local self-government to municipalities; the democratic nature of the regimes that exist in both Denmark and Greenland; the lack of affinity with a foreign country; and last but not least, the fact that home rule was established gradually.

It is remarkable that this case of autonomy has no international ingredient. Yet more interesting, perhaps, is the fact that, although Denmark retains sovereignty, it has not established any means of control and supervision with regard to those matters for which powers have been transferred.

To conclude, the term home rule should be examined. Isi Foighel, who chaired the Commission on Home Rule in Greenland, expressed the following opinion in two of his articles: "One may describe home rule as a particularly *qualified type of self-government.*"[334] This statement is followed by a comparison between home rule and municipal self-government. He did not distinguish between home rule and the general (nonmunicipal) notion of self-government or autonomy. It seems that there is no substantial difference between these notions. Perhaps the term home rule emphasizes the idea that only powers related to internal matters are transferred.

## G. THE PALESTINIANS (THE WEST BANK AND GAZA STRIP)

One of the most famous present-day attempts to establish autonomy (or self-government) concerns the Palestinians. Since 1977 various ideas of autonomy have been studied, suggested, and negotiated. However, it is only since 1993 that this solution has been put into effect.

During the British Mandate in Palestine (1923–48), all the inhabitants of that territory were called Palestinians, both Arabs and Jews. Since the establishment of the State of Israel (1948), however, the name has been used mainly for the Arab inhabitants of the West Bank and the Gaza Strip, as well as for Arab Palestinian refugees. Some authors also use the term for Arabs who live in Israel and have Israeli citizenship. This discussion will focus on the Palestinian Arabs who live in the West Bank and the Gaza Strip (about 1,800,000 in 1995). Opinions differ over the number of Palestinian refugees and displaced persons: In 1948 the number was about 400,000 according to some sources and 700,000 according to others; in 1950 the number of refugees registered with the United Nations Relief and Works Agency (UNRWA) was 960,021. By 1995 their number had grown to about 2.5 million; Israel's population at the end of 1994 was almost 5.5 million.[335]

The area for which autonomy has been foreseen is comprised of two regions: the West Bank and the Gaza Strip. The West Bank is the territory west of the Jordan River that had been part of mandatory Palestine and was annexed by Jordan after the 1948 war. Later, in 1967, it was occupied by Israel in the Six Day War. The West Bank covers about 5,612 square kilometers (2,200 square miles). The area is sometimes referred to as Judea and Samaria, its original geographical designation. The Gaza Strip was also part of mandatory Palestine; it was occupied by Egypt in 1948 and by Israel in 1967. Its area is 365 square kilometers (135 square miles). The area of Israel proper (within the 1949 armistice lines) is 20,770 square kilometers (8,017 square miles). Both the West Bank and the Gaza Strip are directly adjacent to Israel.

This case of autonomy differs in several ways from most of those so far studied. First, the regime has been foreseen to endure for a relatively brief period of five years. Second, it was preceded by a period of zero-sum attitudes, with each party denying the other's existence as a people. Third, unfortunately, vicious acts of violence and terror have been involved. Fourth, autonomy evolved out of a status of military occupation.

### Historical Background

From 1517 until 1918 Palestine (that is, the area known today as Israel, the West Bank and Gaza, and Jordan) was under Turkish rule, like most of the Middle East. During World War I it was occupied by Britain, which was later granted a mandate over the area. Under the Terms of the Mandate agreed upon in 1922 by Britain and the Council of the League of Nations, "the Mandatory shall be responsible for placing the country under such political, administrative and economic conditions as will secure the establishment of the Jewish national home . . . and the development of self-governing institutions, and also for safeguarding the civil and religious rights of all the inhabitants of Palestine, irrespective of race and religion."[336] Accordingly, Britain was to facilitate Jewish immigration and close settlement by Jews on the land,[337] as well as the acquisition of Palestinian citizenship by these incoming Jews.[338] At that time Palestine was inhabited by 757,200 persons, of whom 83,800 were Jews.[339]

In order to accommodate the wishes for self-determination of the non-Jewish inhabitants, Britain, with the consent of the Council of the League of Nations, decided to exclude the areas lying east of the

Jordan River from the application of the above provisions intended to promote Jewish immigration and settlement.[340] Much later this area became the Hashemite Kingdom of Jordan.

Despite some early attempts at cooperation,[341] the Arab national movement in Palestine objected to Jewish immigration to western Palestine and resorted to violence. Due to Arab pressure, in 1939 Britain severely limited both Jewish immigration and the areas where Jews were permitted to acquire land. The closing of the gates of Palestine and other countries deprived many of the Jews of Europe of an asylum from Nazi persecution.

After World War II, only a small number of the European Jews who had survived the Holocaust were permitted to enter Palestine, a fact which led Jews to commit acts of violence and terrorism against the Mandatory administration. In 1947 Britain asked the UN General Assembly to consider the Palestine question. In the same year the General Assembly adopted a resolution recommending the establishment in western Palestine of a Jewish and an Arab State, as well as a *corpus separatum* of Jerusalem with a special international regime to be administered by the United Nations.[342] This resolution received the consent of the national leadership of the Jewish community of Palestine[343] but was categorically rejected by the Arabs,[344] who immediately started to attack Jewish towns and villages.

On 14 May 1948, when the British Mandate over Palestine drew to its end, representatives of the Jewish community in Palestine proclaimed the establishment of the State of Israel.[345] The declaration was followed by an invasion of the new state by the armies of five Arab states. Because of the war, many Palestinian Arabs fled and some were expelled from areas that came under Jewish control. In parallel, about 586,000 Jews from Arab countries poured into Israel. The war ended with armistice agreements. The agreement between Israel and Jordan left the West Bank under Jordanian control[346] and the one with Egypt left the Gaza Strip under Egyptian control.[347] Jordan eventually annexed the West Bank;[348] the Gaza Strip remained under military occupation and in 1962 was granted limited autonomy by Egypt.

The formation of the Palestine Liberation Organization (PLO) was approved in 1964 by the first Arab summit conference. The PLO was intended to organize the Palestinians militarily and politically. Three years later the 1967 Six Day War broke out, and the West Bank and Gaza Strip came under Israeli occupation. These events prompted the PLO to amend its 1964 covenant. The covenant rejected the partition of Palestine; it preached the elimination of the State of Israel by violence and the establishment of a Palestinian state in the whole of Palestine.[349] The PLO is an umbrella organization that includes a number of Palestinian groups, the most important of them being Fatah, headed by Yassir Arafat. Although the organization resorted to cruel acts of terrorism, it was recognized by many states as a national liberation movement and in 1974 was granted observer status at the United Nations.[350]

A first attempt to solve the Palestinian problem by peaceful means was made by Egypt and Israel with the active mediation of U.S. president Jimmy Carter in one of the two 1978 Camp David Accords, "A Framework for Peace in the Middle East."[351] The two parties agreed to conduct negotiations for establishing a regime of full autonomy for five years for the Arab inhabitants of the West Bank and Gaza. Not later than the third year after the establishment of autonomy, negotiations would take place "to determine the final status" of these regions; simultaneously, negotiations would be conducted on a peace treaty between Israel and Jordan. The negotiations for establishing autonomy were to be conducted among Israel, Egypt, and Jordan. It was stipulated that the delegations of Egypt and Jordan "may include Palestinians" from the West Bank and Gaza or other Palestinians as mutually agreed. On the other hand, "the elected representatives" of the inhabitants of the territories would be authorized to take part in the negotiations on the final status of the region in their own right, meaning that the negotiations would be conducted among four parties: Egypt, Israel, Jordan, and the elected representatives from the West Bank and Gaza.

After the conclusion of the 1979 Treaty of Peace between Egypt and Israel,[352] the parties started negotiations on the establishment of autonomy for the Palestinians. These negotiations went on with many interruptions for about three years, but did not lead to an agreement. The main points of disagreement concerned the following questions:[353] Did the Camp David framework envisage a territorial or a personal autonomy? Should the autonomous self-governing authority have the power to make primary legislation, or only regulations? Should east Jerusalem be included in the autonomy arrangements? Who would be responsible for internal security—namely, the fight against terror? What should be the status of the Jewish settlements in the West Bank and Gaza? Who would retain the "source of authority" for the territories? How many organs and how many members should the self-governing authority have? What powers should be transferred from the Israeli military government to the Palestinian authority? In particular, how would powers in the spheres of water and land be divided between Israel and the Palestinians?

The differences of opinion on most of the issues appeared to stem from the parties' conflicting stands regarding the objective of the autonomy regime. Because Egypt saw autonomy as a transitional stage toward full self-determination (that is, toward an independent state), Cairo sought to assure from the beginning that the self-governing authority would possess powers that would lead it to independence. Israel's attitude was different, and it wished to leave all options open. It seems, however, that the failure of those negotiations was due mainly not to differences of opinion, but to the refusal of Jordan and the Palestinians to join in those negotiations.

A few attempts were later made to revive the Camp David formula—for example, President Reagan's initiative of 1982,[354] Secretary of State Shultz's plan of 1988,[355] and Israel's 1989 peace initiative.[356] However, none of them was successful.

In 1988 King Hussein of Jordan announced the disengagement of the West Bank from Jordan in the sphere of law and administration.[357] In the same year the Palestine National Council of the PLO proclaimed the establishment of the State of Falasteen (Palestine).[358] In a press conference Yassir Arafat hinted that the above-mentioned provisions of the Palestine National Covenant had become obsolete, and that a Palestinian state could exist in parallel with Israel.

In the wake of dramatic changes that had occurred in Eastern Europe and under the influence of the 1991 Gulf War, the United States and the Soviet Union invited all parties to the Arab-Israel conflict to the 1991 Madrid Peace Conference;[359] after that meeting negotiations began between Israel and each of its neighbors. In addition, a number of multilateral talks on concerns common to the peoples of the region were started in five working groups. According to the invitation to the conference, the first stage of negotiations with the Palestinians (who were part of a Jordanian delegation) was to address the establishment of interim self-government arrangements for a period of five years. Negotiations on the permanent status would begin in the third year of that regime.

Although the post-Madrid bilateral meetings took place between Israel and a Palestinian delegation that, upon Israel's demand, did not formally include representatives of the PLO, the PLO and Israel conducted secret negotiations in Oslo through the good offices of Norway's minister of foreign affairs. As a result, the parties exchanged letters of mutual recognition in 1993 and signed a Declaration of Principles on Interim Self-Government Arrangements.[360]

### The Regime of Autonomy

The 1993 Declaration of Principles has been the framework for all the negotiations that have since taken place between Israel and the Palestinians. According to the declaration, a timetable has been set for various sets of negotiations intended to lead to a staged transfer of powers from the Israeli military government to the Palestinians, accompanied by a withdrawal and redeployment of Israel's forces.

The first stage concerned the transfer, subject to certain limitations, of most powers in the Gaza Strip and the Jericho area—except for external security, Jewish settlements, Israelis, and foreign relations.[361] This stage, completed in May 1994,[362] also involved a substantial withdrawal and redeployment of Israel's army.

The second stage (not involving changes in the deployment of the army) concerned an early transfer of certain powers in the rest of the West Bank: education and culture, health, social welfare, direct taxation, and tourism.[363] The relevant agreement was signed in August 1994.[364] A year later another batch of powers was transferred: the spheres of labor, commerce and industry, gas and petroleum, insurance, postal services, statistics, local government, and agriculture.[365]

In September 1995 the parties completed the third stage foreseen by the Declaration of Principles—the conclusion of the Israeli-Palestinian Interim Agreement on the West Bank and the Gaza Strip.[366] In accordance with the Declaration of Principles, this agreement provided for a large-scale transfer of powers in the West Bank, preceded by the election of a Palestinian Council. On the eve of those elections, the Israeli army redeployed outside populated areas. Further redeployments to specified locations are to be gradually implemented. The 1995 agreement (discussed below) describes the structure, powers, and number of members of the elected council, the transfer of powers, the redeployment of the Israeli army, and the division of powers in matters of security.

According to the Declaration of Principles, the Council was not to have powers with regard to "Jerusalem, refugees, settlements, security arrangements, borders, relations and cooperation with other neighbors."[367] These matters, which were expressly excluded from the powers of the Council, were intended to be the subject of the negotiations on the "permanent status,"[368] that is, the fourth stage of negotiations, which started in 1996. Those negotiations are to be based on UN Security Council Resolutions 242 (1967)[369] and 338 (1973)[370] and should not to be prejudiced by agreements reached for the interim period.[371]

The transitional arrangements were intended to be in force for a five-year period, to start with the withdrawal from the Gaza Strip and the Jericho area.[372] That withdrawal took place in May 1994, somewhat later than the originally foreseen date; the delay was caused by the complexity of the negotiations.

Of special interest is the division of responsibilities established by the Declaration of Principles in matters of security:[373] According to the declaration, Israel should be responsible for external security, as well as for overall security of Israelis (public order, namely, regular police functions, and internal security—that is, confronting the threat of terrorism), while a Palestinian police force should be responsible for public order and internal security of the Palestinians. The parties have agreed to cooperate and coordinate in security matters.[374] The declaration also foresaw the establishment in Gaza and Jericho of "a temporary international or foreign presence, as agreed upon."[375]

The declaration put much emphasis on the need for cooperation in the various fields of security and economics (water, electricity, energy, finance, transport, trade, industry, labor relations, human resources development, environmental protection, communications, and media).[376] The text also addressed regional cooperation.[377] To enhance the desired cooperation, the document called for the establishment of joint bodies.[378] The parties have agreed to settle disputes by negotiations, leaving the door open for conciliation and arbitration if both parties agree.[379]

The delicate problem of the refugees was also addressed: The "modalities of admission of persons displaced from the West Bank and Gaza Strip in 1967" were to be decided by agreement in a "Continuing Committee" consisting of representatives of Israel, the Palestinians, Egypt, and Jordan,[380] while the other refugees (mainly those of 1948) should be discussed in the negotiations on the permanent status to start in 1996.[381] In this context, one should remember that the problem of the refugees has also been the subject of multilateral negotiations in the framework of one of the fora established by the 1991 Madrid Peace Conference.

Having looked cursorily at the various stages foreseen by the Declaration of Principles, we can now study its implementation in more detail. Although of interest, the first stages are not the focus of this examination. These arrangements—the Gaza and Jericho self-rule established in 1994 and the early transfer of thirteen spheres of powers in the whole of the West Bank—have been superseded by, or incorporated into, the 1995 comprehensive "Interim Agreement."[382] This document (more than three hundred pages long) includes detailed provisions on the election of a Palestinian self-governing council, a staged redeployment of Israeli forces, security arrangements, the transfer of forty spheres of civilian powers from the Israeli military government and its civil administration to the Palestinian authority, legal matters (such as jurisdiction of the courts), economic relations, Israeli-Palestinian cooperation programs, and the release of Palestinian prisoners and detainees.

As mentioned, self-government arrangements were first established in the Gaza Strip and in Jericho. The Israeli forces were redeployed into a "Military Installation Area" along the border of Egypt, and into the areas of the Israeli settlements, including the Gush Katif, Kfar Darom, Nitzanim, and Erez areas.[383] Authority in matters of security has been allocated in accordance with the Declaration of Principles:[384] Israel has responsibility for external security, while internal security and public order are divided between Israel (responsible for overall security of Israelis, the settlements, and the military installation area) and the Palestinian police (responsible for the Palestinians in the Gaza Strip and the Jericho area). A strong police force, the Palestinian Directorate of Police Force, was established to preserve security and public order among the Palestinians.[385]

Special arrangements were made for particularly sensitive areas (for example, the "yellow" areas delineated on a map attached to the agreement[386] and the "Security Perimeter" along the northern and eastern confines of the Gaza Strip)[387] and for joint patrols and mobile units on the principal roads leading to Israeli settlements and to the military installation area.[388] Israel retained full authority over the air space[389] and—subject to certain economic rights and limited police powers of the Palestinians in areas close to the shore—also over the sea.[390] A rather complicated system was devised for assuring both Israeli and Palestinian control at the border crossings to Egypt and Jordan.[391] Furthermore, the Palestinians were assured "safe passage" between the Gaza Strip and the West Bank[392] and the release by Israel of a considerable number of Palestinian prisoners and detainees.[393]

The 1995 Interim Agreement also addressed further redeployment of the Israeli army in four stages. In this respect, the relevant territory of the West Bank was divided into three areas:[394] "Area A" consists of the Jericho area and the main Palestinian cities of the West Bank—namely, Jenin, Nablus, Tulkarem, Kalkilya, Ramallah, Bethlehem, and large parts of Hebron; "Area B" consists of all the other areas populated by Palestinians—about 450 smaller towns, villages, hamlets, and refugee camps; "Area C" consists of those parts of the West Bank very sparsely populated by Palestinians and includes areas of strategic significance for Israel and the Israeli civilian settlements. It was agreed that prior to the elections for the Palestinian Council, which took place on 20 January 1996, the Israeli army would redeploy from Area A and Area B.[395] In addition, after the inauguration of the Council, further redeployments should take place in Area C at six-month intervals, to be completed within eighteen months after the establishment of the Council.[396] Thereafter (1997), the army should be stationed only in the areas of the Israeli settlements and in "specified military locations."

The various stages of redeployment are related to the transfer of powers in the sphere of security, as well as in other areas. Israel is to continue to be responsible for defense against external threats. This includes responsibility for protecting the borders with Egypt and Jordan, as well as defense against external threats from the sea and the air. In addition, Israel is to retain responsibility for the overall security of Israelis and of Israeli settlements, including both internal security and public order. Moreover, Israel is to have "all the powers to take the steps necessary to meet this responsibility."[397]

In Area A the Palestinian Council was granted, with the first phase of redeployment, full responsibility for internal security and public order of Palestinians, as well as all transferable powers in civil affairs (discussed below). In Area B the Council is to be responsible for public order of the Palestinians; in the first stages Israel would still be responsible for internal security. Moreover, Israel has retained the power to protect Israelis and to fight terrorism: "Israel shall have the overriding responsibility for security for the purpose of protecting Israelis and confronting the threat of terrorism."[398] Later, responsibility for internal security in Area B should be transferred to the Council.[399] Civil powers were transferred to the Council in respect of Area B without reservation during the first phase of redeployment.[400]

In Area C—very sparsely populated by Palestinians—Israel initially should retain full responsibility for both internal security and public order, as well as for civil matters related to territory, while the Palestinian Council should have powers in civil spheres not related to territory.[401] Powers concerning public order and internal security of Palestinians, as well as civil powers related to territory, should be transferred gradually in Area C.[402]

In the sphere of security, as in other areas, close cooperation between Israel and the Palestinian authorities has been planned, including joint patrols and joint mobile units.[403] The security annex (Annex 1) specifies the deployment of the Palestinian police, its weapons and equipment, and its rules of conduct.

As in security matters, the civil powers of the Palestinian Council have been delineated by reference to territory, people, and subject matter:[404] Territorially, the powers of the Council should extend to the Gaza Strip and to Areas A, B, and C in the West Bank (in Area C, the transfer of powers is gradual), but they should not apply to Israeli settlements and Israeli military locations. As to the people subject to its jurisdiction, the Council's powers should not, in principle, apply to Israelis. The list of the powers transferred to the Palestinians includes forty subject matters. Israel has retained full civil jurisdiction over the Israeli settlements and military locations, and temporary jurisdiction over territory-related matters in Area C. In addition, all Israelis, wherever they may be in the relevant areas, are subject to Israeli authority, and civil powers not specifically transferred to the Palestinians remain with Israel.

Subject to the above limitations, the following civil powers have been transferred to the Palestinian Council:[405] agriculture; archaeology; assessments; banking and monetary issues; civil administration employees; commerce and industry; comptrol; direct taxation; education and culture; electricity; employment; environmental protection;[406] fisheries; forests; gas, fuel, and petroleum; government and absentee land and immovables; health (including vaccination); indirect taxation; insurance; interior affairs; labor; land registration; legal administration (including the judicial system, registration of companies, and protection of intellectual property rights); local government; nature reserves; parks; planning and zoning; population registry and documentation (including the right to issue passports); postal services; public works and housing; quarries and mines; religious sites;[407] social welfare; statistics; surveying; telecommunications; tourism; transportation (including drivers' and vehicle licensing, traffic supervision, vehicle maintenance, transportation of dangerous substances, public transportation, and meteorology); treasury (matters of budgets, revenues, expenses, and accounts); water and sewage (including allocating and protecting water resources and preventing pollution).

In some of these spheres, the transfer was subject to certain limitations. For example, the Palestinian postal authority should only design stamps "in the spirit of the peace."[408] In matters of population registry, the Palestinian authority must coordinate its activity very carefully with Israel.[409]

Although in principle the Palestinian authority was not granted powers and responsibilities in the sphere of foreign relations, the PLO was authorized to sign certain categories of agreements with states or international organizations for the benefit of the Palestinian authority: economic agreements; agreements with donor countries; agreements for implementing regional development plans; and cultural, scientific, and educational agreements. For the purpose of implementing the agreements, representative offices other than embassies and consulates may be established in the Gaza Strip and the West Bank.[410]

Before we continue to analyze the powers of the autonomous Palestinian entity, a short survey of its institutions is warranted. In accordance with the 1995 Interim Agreement, on 20 January 1996 elections were simultaneously held for the Palestinian Council and for the chairman of the Executive Authority of the Council. The expression used in the agreement for the latter is *Ra'ees*, an Arabic word that can be translated both as president (the preference of the Palestinians) and as chairman (the preference of the Israelis).[411] These elections were held under international observation. The observers included representatives many countries and international organizations. The European Union agreed to coordinate the observation.

The Palestinians elected a Council with eighty-eight members.[412] In principle, this organ has been the bearer of all the powers of the Palestinian entity. It is, of course, authorized to legislate, but it is not authorized to adopt legislation that exceeds its powers or is inconsistent with agreements between Israel and the Palestinians.[413] All legislation should be communicated to the Israeli side of a joint legal committee. Israel was not given a right to veto Palestinian legislation;[414] however, the Palestinian *Ra'ees* was requested not to promulgate legislation of the Council if it was adopted *ultra vires* or was not consistent with the agreements.[415]

The Executive Authority of the Council is headed by the elected *Ra'ees*. The other members are proposed to the Council by the *Ra'ees* and need the approval of the Council. The 1995 Interim Agreement makes no mention of the number of members of the Executive Authority. It was, however, foreseen that the *Ra'ees* could appoint to the authority some individuals, not exceeding 20 percent of the total membership, who are not members of the Council. They must have a valid address in the area that is under the jurisdiction of the Council.[416] Acts of the *Ra'ees* and of the Executive Authority or its members are subject to judicial review by the competent relevant Palestinian court of justice.[417]

The Interim Agreement also allows the council to establish an independent judicial system.[418] Annex IV of the Interim Agreement addresses the jurisdiction of the courts in criminal and civil matters, as well as questions of legal assistance and the transfer of suspects.[419] Basically, in criminal cases Israel has jurisdiction over all offenses committed by Israelis and over all offenses committed in the Jewish settlements or in the military installation area, except for offenses not related to Israel's security interests committed by and against Palestinians and their visitors. In addition, Israel has retained some criminal jurisdiction for security offenses in certain areas.[420] The Palestinian courts have criminal jurisdiction over offenses committed by non-Israelis, except for the above-mentioned localities where jurisdiction was reserved for Israel.[421]

In civil matters, the Palestinian courts have jurisdiction over Israelis only if the subject matter of the action is either an ongoing Israeli business situated in the territory or "real property" located there. In other cases, the consent of the Israeli party can endow the Palestinian court with jurisdiction.[422] The enforcement of all judgments against Israelis may be effected by Israel only.[423] The Palestinian courts do not have jurisdiction for actions against the State of Israel or its organs and agents.[424]

Of special interest is Annex V, the Protocol on Economic Relations, which was negotiated at an early stage in Paris. It was first applied to the Gaza Strip and Jericho area,[425] but the parties agreed that later its provisions would also apply to the rest of the West Bank.[426] In principle, the Palestinian authority has been authorized to handle economic matters. However, in order to encourage the Palestinian economy and to prevent smuggling and competition between Israel and the self-government areas, certain arrangements were agreed upon. Analyzing all these arrangements would be beyond the scope of this chapter;[427] therefore, only the main points are summarized.

A free flow of both industrial and agricultural products between Israel and the Palestinians has been foreseen, subject to local legislation (for example, on matters of standards).[428] The markets for certain agricultural produce would open gradually: poultry, eggs, potatoes, cucumbers, tomatoes (mainly exported by the Palestinians), and melons (mainly exported by Israel).[429] Detailed provisions on preventing animal and plant disease are also included.[430]

Israeli rates of customs duties should apply as a minimum to goods imported into the autonomous area from other countries, as should Israeli regulations on classification and valuation.[431] But the Palestinian authority has been granted discretion with regard to the importation of certain goods: these include a number of categories of goods produced in Arab countries and certain items imported from all Arab, Islamic, and other countries, without having necessarily been produced there. (Some of the items appear on both lists). However, in both cases the amount imported should correspond to the needs of the Palestinian market.[432] In addition, the Palestinian Council has been authorized to import some items, with full discretion regarding the rates of customs and with no quantitative limit. This discretion should apply to certain basic food items and other goods needed for the Palestinian economic development program.[433] The Palestinians have also been authorized to determine their own rates of customs and purchase tax for imported motor vehicles; they were permitted to import used passenger cars (not more than four years old), although such importation into Israel has not been allowed. Certain vehicle standards must, however, be observed.[434] A value-added tax (VAT) of 15 to 16 percent should be imposed on all goods and services, whether locally produced or imported.[435]

The Palestinian authority has been authorized to export both agricultural and industrial produce to external markets.[436] It has also been granted the power to impose direct and indirect taxes, but as mentioned, VAT should be at a rate of 15 to 16 percent and the purchase tax should be similar to the one imposed by Israel.[437]

Israel committed itself to transferring to the Palestinian Authority 75 percent of the revenues from income tax collected from Palestinians employed in Israel and the full amount of income tax collected from those employed in the settlements, as well as other tax revenues.[438] Detailed provisions were included in the agreement to prevent both overlapping and loopholes in the sphere of taxation.[439]

While attempting in principle to "maintain the normality of movement of labor between them," each side has been allowed to "determine from time to time the extent and conditions of the labor movement into its area."[440]

The Palestinians were authorized to establish a monetary authority, with the main function of regulating and supervising the banks operating in the self-governing areas.[441] It should also control foreign exchange transactions, regulate the capital market, and "act as lender of last resort for the banking system" in the autonomous area. However, it was not granted the main power usually vested in central monetary institutions, namely, the right to issue money. The Israeli currency (shekel) should be one of the circulating currencies in the areas and should be acceptable as payment for all purposes. Moreover, banks in the areas should accept deposits in Israeli currency.[442]

To what economic model do the provisions of the Interim Agreement correspond? According to Ephraim Kleiman, "quantitatively speaking, the agreed arrangement is first and foremost a customs union. But . . . it contains also an element of a common market. . . . [I]t combines also, albeit for limited quantities only, some elements of a Free Trade Area Agreement."[443]

In all the various spheres—security, civil affairs, legal matters, and economics—elaborate mechanisms for liaison, cooperation, consultation, and coordination between Israel and the Palestinian Authority have been established,[444] and Annex 6 encourages close cooperation in many fields. The parties committed themselves to exercising their respective powers "with due regard to internationally accepted norms and principles of human rights and the rule of law,"[445] and to abstain from "incitement, including hostile propaganda, against each other."[446] In addition, they committed themselves not to take any step that would change the status of the autonomous areas, pending the outcome of the permanent status negotiations. This means that Israel is precluded from annexing the areas and the Palestinians may not declare independence.[447]

The agreement did not address the question of sovereignty over the autonomous areas. As to the question of who retains the residual powers, perhaps an implied answer may be found in the provision that states that "Israel shall continue to exercise powers and responsibilities not so transferred [to the Council]."[448]

The PLO undertook to convene the Palestine National Council within two months of the inauguration of the new Council, in order to formally approve the necessary changes in the Palestinian covenant[449]— a commitment already included in the 1993 exchange of letters between Israel's prime minister and Yassir Arafat,[450] as well as in the exchange of letters that accompanied the conclusion of the 1994 Gaza-Jericho agreement;[451] however, those texts included no timetable. The Palestine National Council met in Gaza on 24 April 1996 and voted to repeal those provisions of the Palestinian covenant which were in conflict with the letters of reciprocal recognition exchanged between the government of Israel and the PLO in September 1993. The resolution authorized the legal committee of the council to draft a new covenant and to submit it to the central committee of the PLO.[452]

## Concluding Remarks

At the beginning of the discussion of this case four characteristics were mentioned: the fact that autonomy is foreseen for a limited period, the zero-sum attitude that preceded it, the acts of violence, and the fact that it evolved out of a military occupation. Detailed analysis has shown a few additional features. Like certain other regimes of autonomy, this one has been established in stages; however, the gradualism has been applied not only to the extent of the powers to be transferred, but also (and mainly) to the geographical areas in which the autonomy should be established. Another interesting feature is that the powers of the self-governing authority have been delineated according to three criteria: the territory where they apply, the persons who are subject to them, and the actual contents of the powers. As another characteristic, within the autonomous areas there are to be enclaves—the Israeli settlements and the military locations—to which the regime should not apply.

The area and the population are relatively large in comparison to Israel itself and are adjacent to it. The parties have envisaged a very broad autonomy for a limited period. However, there is no indication in the texts on the options that might be considered at the end of the interim period. While it is clear that most of the Palestinians strive for independence, many Israelis probably prefer a status short of independence, due to the security risks.

At the time these lines are being written, it is too early to predict whether this case can be described as a success. On the one hand, according to public opinion polls the majority of the population in both Israel and the autonomous territories seem to favor the arrangement, but there is a danger that the terrible assassinations and acts of terrorism by extremists could undermine it. Moreover, the movement of goods and of people has been considerably hampered due to a closure that Israel imposed for security reasons in the wake of various terrorist attacks on civilian buses. The change in government in Israel that followed the elections of 29 May 1996 may also have a negative effect on the development of the regime of autonomy in the West Bank and Gaza, in particular on the timetable foreseen. According to some proposals, the parties, instead of continuing to negotiate on the implementation of self-government, should as soon as possible hold intensive negotiations on the final status.

Whereas the 1978 Camp David framework[453] spoke of autonomy, the negotiators in the 1990s used the term self-government. However, it seems that the change in terminology is due to the Palestinians' aversion to the Camp David process and not to a real difference between the two concepts.

# PART IV

CONCLUSIONS

*What lessons can be learned from the above analysis of the concept of auton-omy and of a number of cases? In the following concluding chapters an attempt is made to examine whether there exists a right to autonomy. This examina-tion is followed by some guidelines on issues that are relevant for the establish-ment of a regime of autonomy and a tentative list of factors that may increase the prospects for success. These developments are intended to help the "auton-omy builders," whether territorial or personal. Lastly, an attempt is made to evaluate the usefulness of the concept of autonomy.*

# 10

# THE QUEST FOR AUTONOMY

The dangers inherent in a considerable number of situations of ethnic conflict have been increasing: for example, in Sri Lanka, in Kashmir, in Chechnya, and in southeast Turkey. The illusion of the single-nation state has long been shattered.[1] It is a truism that the great majority of existing states are inhabited by people of different ethnic allegiances. Ethnicity is a phenomenon that far predates the establishment of the modern state system, and it will probably survive it. At a fundamentally human level, ethnicity is the sense of solidarity and allegiance of individuals to those who share their color or their appearance, their language, their religion, or their tradition, an affinity that has been termed "primordial attachment."[2] Ethnic solidarity fulfills the individual's need for identity, affiliation, and self-esteem, which, in turn, enhance a sense of security.[3] To use more political language, it is "the self-assertion of ethnic groups, ranging from primary cultural, religious, and educational endeavors, via political organization, to the ultimate step of struggling for territorial or state power."[4]

Ethnic consciousness has grown considerably in the past thirty years due to several developments. The recognition first of certain minority rights, then of the right to self-determination of peoples, and finally of the rights of indigenous groups was probably prompted by the increase in ethnicity, but that recognition has, in turn, enhanced ethnic consciousness. Another important development has been the achievement of independence by a great number of colonies: Under colonial rule, ethnic differences among the local population had been muted in many cases; with the advent of independence, ethnic allegiances surged, sometimes leading to violence.[5]

Rapid secularization, democratization, and urbanization have also had their impact on ethnic feelings: The nation or ethnic group has become the substitute for religion, and democracy has further emphasized the importance of the nation.[6] Last, but not least, the end of the Cold War has caused ethnic and religious frictions to resurge: The East-West rivalry and the accompanying constant danger had been overarching considerations that kept differing groups together. Once this danger had disappeared or decreased, the previously suppressed identities reasserted themselves. Heterogeneity—though often based on ethnic phenomena—can also have economic origins (as in the situation that may occur when market-oriented Hong Kong and Macao revert to communist China by the end of this century).

To the objective situations of diversity that may require accommodation between the central power and local or ethnic aspirations, one must add the widespread dissatisfaction of people with the inefficiency and remoteness of the large-scale, bureaucratic state.[7]

These trends have increased the awareness of, and claims for, minorities' rights, indigenous peoples' rights, and peoples' right to self-determination. The international community still hesitates to grant minorities group rights in general and autonomy in particular; however, it seems that a tendency can be discerned toward granting indigenous populations a certain degree of self-government. A people's right to self-determination is rather problematic. As Robert Lansing, President Wilson's secretary of state, wrote: "Will it not breed discontent, disorder and rebellion? . . . The phrase is simply loaded with dynamite. It will raise hopes which can never be realized. It will, I fear, cost thousands of lives. . . . What a calamity that the phrase was ever uttered! What misery it will cause!"[8] This danger is demonstrated daily by the myriad claims to self-determination—often accompanied by acts of violence by long-suppressed ethnic, religious, and other groups—which, if granted, would destroy many existing states and would splinter the world into thousands of nonviable ministates. The lack of a clear distinction between the concept of "people" and of minorities or ethnic groups has contributed to the confusion.

Due to its ambiguity, some authors prefer not to consider self-determination as a legal right;[9] others have limited its external aspect to cases of colonialism, to foreign or alien domination, and to entire populations of a given state,[10] while emphasizing its internal aspect of representative democracy.[11] Moreover, according to the Badinter Arbitration Commission, which gave its opinion on matters related to the breaking up of the Yugoslav federation, the right of self-determination is a principle that protects human rights; by virtue of that right each individual may choose to claim membership in an ethnic, religious, or linguistic community.[12]

A somewhat related perspective has been adopted by those authors who recommend that claims for self-determination and minority rights be settled on a nonterritorial and nonstatist basis: In parallel with states, there should be established a system of nations, coupled with a decrease of state sovereignty, with a new allocation of powers, with functional borders, and with a distinction between citizenship—a link to the state—and nationality—a link to a nation.[13]

At present, however, claims for self-determination are still linked to territory. Thus, a much-debated question has been whether self-determination justifies secession from an existing noncolonial, nonforeign state. A wholesale right of secession (or full self-determination) has to be rejected—not only because of the havoc that its implementation would cause, but also because it cannot solve the problem of ethnic diversity, since ethnic groups are often geographically interspersed.

It thus seems preferable to solve ethnic problems by looking for appropriate solutions within the state. Indeed, various authors have emphasized that aspirations for self-determination and ethnic friction can also be met by measures short of secession.[14] Among the proposed solutions, two main systems may be identified: "consociationalism" or power sharing, on the one hand, and systems of diffusion of power from the center to the periphery, on the other hand. The power-sharing model is closely associated with Arend Lijphart.[15] His system consists of four elements: the participation of the representatives of all significant groups in the government of the country; a high degree of autonomy for these groups; proportionality; and minority veto. The first element means jointly exercising governmental (particularly executive) power, for example, through a grand coalition cabinet. Issues that are not of common concern should be left for each group to decide for itself, in the framework of autonomy, the second element. "If the groups have a clear territorial concentration, group autonomy may be institutionalized in the form of federalism. If the groups are intermixed, autonomy will have to take nonterritorial forms or a combination of territorial and nonterritorial forms." Proportionality, the third element of power sharing, is to serve as the basic standard of political representation, public service appointments, and allocation of public funds. The fourth characteristic, the minority veto, would be the minority's ultimate weapon to protect its vital interests; however, it should use this power only rarely, and then only on issues of fundamental importance.[16] Although not mentioned by Lijphart, it appears that Switzerland is a good example of power sharing.[17]

Lijphart mentions nine other factors that are favorable to the success of power sharing, but none is indispensable:

- the absence of a majority ethnic group;
- the absence of large socioeconomic differences among the groups;
- the rough equivalence in size of the groups;
- a relatively limited number of groups;
- a relatively small total population;
- the presence of external dangers that promote internal security;
- overarching loyalties that reduce the strength of particularistic ethnic loyalties;
- geographic concentration of the ethnic groups; and
- prior traditions of compromise and accommodation.[18]

It follows that autonomy is an important element in Lijphart's thesis.

The second means of solving ethnic conflicts without secession involves the diffusion of powers. This solution can take various forms, including federalism, decentralization, self-government, associate statehood, self-administration, and autonomy. Some authors use autonomy as a generic term for all these institutions. This author, however, has tried to distinguish between autonomy and the various other schemes.

This leads us to a recapitulation of the meaning of autonomy.

The term autonomy has been used by various politicians and authors with different, though related, meanings. For some, it is the right to act upon one's own discretion; for others, it is synonymous with decentralization. After investigating various cases and opinions of experts, this author would summarize certain concepts related to autonomy as follows:

- Territorial political autonomy is an arrangement aimed at granting a certain degree of self-identification to a group that differs from the majority of the population in the state, and yet constitutes the majority in a specific region. Autonomy involves a division of powers between the central authorities and the autonomous entity. The powers of the entity usually relate to matters of culture, economics, and social affairs. The extent of transferred powers varies widely, ranging from a minimum to almost the totality of powers. The autonomous authorities usually have the powers of legislation, administration, and adjudication. In some cases, however, autonomy has not included the right to adjudicate.

Not all powers are divided between the center and the region; undivided powers may either be shared or exercised in parallel. The acts of the autonomous authorities are not subject to full control by the central government, but the latter may veto them in severe cases, such as excess of power.

Autonomy, by its very nature, requires cooperation and coordination between the central authorities and the local ones. In many instances, introducing changes into a system of autonomy requires the assent of both the center and the local authorities.

As has been shown, cases of autonomy differ greatly and hence some diverge from the above description in certain aspects.

- Administrative autonomy is limited to matters of administration and thus resembles decentralization.
- Personal autonomy applies to all members of a certain group within the state, irrespective of their place of residence. It is the right to preserve and promote the religious, linguistic, and cultural character of the group through institutions established by itself. These institutions are authorized by the state to make binding decisions and impose taxes.

Having studied the nature of autonomy and several cases of its implementation, the question arises whether a legal right for autonomy exists, and if so, for whom. So far, no binding international document of general application establishes a right to receive—or an obligation to bestow—autonomy.[19] The Declaration of the Rights of Indigenous Peoples would grant such a right, but it has not yet (March 1996) been adopted by the UN General Assembly. Moreover, unless included in a treaty, it will not be binding. It has been claimed that certain provisions in the 1966 International Covenant on Civil and Political Rights should be interpreted as implying at least "qualified support for some forms of autonomy":[20] Article 1 establishes the right to self-determination and Article 25 provides for the right of citizens to political participation; the rights of minorities to enjoy and develop their own culture are enshrined in Article 27. Thus, Nirmala Chandrahasan relied on these provisions in asserting the existence of a right to autonomy:

> This article takes the view that the rights of political participation and self-determination may be interpreted as recognizing a collective right to some form of autonomy, which we will term internal self-determination, in respect of ethnically distinct minorities that possess a homeland, i.e., occupy a distinct territory where they constitute the majority.[21]

However, it is doubtful whether one may give those provisions such a broad interpretation that they would include a right to autonomy. That interpretation would hardly be "in accordance with the ordinary meaning to be given to the terms of the treaty in their context and in the light of its object and purpose."[22]

According to Henry J. Steiner, a right to autonomy does not exist; however, in certain situations autonomy may constitute "a practical necessity, a 'least worst' solution that is surely preferable to ongoing violence and systemic oppression."[23] Nonetheless, "the rhetoric of rights may here be inappropriate, even misleading. Elaboration of principles indicating the circumstances that justify minority claims may be preferable."[24]

Hurst Hannum, on the other hand, seems to perceive a right to autonomy:

> It is the suggestion of the present book that a new principle of international law can be discerned in the interstices of contemporary definitions of sovereignty, self-determination, and the human rights of individuals and groups, which will support creative attempts to deal with conflicts over minority and majority rights before they escalate into civil war and demands of secession. . . . This right to autonomy recognizes the right of minority and indigenous communities to exercise meaningful internal self-determination and control over their own affairs in a manner that is not inconsistent with the ultimate sovereignty—as that term is properly understood—of the state.[25]

This right may be asserted more aggressively in case of discrimination or marginalization of the group.

The Draft Convention on Self-Determination through Self-Administration prepared in April 1994 by the Permanent Mission of the Principality of Liechtenstein to the United Nations[26] would involve the granting of limited autonomy to "communities," but the draft has not yet been adopted by states.

On the basis of our earlier analysis,[27] it appears that the international community has thus far refused to recognize a general right to autonomy for minority groups. Since the deliberations in various international bodies have shown that many states oppose the granting of such a right, it is doubtful whether one may conclude by analogy or by implication that such a right nevertheless does exist.

The community of nations is perhaps more inclined to recognize a right of indigenous populations or peoples for autonomy, because a number of states have included such a right in their constitutional legislation.[28] This right, as well as a right to self-determination, has been included in the Declaration on the Rights of Indigenous Peoples, but it is not known whether the UN General Assembly will adopt that declaration and what changes will be introduced into it before its adoption. Furthermore, such a declaration per se would have no binding force.

On the other hand, "peoples" certainly have the right to autonomy since they have been granted the right to self-determination. Moreover, as noted above,[29] autonomy may be the compromise solution in those cases where a people is not granted full self-determination, including the choice of independence.

An analysis based on the distinction between minorities, indigenous groups, and peoples—although prima facie quite convincing—is not practical: As demonstrated, the term "people" has no clear and recognized definition. Most indigenous groups and many minorities could easily fit into the concept of "peoples." Hence, it is almost impossible to decide which group constitutes a people and as such should enjoy the right to self-determination and which group does not.

To conclude, it seems that except for "peoples" (whatever this term may mean), international law has not yet established a right to autonomy. However, an interesting compromise solution has been mentioned by Thomas Buergenthal:[30] The various groups would have a right, and the relevant states would have a concomitant obligation, to *negotiate* the possibility of establishing a regime of autonomy.

# Establishing an Autonomous Regime: Issues to Consider

Equipped with the results of both a theoretical analysis of autonomy and a specific examination of some cases, we may now venture to deal with practical questions: What are the main subjects that those who consider establishing an autonomy may have to address? What are some of the available options or alternatives? It should be emphasized that the following discussion does not purport to deal with all the relevant questions, nor are the lists of options given below exhaustive. The following material is based on the cases analyzed in part III, on the theory of autonomy, on interviews, and on personal experience.

## The Diversity of the Cases

Let us start by repeating that each case is different and is influenced by history, geography, tradition, economic situation, strategic considerations, the nature of the group that desires autonomy, and the reason for the establishment of the regime. Therefore precedents should not be followed automatically. Inventive thinking and bona fide negotiations should help to find workable solutions.

## Modes of Establishment of Autonomy

Several questions relating to the mode of the establishment of autonomy have to be considered. Should the regime be established by an

international convention, and, if so, who should be the parties to negotiate and sign it? Possible candidates are the central state, another state
with which the relevant ethnic group has a cultural or linguistic affinity, major regional or global powers, representatives of the ethnic
group itself, or an international organization, whether regional or universal. However, most states may be reluctant to let other countries
have a say in a matter that the state prefers to consider as an internal question.

The autonomy can also be established by an appropriate act of the
central state itself, for example, the introduction of the relevant provisions into the constitution or adoption of an organic law or ordinary
laws. There may also be a combination of international and national
acts. The regime will probably gain additional legitimacy if it is also
approved by a vote or a referendum of the residents of the area. Such
a procedure raises several questions: Who among the local inhabitants
may participate in the vote? How long should a person have lived in
the area to qualify for participation in the popular vote? Should people
who used to live in the area, but who left because of the ethnic conflict,
be consulted?

## TERRITORIAL, PERSONAL, OR MIXED AUTONOMY?

Does the situation call for a territorial, a personal, or a mixed autonomy? Territorial autonomy may be the appropriate solution where
members of the ethnic group constitute a considerable majority in a
certain region; but ethnic minorities are often interspersed, and in that
case only personal autonomy may be possible. When the group is the
majority in a certain area, but is interspersed in other areas, a mixed
territorial and personal regime may be considered.

## DEFINITION OF THE REGION OR THE PEOPLE

Closely related to the preceding question is the need to define the area
(in case of territorial autonomy) and the people (in case of personal
autonomy) to which the regime should apply. Logically, the boundaries
of a region subject to territorial autonomy should include as many
members as possible of the ethnic group for which the autonomy is
established, and as few people as possible who do not belong to the
group. However, when determining the boundaries, one may also have

to take into consideration that due to the movement of people, majorities and minorities may change.

Another matter to consider is whether territorial autonomy should apply to all the residents of the area in question or only to members of the group for whose sake the regime is established.

When defining the people who belong to a specific ethnic or religious group—a question relevant mainly for personal autonomy, but also for the territorial autonomy of indigenous groups (for example, the right to live on a reservation)—several approaches can be taken. One, which is usually rejected, would authorize the central government to establish the relevant criteria; another would leave the decision with representatives of the group; and a third would leave the choice to each individual. A solution could also be based upon a combination of these alternatives. A somewhat related question is whether personal autonomy should apply to all the members of the minority group in the country or only to those who live in certain areas where they constitute a large minority.

## VARIABLES RELATED TO TIME

Another matter to be considered are the variables related to time. Should the autonomy be established in the whole area and in all spheres simultaneously, or is it preferable to establish it in stages? What are the conditions for passage from one stage to the next one?

In some cases it must be decided whether autonomy should be a permanent solution or merely a provisional measure. The extent of the powers granted to the autonomous authorities may depend on whether the regime is intended to be permanent or provisional.

If a temporary autonomy is established, a few additional questions arise: Should the duration of the autonomy be determined in advance by a fixed time limit, or should it depend on other circumstances? Other questions relate to the arrangements that should follow the interim autonomy regime. These arrangements can be agreed upon in advance at the time the autonomy is established, or several options may be foreseen. If several options are outlined, a procedure should be established for choosing among them. If no indication is given on the content of the final arrangements, there may be a need for provisions that lay out the procedure to be followed in order to agree upon and establish these arrangements.

## THE INSTITUTIONS OF THE REGIME OF AUTONOMY

When a regime of autonomy is established, one has to decide what are to be its institutions, how the members should be appointed, and what should be the limitations on their powers.

If a territorial political autonomy is to adopt its own constitution, provision must be made for a constituent assembly. In addition, one has to lay down whether this constitution will require the approval of an organ of the central government, a local referendum, or perhaps both.

The legislature of the territorial autonomy is usually a representative body elected periodically by the local population. Several questions related to this organ have to be dealt with. Does the central government have the authority to dissolve this autonomous legislature, and, if so, under what circumstances? Should (as is often the case with autonomies) the laws adopted by this legislature require approval by an organ of the central government, and, if so, which organ? Moreover, one has to enumerate in advance the grounds that will justify the denial of such approval (that is, the application of a veto). Possible reasons for refusing to approve a law may be excess of power, incompatibility with the state's constitution or with its international obligations, or endangering of the state's security or its vital interests. One must also establish what organ (the supreme court or the constitutional court of the state, for example) has to be consulted to determine whether the use of the veto power is warranted in a particular case, and what is to be the effect of this veto: Should the law be definitively rejected, or may it be reintroduced to the autonomous legislature and eventually adopted by a qualified majority?

A parallel or complementary question is whether a procedure should be established by which the legislature of the center would be prevented from encroaching upon the powers of the autonomy's legislature.

As with all political entities, the head of the executive branch in an autonomous regime can be elected either by the population or by the members of the local legislature. There may also be a need to obtain the confidence of the legislative assembly. The central government may also have a say in the designation of the head of the executive branch: That person may be appointed by the center with the approval of the local legislature, or vice versa. Parallel procedures may be envisaged for dismissal.

The powers and responsibilities of the local executive organ may be limited to implementing laws of the autonomous area; but they may also encompass the implementation of laws and regulations of the central government. Moreover, one can imagine a phased system under which originally the local executive is only in charge of local legislation but the central government may delegate to it certain powers related to the implementation of powers of the state.

When considering the judiciary, the preliminary question is whether the specific regime under discussion should have its own system of courts. At least three possibilities have to be considered: (1) the central state remains in charge of all matters of adjudication; (2) the whole sphere is transferred to the autonomous body; and (3) two parallel systems for the administration of justice are established, one dealing with matters within the competence of the autonomous area, the other linked to the judiciary of the state and handling matters reserved for the central authorities. The division of powers between the two sets of courts could also have a personal element: People who do not belong to the group for which the autonomy was established may be permitted to have their grievances decided by the courts established by the central authorities.

Provisions would have to be made for cases where there is disagreement on the question which court system has jurisdiction over a certain dispute. One could also consider granting the possibility of appealing on certain points against decisions of the highest instance of the autonomy's judiciary to the supreme court of the state. If such action is permitted, one has to decide whether the state's supreme court should have a special chamber to deal with appeals from the autonomous area, and whether the bench of this chamber should include jurists that belong to the ethnic group for which the autonomy was established. The local judges of the autonomous region can be appointed locally; some of them may need the approval of the central authorities.

The official who represents the central government in the autonomous area can be appointed either by the center alone or by the center with the approval of the local legislature (or its chairperson). The representative's task should be to oversee the implementation of laws and policies in the spheres reserved for the state. The smooth functioning of an autonomy depends to a considerable extent on the wisdom and tact of this official.

Those who intend to set up a regime of autonomy should also consider favorably the establishment of a joint organ that has the competence to address matters that require coordination and cooperation between the center and the autonomous region.

In the case of personal autonomy, the relevant institutions and their powers will of course be very different, because the group will only have competence to regulate and administer in a limited number of spheres. There may, nevertheless, be room for a body of representatives with an executive board. Moreover, an organ that would represent the minority in dealing with the central authorities is needed.

Normally, personal autonomy does not include the power to adjudicate. However, if the relevant group is a religious one, its tribunals may have jurisdiction on certain matters of personal status. In such a case it will be necessary to regulate a few subjects: the composition of the tribunals and the mode of appointment of the judges; the jurisdiction of the tribunals *ratione personae* and *ratione materiae* (namely, what persons and what subjects would be within that jurisdiction) and, in particular, whether they have compulsory jurisdiction or jurisdiction that depends on the consent of the parties; the laws to be applied by the tribunal (only the religious system of laws or also relevant state laws); whether their decisions require confirmation by a court of the state or are subject to its control; and whether jurisdiction is exclusive or parallel.

## A GENERAL CLASSIFICATION OF POWERS

As mentioned earlier,[1] some of the powers will remain with the center, while others will be transferred to the autonomous authorities; some will require joint action by the two, and still others will be held by both the center and the region so that both can act in those spheres independently.

When establishing a regime of autonomy, these classifications may help divide power. In addition, there might be a fifth category of powers: those that belong to neither the center nor the region, but are vested in or transferred to an international organization (for example, the European Union).

## THE DIVISION OF POWERS IN SPECIFIC AREAS

With the general classification in mind, we can now proceed to an exploration of the specific powers that have to be addressed. It should be emphasized that what follows is not an exhaustive list of powers that have to be considered, and hence other matters may also require a settlement. On the other hand, there may be cases of autonomy where some of the powers explored in the following pages may not be relevant.

## Security

When deciding who should be in charge of security, a distinction can be made among external security, internal security (that is, confronting the threat of terror or subversion), and public order (preventing crimes). External security is always left within the responsibility of the central government. The term, however, can be subject to differing interpretations and, hence, should be defined in advance.

Public order is the domain of a police force, which is often under the control of the local authorities. It may, however, be necessary to grant to the police or the army of the central authorities some power to intervene—upon their own initiative or at the request of the autonomous authorities—in the autonomous area in case of emergency. Joint activities in the sphere of security (such as joint patrols in certain areas) should also be considered.

In addition to the basic distinction among external security, internal security, and public order, the division of powers and responsibilities could also be based on a territorial distinction—that is, certain areas would be within the responsibility of the center and others within the powers of the autonomous authorities. Moreover, one could also add a personal division: certain persons would be protected by the central authorities, and others by the autonomous ones.

Since the various aspects of security are interrelated, it may be helpful to establish a joint security committee that handles cooperation and the division of responsibilities.

## Foreign Relations

Although in most cases of autonomy foreign relations are in principle reserved to the central authorities, a number of possible variations should be considered. The central government is usually in charge of the treaty-making power, but the autonomous area may be granted a limited right to conclude treaties in a number of spheres (such as economic or cultural matters). The autonomous entity may also be allowed to conclude agreements limited not by subject matter, but by the identity of the other party—for example, the autonomous area may be permitted to conclude agreements only with neighboring states. These activities may or may not require the authorization or approval of the central authorities.

Similarly, the center may commit itself to consult the regional authorities before it concludes agreements that may have an impact on the region. It may even include members of the regional group in the delegation that negotiates the agreement.

The implementation of a treaty may require introducing changes into the laws in a sphere in which powers have been transferred to the autonomous entity. When establishing the autonomy, one must decide whether the legislature of the state will be empowered to introduce these changes or whether only the local legislature will be authorized to effect this incorporation.

Although an autonomous entity does not usually have the right to establish embassies or consulates, it may be permitted to open offices in foreign countries for developing relations in the spheres in which it does have authority (for instance, trade and tourism).

Several options exist when considering membership in international organizations. Although states are the main members of intergovernmental organizations, an autonomous entity may have a certain influence in this sphere. One can imagine at least three possibilities: (1) The autonomous entity—by virtue of its being part of the central state—is automatically a member of all, and none but, the organizations in which the central state participates (in such a situation, the autonomous entity's membership would not be separate from the central state's); (2) the entity is allowed not to be a member of such an organization; and (3) the entity may be allowed to be a member of an organization, even if the center is not. Such "autonomous" membership would of course be limited to organizations of a technical or economic nature. The status of the autonomous entity in the organization would probably be different from the status of a state, which can be a full member. Both nonparticipation in an organization in which the center is a member and membership in an institution without the center would normally require the consent of the central authorities.

### Economic Matters

The division of powers is perhaps hardest to define in this area. The economic realm includes, inter alia, commerce, trade (within the autonomous area, between the area and the rest of the state, and between the area and foreign countries), industry, agriculture, tourism, natural resources, land, public works, and roads and highways. For each sphere of economic activity, there are a variety of possible approaches, in addition to the five general categories mentioned above.

- While reserving the power to the center, the state could commit itself to consult the autonomous authorities before adopting any measures that would have an impact on the local situation.
- The center could retain control, but permit the autonomous entity to initiate or recommend activities in the area.
- The autonomous authorities could have powers limited territorially to the autonomous area (such as trade within the area).
- The autonomous entity could be authorized to act in those spheres within the framework of a general policy established by the central government.

Matters of land ownership and of traditional economic activities are of particular importance to indigenous populations and would require careful consideration.

Natural resources have been a bone of contention in several cases of autonomy. Different solutions may be adopted for above-ground resources, on the one hand, and underground minerals, on the other hand. With regard to fishing, a distinction can be made among fishing in a river or lake that is wholly in the autonomous area, fishing in waters that are common to this area and to other parts of the state, fishing in the territorial sea (up to 12 miles from the coast), and fishing in the exclusive economic zone (up to 200 miles from the coast).

### Water and Energy

Although control over water and energy can be divided according to one of the principles described above, one should note the special character of these two resources. Since the autonomous area and the rest of the state may have common or interdependent aquifers, this area will usually require coordination and cooperation. In those parts of the world where water is scarce, it is particularly important to establish a system of dividing and controlling water resources. Moreover, since the availability of water and the need for this precious resource are often subject to change, a procedure should be agreed upon for introducing the necessary changes. A joint organ should review requests for permits to undertake development projects. Furthermore, water sources are in constant danger of pollution. Hence, the agreement on autonomy should also include provisions for protecting joint water sources against contamination.

Cooperation and coordination may also be needed in matters of energy. Due to the high cost of producing energy, the autonomous area may not be able to provide its energy independently. Moreover, the sources of the area's energy may be beyond its territory, or vice versa— the sources of the energy of other parts of the state may be located in the autonomous area.

### Communication and Transportation

While intraregional communication and transportation can easily be transferred to the autonomous entity, a different solution may have to be found for interregional or interstate activities. Since strong interests of the central government may be involved, it may wish to reserve these powers to itself, including ancillary matters such as maritime ports and airfields. However, various possibilities of cooperation and consultation may be considered.

The sphere of communication also includes telecommunications. If the autonomous area is allowed to operate its own radio and television transmitters, the parties have to make arrangements to allocate frequencies.

It may be more efficient to have postal services within the responsibility of the central authorities. However, if the parties agree to transfer these powers to the autonomous area, detailed provisions should prevent unfair competition between the services of the autonomous area and the state at large. In addition, cooperation has to be established with regard to interregional and international postal service.

### Protection of the Environment

The importance of cooperating to prevent water pollution has already been mentioned. But arrangements must be made to protect the environment in a larger context. This matter cannot be addressed on a strictly local basis and requires coordination with the state. Moreover, environmental issues are increasingly subject to international cooperation, perhaps justifying an increased role for the central government. On the other hand, because international bodies establish many of the rules that have to be obeyed by both the center and the autonomous region, it is immaterial whether the center or the region is in charge of legislation in this sphere. Questions related to protecting the environment are of particular importance in those cases where autonomy is granted to an area inhabited by indigenous populations.

## Matters of Culture

The acquisition of powers in the sphere of culture is one of the core wishes of most claims for autonomy. The main elements of culture are religion, education, and language. The right of an ethnic group to regulate its religious life is usually recognized—subject, of course, to general standards of public order and human rights. The situation may be a little tricky if some places that are holy for the majority of the population of the state are located in the autonomous area and vice versa. Provisions have to be made for freedom of access and freedom of worship.

The questions that surround the issue of education may be more complex: Who has authority to decide on the construction of new schools? Who employs and supervises the teachers? Should there be both state schools and schools of the autonomous entity within the autonomous region? What will be the language of instruction in the schools? Will the official language of the state have to be taught in the autonomous schools, and from which grade on? What levels of education are included in the powers of the autonomous region—kindergarten, elementary school, high school, higher education? Is the autonomous entity free to establish its own curriculum, or does it have to meet some requirements of the state? Are the diplomas of the establishments of the autonomous entity recognized by the state, and vice versa?

Questions related to the issue of language can also have many alternative solutions. Autonomy, of course, involves as a bare minimum the permission to use the language of the ethnic group for which the autonomy was established. Moreover, this language may be recognized either as the only official language or as a second "official" or "national" language in the region. The use of this language may be either compulsory or optional in dealings with the autonomous authorities and perhaps also with the local organs of the central government.

In this context, reference should be made to the European Charter for Regional or Minority Languages, adopted by the Committee of Ministers of the Council of Europe in 1992.[2] It establishes an obligation for states to protect and promote regional and minority languages by education and research and by permission to use those languages in official legal documents, as well as in legal proceedings, in the media, and in economic life. In particular, all discrimination with regard to the use of those languages must be eliminated.

### Social Matters

This topic includes questions of public health, welfare, social security, and labor. Usually, the autonomous region is granted powers in these spheres, but each area must be examined to determine whether the local arrangements should be completely independent or whether they should conform to some general guidelines established by the central government. In particular, when these services are subsidized by the center, they may have to be adapted to the latter's guidelines. As in most other spheres, cooperation and coordination are necessary.

In the realm of labor, it is important to decide whether the local labor exchanges should have the right to grant preference to those candidates who live in the autonomous area, or whether they should have to treat all candidates with complete equality.

### The Legal System

When establishing an autonomy one has to determine which legal system should apply in the various areas of the law (private law, criminal law, commercial law, and so forth). One possibility would be that a special legal system adopted by the autonomous legislature would be applicable, except for those matters regulated by the center (in view of the spheres in which the latter has jurisdiction). The opposite may also be an option, that is, the laws of the center apply, except for the spheres specifically within the powers of the autonomous area. A common variation recognizes the right of the region to legislate on various legal matters, within the framework of general principles established by the center.

In those spheres in which the center is in charge of the legal system that applies in the autonomous area, the question arises whether one and the same set of laws should apply in the whole country or whether the central authorities may adopt special laws for the autonomous area, taking into account its particular social and ethnic makeup (for example, Denmark has adopted a special criminal code for Greenland). It appears that such a differentiation would be quite legitimate and would not be considered illegal discrimination, in view of the opinion expressed by the Human Rights Committee established under the 1966 International Covenant on Civil and Political Rights. In its general comment on discrimination, the committee stated that "[t]he enjoyment of rights and freedoms on an equal footing . . . does not mean identical treatment in every instance. . . . [N]ot every differentiation of treatment will constitute discrimination, if the criteria for such differentiation are reasonable and objective and if the aim is to achieve a purpose which is legitimate under the Covenant."[3]

Since there may be areas of parallel powers of the center and the region, guidelines should be established in advance in case of a contradiction between rules of these two sources. It should also be decided in advance whether the laws of the autonomous parliament may diverge from all or some of the provisions of the constitution and the laws of the state. Provisions on the applicable legal system should also include directives on legal assistance and on the transfer or extradition of criminals between the autonomous area and the rest of the state.

If autonomy is granted to an indigenous group, special provisions may allow the group to live by its traditional customs. It will be necessary to decide in advance in what spheres and under what conditions the tribal customs should be applicable.

## Powers in Financial Matters

This group of powers includes questions related to currency, foreign trade, banking, customs, and taxation. Although in most cases these powers (except for taxation) are reserved for the central government, a different solution could be based on the various alternatives outlined above in the section on economic powers.

With regard to taxes, one has to decide who has the power to impose them and who has the responsibility for collecting them. Distinctions may be made between local taxes and national ones, between direct and indirect taxes, and between taxes on income and those on property located in the autonomous area. If the autonomous area has powers of taxation, measures have to be adopted to coordinate between the taxes imposed in the autonomous area and the state at large, in order to prevent smuggling. This, of course, mainly concerns indirect taxes, like value-added tax and customs duties. In addition, the parties must coordinate and cooperate to prevent tax avoidance and tax evasion.

### Residual Powers

Since it is practically impossible to solve in advance all issues that may come up, it is important to include in the autonomy arrangements a provision on residual powers, establishing who is authorized to deal with matters that have not been regulated in advance. There are at least four possible solutions:

1. Residual powers are reserved for the center.
2. They belong to the autonomous authorities.
3. They should be allocated to either the center or the region on the basis of resemblance to and analogy with other powers that have been expressly allocated.
4. They should be exercised by a joint body.

### The Division of Powers in the Case of Personal Autonomy

So far, our review of possible modes of division of powers has centered on territorial political autonomy. The situation is quite different with regard to personal autonomy. In these cases, the relevant powers are mainly in the sphere of religion, education, and language. A group that enjoys personal autonomy usually has the right to regulate its religious life and institutions, subject to public order and certain standards of human rights.

In cases where personal autonomy is granted to a religious group, it has to be decided whether the religious authorities of that group should have certain powers and jurisdiction over members of the group, for example, in some matters of personal status. The specific questions that have to be dealt with have been examined above, in the context of the power to adjudicate.

Educational matters have to be settled in a manner similar to that mentioned above in the context of territorial autonomy. If the group is granted the right to run its own schools, several questions may arise: Should these schools be subsidized by the state? What should be the balance between instruction in the official language of the state and in the language of the minority in those schools? What levels of education (kindergarten, elementary school, high school) are included in the right to establish the group's own schools? What should be the balance between those parts of the curriculum that the minority may establish and those parts that have to conform to the general curriculum of the state?

Issues connected with the language of the minority have also been discussed in the relevant passage on territorial autonomy. There is no doubt that people may use their own language, but should it be used in the media and in dealings with organs of the state? The answers to this question will usually depend on the relative number of the members of the minority group in a certain area or, to use the language of the European Charter for Regional or Minority Languages, "the geographical area in which the said language is the mode of expression of a number of people justifying the adoption of the various protective . . . measures."[4]

## THE QUESTION OF SOVEREIGNTY

Another issue that should be addressed when establishing an autonomy concerns sovereignty. In most of the past and present schemes of autonomy, sovereignty has been vested in the central state. However, different solutions could also be considered. Sovereignty could be suspended, divided, shared, or be of a functional character. As mentioned above in the chapter on autonomy and sovereignty,[5] the notion of sovereignty has undergone great changes and has become flexible.

## THE PROTECTION OF HUMAN RIGHTS

The place of human rights in the autonomous system is very important. Within the autonomous territory there may live people of ethnic groups other than the one that is the majority in that region, either members of the group that is the majority in the state or members of another minority. When establishing an autonomy, the rights of these groups must be guaranteed. Moreover, certain basic rights of members of the group for which the autonomy is established must be protected, regardless of the traditions of the group.

How can these basic rights be ensured? The text may include a reference to "public order" (or *"ordre public"*), to the fundamentals of human rights applicable in the central state, or to certain international standards of human rights (for example, the two 1966 international covenants or the various human rights documents of the OSCE). Another possibility would be to refer to international standards of human rights, without specifying particular documents.

## PARTICIPATION IN THE PUBLIC LIFE OF THE STATE

Should the inhabitants of the autonomous region take part in the public life of the central state? And, if so, how should they participate? They may have the right to full participation in the organs of government of the center; they may be completely excluded; or they may be authorized to take part only in certain activities or be only partly represented.

The answers to these questions may have some correlation with the question of sovereignty, of the citizenship of the inhabitants of the autonomous region, and of the extent and scope of the powers of the autonomous entity.

## POWER TO AMEND THE AUTONOMY ARRANGEMENTS

How should the arrangements for autonomy be changed or amended? Who should have the power to introduce those changes? Again, there are several options. The power of amendment could be reserved exclusively for the central state authorities; it could be a power to be exercised jointly by the center and the region; it may be subject to the approval of an international body.

## CITIZENSHIP

Provisions on the citizenship of the residents of the autonomous area must also be considered. The appropriate solution will depend on the specific circumstances of the case. If the central state is the sovereign, the residents would normally be its citizens, but provision may be made for adding the name of the autonomous region to the passport. The residents may also be free to have the citizenship of another state or dual nationality. It is rare for an autonomous region to have its own passports (like the Palestinians).

## PRESERVATION OF THE SPECIAL CHARACTER OF THE AREA

Should provisions be adopted to preserve the special ethnic character of the autonomous region? The local population may be keen on adopting such measures, while the central government may prefer that the door be left open for demographic changes, in order to bring the area closer to the mainstream character of the state. The cases include contradictory situations. In the case of the Åland Islands, the autonomy arrangements go to great lengths to preserve the distinctive character of the population; on the other hand, in the case of Tibet, the Chinese authorities have planned for the large-scale movement into the area of Chinese (Han) people. One can also envisage a system that permits free movement of individuals, but prohibits state intervention.

Measures to keep others out of an autonomous area may enhance the preservation and the development of the local ethnic group's tradition, culture, and language. On the other hand, such measures create closed and self-centered societies. Moreover, such measures could also be considered contrary to the right to freedom of movement, which is a recognized human right. When establishing autonomy, these different and contradictory considerations have to be taken into account.

## FINANCING THE AUTONOMOUS ENTITY

How should the autonomous entity be financed? This question is, of course, of the utmost importance. The answer depends on the economic situation of the central authorities and of the autonomous area. Granting the local authorities an appropriate portion of the taxes collected from the local population would be reasonable. The specific share to be allotted to the local authorities could be established in view of the services supplied by the center and the region, respectively. This share could be agreed upon in advance or could be the subject of periodic negotiations.

Circumstances may also warrant providing additional financial support from the center to the periphery. These subsidies can be granted on a specific basis, for certain projects, or as a block grant. In the latter case, the autonomous entities have much more discretion in using the funds.

May the autonomous authorities receive financial support from outsiders? To what extent? On the one hand, such assistance would help the autonomous institutions to function and fulfill their duties; on the other hand, the central government may view it as an interference in the relations between the center and the autonomous entity. In answering these questions, a distinction could be made among assistance from foreign individuals and corporations, from nongovernmental organizations, from international governmental organizations, and from foreign states.

## DISPUTE SETTLEMENT

Another important matter to be considered is the mode and mechanism for settling disputes between the central government and the autonomous entity. Should such disputes be settled by diplomatic means (negotiation, mediation, enquiry, or conciliation) or by a judicial procedure (arbitration or adjudication)? Different modes could be established for different kinds of disputes, but it must be clear who decides to which category a specific dispute belongs. One could also imagine a two-tiered arrangement, namely, starting with one procedure (such as conciliation), with a possible right of appeal to another procedure (such as adjudication). The first attempt would always involve direct negotiations.

One has also to determine what organ should be empowered to settle the disputes. Should it be an international body, or a joint body with members from both the central authorities and the regional ones? Or should it be the highest court of the state? If the task of settling disputes is entrusted to a nonpermanent organ, one has to establish in advance the composition of the ad hoc body and the procedures it should follow.

## SUPERVISION BY THE CENTER

How and to what extent may the central government supervise the activities of the autonomous entity? As mentioned earlier,[6] the center does not have a general power of control, as it would have in case of decentralization. Nevertheless, it follows from some of the above analyses that the center may keep certain means of supervision or direction. Thus, fiscal measures may serve as an efficient means of control (through periodic negotiations on the allocation of resources to the autonomous entity). The need for confirmation of the laws of the autonomous entity and the important—though limited—power of veto of the center can be quite significant. Moreover, the power reserved to the central government to appoint or confirm some of the key figures of the self-governing authorities may give the center considerable leverage.

When dividing powers, the center can retain some of the more important competences. Alternatively, the arrangement could provide that the local authorities may act in a certain sphere only within general guidelines established by the center or in accordance with national planning. The center may also retain the residual powers. An important, perhaps less known, means of control exists if the judicial organ of the central state plays a leading role in the settlement of disputes between the autonomous region and the center.

Another matter to be considered is whether the central organs should be authorized to act instead of the autonomous ones in case the latter do not function or do not fulfill their responsibilities. Moreover, should the central government have the power to impose sanctions on the local authorities (for example, to dissolve the legislature of the autonomous entity or to dismiss its executive organ)? All these possibilities must be considered when establishing a regime of autonomy.

## RELEVANT CIRCUMSTANCES

So far, we have examined a great number of matters and options. The choice of the specific solution may depend on a number of geographic, historical, political, and demographic circumstances. For practical reasons, the geographic proximity or remoteness of the center of the state in relation to the autonomous region may have to be taken into consideration. In addition, the past relations between the center and the periphery may determine some of the content of the regime. For instance, the autonomous region may have had the status of a colony; it may have been an independent but weaker state; it may have been transferred from one state to the other; it may have been one of several semi-independent units that merged into a unitary state; or it may have been detached from a state and become internationalized.

Another significant parameter is the question of sovereignty. Autonomy arrangements will probably depend considerably on the determination of who has sovereignty over the autonomous area. As mentioned earlier, sovereignty can reside with the center, it can be suspended or shared, or it can be of a functional nature. A related question is whether the area was or is the object of a territorial dispute.

The basic ideology and international outlook or alignment of the center and the autonomous entity will also have an impact upon the extent of the autonomy arrangements. It may be expected that if there is parallelism or similarity between the attitudes of the central government and those of the autonomous authorities, the former is likely to be disposed to grant the latter extensive powers. On the other hand, if there is a sharp discrepancy, the center will hesitate to divest itself of major powers, in particular in security matters.

The nature of the group that is granted autonomy has also to be borne in mind. An ethnic or linguistic minority may be satisfied with few powers or with personal autonomy; a group that considers itself to be a "people"—whatever that may mean—will seek maximum powers and responsibilities.

The type of the autonomy to be granted will depend on the demographic composition of the autonomous area: Is it inhabited mainly by one ethnic group, or are there members of more than one group? If there are several groups, what is the numerical ratio among them? What are the relations among the various groups, and how does each group relate to the center? What is the ratio between the minority for whom the autonomy is granted and the members of the majority in the state who live in the autonomous area?

Finally, the division of powers in matters of security will depend on whether the regime of autonomy is welcomed by all the members of the group, or whether some are not satisfied and may resort to violence.

# 12

## FACTORS THAT MAY INCREASE
## THE PROSPECTS FOR SUCCESS

Although each case of autonomy is different, it seems that certain ingredients may generally be counted on to enhance the chances of success.

1. A regime of autonomy should be established with the consent of the population intended to benefit from it. (Thus, due to the objection of the Palestinians, the autonomy negotiations between Egypt and Israel from 1979 to 1982 were doomed to failure.) However, sometimes a population that at first only reluctantly accepts a regime of autonomy, later comes to favor it (as happened in the Åland Islands).

2. The regime should be established with the consent, express or implied, of a foreign state to which the autonomous group may have an ethnic or other affiliation. (Thus, Sweden's positive attitude has contributed to the success of the regime of the Åland Islands.)

3. The regime should be beneficial for both the state and the population of the autonomous region.

4. The local population should be permitted to enjoy the formal or symbolic paraphernalia of self-determination, such as a flag, an anthem, and an officially recognized language. (Most of the successful autonomies enjoy these privileges, including the Åland Islands, Greenland, and the Faroe Islands.)

5. The division of powers should be defined as clearly as possible. (The texts concerning the Åland Islands, South Tyrol/Alto Adige, Memel-

Klaipeda, Eritrea, and the Palestinians are quite detailed; however, although the documents concerning Greenland and the Faroe Islands are rather short, their autonomy has nevertheless been a success.)

6. If activities of the central government in spheres that are under its authority directly affect the autonomous region, the local authorities should, if possible, be consulted. (This practice is particularly conspicuous in the case of the Åland Islands and Greenland.)

7. An organ for cooperation between the central government and the local authorities should be established. Its composition, powers, responsibilities, and procedures should be established, as far as possible, in advance. (Thus, the Åland Delegation has prevented many misunderstandings, and the numerous organs of cooperation planned for Israel and the Palestinians may have a beneficial effect.)

8. Modes and mechanisms for settling disputes between the center and the local authorities should be established, with a maximum of detail. (However, when relations between the center and the autonomous authority are good, disputes can often be prevented at an earlier stage by the organs of cooperation.)

9. Under certain circumstances it may be preferable to establish the autonomy in stages, that is, to transfer the relevant powers (and perhaps also the territory involved) gradually. (Gradualism was particularly efficient in the cases of Greenland and the Palestinians.)

10. The prospects for success are greater if both the central government and the autonomous authorities are based on democratic regimes. (As examples one may refer to Puerto Rico, Greenland, and the Åland Islands.)

11. Every regime of autonomy must include guarantees for the respect of human rights, including the principle of equality and non-discrimination among all the inhabitants. Similarly, a minority that lives within an ethnic group that has been granted autonomy should enjoy minority rights. (This is particularly important in cases where there are considerable ideological or traditional differences between the center and the autonomous population on matters of human rights—for example, the status of women and the rights of the child.)

12. A rather similar stage of economic development and standard of living in the autonomous region and in the state as a whole may enhance the chances of success. (Thus, Denmark's efforts to raise the standard of living in Greenland have helped to make this autonomy a suc-

cess, while the economic and social differences between the north and the south may have contributed to the failure of the autonomy in southern Sudan.)

13. If autonomy is established for a limited period, the procedure to be followed at the end of that period should be established. If possible, a list of tentative options to be considered at that stage should be drafted.

14. If the autonomy arrangement includes a commitment to certain rules of behavior, it may be helpful if those rules can be based on international norms (as is the case with the references to international standards of human rights, health, and environmental protection included in the texts relating to the Palestinians).

15. The most important and indispensable condition for a successful autonomy is a prevailing atmosphere of conciliation and goodwill. This condition must be generated by an energetic and sustained effort to explain and to engage in patient dialogue. (So far, no arrangements of autonomy have succeeded in a hostile atmosphere. The atmosphere may, however, improve with time, as happened in the Åland Islands.)

16. Autonomy should be established before the relations between the majority in the state and the majority in the region deteriorate considerably. If there is hatred and frustration, it is too late, and autonomy will not be able to soothe the strained atmosphere.

# 13

# AUTONOMY: AN APPRAISAL
# OF THE PROS AND CONS

Opinions on autonomy vary remarkably. Although some consider it to be futile and unworkable,[1] others have expressed the opinion that it "remains a useful, if imprecise, concept within which flexible and unique political structures may be developed to respond to that complexity."[2]

It is true that autonomy is often "reluctantly offered and ungratefully received."[3] It is usually a compromise solution, and it often does not correspond to the original wishes of any of the parties involved. In many cases, the central government hesitates to grant autonomy for various reasons:

- the fear that autonomy may lead to secession;
- the consideration that granting autonomy to a certain region or group would constitute discrimination against the other inhabitants;[4]
- the concern that granting autonomy may lead to the violation of certain interests or values of the state as a whole (for example, behavior that could harm the environment or the imposition of punishments that do not conform to the moral values of the majority of the population); and
- the risk that autonomy might induce the intervention of a foreign state to which members of the autonomous group have an ethnic or other affiliation.

The members of the group for whom the autonomy is established often view it as a lesser evil, generally preferring complete secession.

Nevertheless, various countries have resorted to autonomy in order to accommodate diversity and heterogeneity. In some cases the scheme functions properly, in others it more or less works; but sometimes autonomy does not function and does not lead to the hoped-for peaceful coexistence.

Not all minorities or groups need autonomy. Many problems of minorities can be solved within the framework of general rules of human rights without autonomy, such as the prohibition of discrimination and the right of citizens to political participation. If there is a need for further collective arrangements, autonomy should be among the possibilities to be considered. Autonomy is not a panacea, but only a tool or a framework that can constitute an adequate compromise if the parties are looking for one. By definition, compromise involves mutual concessions and, therefore, in most cases none of the parties will be fully satisfied by the compromise. Autonomy cannot create the wish for compromise, but it can help shape its content. Like any tool, it must be used in accordance with the special circumstances of each case.

One of the great advantages of autonomy is its flexibility. It includes a wide range of possibilities—from a minimum of competence, on the one hand, to a great number of powers just short of full independence, on the other hand.

When establishing an autonomy, one should be careful that it does not lead to complete separateness or to a cultural ghetto: "States composed of segregated autonomy regimes would resemble more a museum of social and cultural antiquities than any human rights ideal."[5]

The structure of the international community is going through a period of transformation due to various factors discussed above,[6] in particular the trend toward fragmentation within the state and the increasing role and powers of international organizations. The existence of an overarching international body with powers above both the state and the autonomous region can perhaps mitigate the effects of the regionalization, making it easier for the center to divest itself of some of its powers in favor of the autonomous region.

◆ ◆ ◆ ◆ ◆

May I express the hope that this study may contribute to the search for peaceful solutions that preserve the unity of the state while satisfying the aspirations of certain groups that wish to preserve and promote their own way of life. Two admonitions must, however, be repeated: *ceterum censeo,* first, each case is different, and second, no system of coexistence can work unless the people involved have peaceful intentions.

# NOTES

## 1. EASING ETHNIC TENSIONS

**1.** See, for example, Malcolm N. Shaw, "The Definition of Minorities in International Law," *Israel Yearbook on Human Rights* 20 (1990): 13–43. See also *Compilation of Proposals Concerning the Definition of the Term "Minority,"* UN Doc. E/CN.4/1987/WG.5/WP.1, 14 November 1986. For a description of the various minorities, see Georgina Ashworth, ed., *World Minorities,* 3 vols. (Sunbury, England: Quartermaine House Ltd., 1977–80); Minority Rights Group, ed., *World Dictionary of Minorities* (Chicago: St. James Press, 1990); Minority Rights Group, *Minority Rights Group: Report* (London: Minority Rights Group; 6 issues/year). See also Joseph V. Montville, ed., *Conflict and Peacemaking in Multiethnic Societies* (Lexington, Mass.: Lexington Books, 1990); Ted Robert Gurr, *Minorities at Risk: A Global View of Ethnopolitical Conflict* (Washington, D.C.: United States Institute of Peace Press, 1993); Jochen A. Frowein et al., eds., *Das Minderheitenrecht europäischer Staaten,* 2 vols. (Berlin: Springer, 1993–94).

**2.** Francesco Capotorti, "Minorities," in Rudolf Bernhardt, ed., *Encyclopedia of Public International Law,* vol. 8 (1985), 385–395 at 385. The main elements of this definition have also been adopted by others. See, for example, Adeno Addis, "Individualism, Communitarianism, and the Rights of Ethnic Minorities," *Notre Dame Law Review* 66 (1991): 1219–1280 at 1261. The Declaration on the Rights of Persons Belonging to National or Ethnic, Religious and Linguistic Minorities, adopted by the UN Commission on Human Rights on 21 February 1992 (Resolution 1992/16) and by the UN General Assembly on 18 December 1992 (Resolution 47/135), does not include any definition. The term usually relates to people who are citizens of the state in which they reside and where they constitute a minority group. See G. Gilbert, "The Legal Protection Accorded to Minority Groups in Europe," *Netherlands Yearbook of International Law* 23 (1992): 67–104 at 72.

**3.** On this regime, see, for example, Jacob Robinson et al., *Were the Minorities Treaties a Failure?* (New York: Institute of Jewish Affairs, 1943); Louis B. Sohn and Thomas Buergenthal, *International Protection of Human Rights* (Indianapolis: Bobbs-Merrill, 1973), 213–306; Jacob Robinson, "International Protection of Minorities: A Global View," *Israel Yearbook on Human Rights* 1 (1971): 61–91; Richard B. Bilder, "Can Minorities Treaties Work?" *Israel Yearbook on Human Rights* 20 (1990): 71–92 at 74–79; and Carol Weisbrod, "Minorities and Diversities: The 'Remarkable Experiment' of the League of Nations," *Connecticut Journal of International Law* 8 (1993): 359–406.

**4.** For an analysis of this provision, see Louis B. Sohn, "The Rights of Minorities," in Louis Henkin, ed., *The International Bill of Rights: The Covenant on Civil and Political Rights* (New York: Columbia University Press, 1981), 270–289; Patrick Thornberry, *International Law and the Rights of Minorities* (Oxford: Clarendon, 1991), 141–247. For the "General Comment" on Article 27 by the Human Rights Committee established under the convention, see UN Doc. CCPR/C/21/Rev. 1/Add. 5 (1994).

**5.** For example, the 1989 Convention on the Rights of the Child (Article 30); the 1948 Convention on the Prevention and Punishment of the Crime of Genocide; the 1960 UNESCO Convention against Discrimination in Education; the 1965 International Convention on the Elimination of All Forms of Racial Discrimination; the 1981 UN Declaration against Intolerance and Discrimination Based on Religion or Belief. Within the European context, one may also refer to the Resolution of the European Parliament of 16 October 1981, known as the Community Charter of Regional Languages and Cultures and the Charter of the Rights of Ethnic Minorities; the European Charter for Regional or Minority Languages, adopted by the Committee of Ministers of the Council of Europe on 5 November 1992, European Treaty Series, no. 148, reproduced in Hurst Hannum, ed., *Documents on Autonomy and Minority Rights* (Dordrecht, The Netherlands: Nijhoff, 1993), 86–101; and the Framework Convention for the Protection of National Minorities, adopted by the Council of Europe on 1 February 1995, reproduced in *International Legal Materials* 34 (1995): 351–359.

**6.** For an outline of the CSCE's activities in this area, see Felix Ermacora, "Rights of Minorities and Self-Determination in the Framework of the CSCE," in Arie Bloed and Pieter van Dijk, eds., *The Human Dimension of the Helsinki Process: The Vienna Follow-up Meeting and Its Aftermath* (Dordrecht, The Netherlands: Nijhoff, 1991), 197–206; Mala Tabory, "Minority Rights in the CSCE Context," *Israel Yearbook on Human Rights* 20 (1990): 197–222, reprinted in Yoram Dinstein, ed., *Protection of Minorities and Human Rights* (Dordrecht, The Netherlands: Nijhoff, 1992), 187–211.

**7.** "Document of the Copenhagen Meeting of the Conference on the Human Dimension of the CSCE," *International Legal Materials* 29 (1990): 1306–1321. The document was comprehensively analyzed in the following articles: Thomas Buergenthal, "The Copenhagen CSCE Meeting: A New Public Order for Europe," *Human Rights Law Journal* 11 (1990): 217–246; Hurst Hannum, "Contemporary Developments in the International Protection of the Rights of Minorities," *Notre Dame Law Review* 66 (1991): 1431–1448 at 1439–1443; and Arie Bloed, "A New CSCE Human Rights 'Catalogue': The Copenhagen Meeting of the Conference on the Human Dimension of the CSCE," in Bloed and Dijk, *Human Dimension,* 54–73.

**8.** Some states represented at the conference, such as Italy, were in favor of a more far-reaching provision that would have established a right to autonomy for minority groups who are a majority in a certain region. See Vincent Ramelot and Eric Remacle, *L'OSCE et les conflits en Europe, les dossiers du Grip* (Brussels: Institut européen de recherche et d'information sur la paix et la sécurité, 1995), 42–43.

**9.** CSCE, Report of the CSCE Meeting of Experts on National Minorities (Geneva, 1991), CSCE/REMN.20 of 19 July 1991. The author wishes to express her thanks to Ambassador Max Kampelman for having provided this document to her.

**10.** Document of the Moscow Meeting of the Conference on the Human Dimension of the CSCE, Moscow, 30 October 1991. The author wishes to express her thanks to Dr. David Stewart for having provided this document to her.

**11.** *International Legal Materials* 31 (1992): 1385–1420 at 1395–1399.

**12.** UN General Assembly, Resolution 47/135. For an analysis of this declaration, see Natan Lerner, "The 1992 UN Declaration on Minorities," *Israel Yearbook on Human Rights* 23 (1993): 111–128. The hope has been expressed that, once a declaration has been adopted, a binding convention may follow. See Stephen Roth, "Towards a Minority Convention: Its Need and Content," *Israel Yearbook on Human Rights* 20 (1990): 93–126.

**13.** Council of Europe, Framework Convention. See also Florence Benoît-Rohmer, "La Convention-cadre du Conseil de l'Europe pour la protection des minorités nationales," *European Journal of International Law* 6

(1995): 573–597; and Florence Benoît-Rohmer, *The Minority Question in Europe: Texts and Commentary* (Strasbourg: Council of Europe, 1996), 121–151.

**14.** Marc Weller, "The International Response to the Dissolution of the Socialist Federal Republic of Yugoslavia," *American Journal of International Law* 86 (1992): 569–607 at 583. For an outline of developments in the area, see also *Report of the Secretary-General Pursuant to Paragraph 3 of Security Council Resolution 713 (1991)*, UN Doc. S/23169, 25 October 1991.

**15.** The EPC was established by Title II of the Single European Act of 1986.

**16.** *International Legal Materials* 31 (1992): 1485–1487 at 1486; Weller, "The International Response to the Dissolution of Yugoslavia," 587.

**17.** Weller, "The International Response to the Dissolution of Yugoslavia," 593; *International Legal Materials* 31 (1992): 1497–1499 at 1498 (Opinion no. 2 of 11 January 1992).

**18.** Alain Pellet, "The Opinions of the Badinter Arbitration Committee: A Second Breath for the Self-Determination of Peoples," *European Journal of International Law* 3 (1992): 178–185 at 183; *International Legal Materials* 31 (1992): 1492–1497 at 1496 and 1497 (Opinion no. 1).

**19.** Pellet, "Opinions of the Badinter Arbitration Committee," 184; *International Legal Materials* 31 (1992): 1497–1499 at 1498 (Opinion no. 2 of 11 January 1992).

**20.** Weller, "The International Response to the Dissolution of Yugoslavia," 592; Pellet, "Opinions of the Badinter Arbitration Committee," 184; *International Legal Materials* 31 (1992): 1494–1499 at 1496, 1498, and 1499 (Opinions no. 1 and no. 2 of 11 January 1992).

**21.** Proposed constitutional structure for Bosnia and Herzegovina, submitted in the framework of the International Conference on the Former Yugoslavia (in which the United Nations, the European Community, the CSCE, and other organizations participated), reproduced in Annex VII to the *Report of the UN Secretary General on the International Conference on the Former Yugoslavia*, UN Doc. S/24795, 11 November 1992; *International Legal Materials* 31 (1992): 1584–1594.

**22.** Section 15 of the 1990 Constitution of Croatia, and Sections 3–59 of the 1991 Constitutional Law of Human Rights and Freedoms and the Rights of National and Ethnic Communities or Minorities, in Albert P. Blaustein and Gisbert H. Flanz, eds., *Constitutions of the Countries of the World* (Dobbs Ferry, N.Y.: Oceana, 1991), binder 5, release 92-3, 33, 37–38, 139–160; Sections 45–50 of the 1992 Constitution of the Federal Republic of Yugoslavia, in Blaustein and Flanz, *Constitutions*, Supplement, binder 3, release 94-2, 13–14; Section 48 of the 1991 Constitution of Macedonia, in Blaustein and Flanz, *Constitutions,* binder 11, release 93-7, 1, 17; Sections 61–65 of the 1991 Constitution of Slovenia, in Blaustein and Flanz, *Constitutions,* binder 17, release 92-6 1, 11–13.

**23.** Sections 5–58, 1991 Constitutional Law of Human Rights and Freedoms.

**24.** Section 64, 1991 Constitution of Slovenia.

**25.** *International Legal Materials* 35 (1996): 75–183.

**26.** Ibid., Annex 4, 117.

**27.** Ibid., Annex 6, 130.

**28.** Section II(2), Constitution of Bosnia and Herzegovina.

**29.** Recently, the number of publications on this subject has grown considerably; only the most important ones will be mentioned here. Report by Jose R. Martinez Cobo, Rapporteur, *Study of the Problem of Discrimination against Indigenous Populations,* UN Doc. E/CN.4/Sub.2/1986/7, Adds. 1–4, 1986. The conclusions and recommendations of this study have been published in UN Sales no. E.86.XIV.3. See also Hurst Hannum, *Autonomy, Sovereignty, and Self-Determination: The Accommodation of Conflicting Rights* (Philadelphia: University of Pennsylvania Press, 1990), 74–103; Gudmundur Alfredsson, "Indigenous Populations," in Bernhardt, *Encyclopedia of Public International Law,* vol. 8 (1985), 311–316; Raidza Torres, "The Rights of Indigenous Populations: The Emerging International Norm," *Yale Journal of International Law* 16 (1991): 127–175; Chris C. Tennant and Mary Ellen Turpel, "A Case Study of Indigenous Peoples: Genocide, Ethnocide and Self-Determination," *Nordic Journal of International Law* 59 (1990): 287–319; Thornberry, *International Law and the Rights of Minorities,* 331–382; Catherine Brölmann and Marjoleine Y. A. Zieck, "Indigenous Peoples," in Catherine Brölmann et al., eds., *Peoples and Minorities in International Law* (Dordrecht, The Netherlands: Nijhoff, 1993), 187–220; Bradley Reed Howard, "Human Rights and Indigenous People: On the Relevance of International Law for Indigenous Liberation," *German Yearbook of International Law* 35 (1992): 105–156; Russel Lawrence Barsh, "Indigenous People in the 1990s: From Object to Subject of International Law?" *Harvard Human Rights Journal* 7 (1994): 33–85.

**30.** Martinez Cobo, UN Sales no. E.86.XIV.3, 29, paragraphs 379–382.

**31.** See, for example, the 1994 Draft Declaration on the Rights of Indigenous Peoples, prepared by the Working Group on Indigenous Populations of the Sub-Commission on Prevention of Discrimination and Protection of Minorities, UN Doc. E/CN.4/Sub.2/1994/56, 28 October

1994, Preamble and Article 3. The declaration was adopted by the Sub-Commission on 26 August 1994. The UN Commission on Human Rights, by Resolution 1995/32 of 3 March 1995, decided to establish an "open-ended inter-sessional Working Group" for further elaboration of the draft, UN Doc. E/CN.4/1995/L.11, Add. 2, 3 March 1995.

On the right of self-determination of indigenous peoples, see also Erica-Irene A. Daes, "Some Considerations on the Right of Indigenous Peoples to Self-Determination," *Transnational Law and Contemporary Problems* 3 (1993): 1–11; Gudmundur Alfredsson, "The Right of Self-Determination and Indigenous Peoples," in Christian Tomuschat, ed., *Modern Law of Self-Determination* (Dordrecht, The Netherlands: Nijhoff, 1993), 41–54.

In order to exclude indigenous groups from those that have a right to self-determination, sometimes an attempt is made to describe them by the term *people* in the singular, which would merely mean a number of persons, while *peoples* in the plural would refer to groups that do have the right of self-determination. See, for example, Alfredsson, "Right of Self-Determination," 46; and *Consideration of a Permanent Forum for Indigenous People,* report of the workshop held in accordance with Commission on Human Rights Resolution 1995/30 (Copenhagen, 26–28 June 1995), UN Doc. E/CN.4/Sub.2/AC.4/1995/7, 12 July 1995, paragraph 15, 5; *Discrimination against Indigenous Peoples,* report of the Working Group on Indigenous Populations on its 12th session, UN Doc. E/CN.4/Sub.2/1994/30, 17 August 1994, 14.

**32.** Convention (No. 169) Concerning Indigenous and Tribal Peoples in Independent Countries (1989), *International Labour Office Official Bulletin,* ser. A, 72, no. 2 (1989): 59, reprinted in *International Legal Materials* 28 (1989): 1382.

**33.** Working Group on Indigenous Populations, 1994 Draft Declaration on the Rights of Indigenous Peoples. For an analysis of this draft declaration, see Catherine M. Brölmann and Marjoleine Y. A. Zieck, "Some Remarks on the Draft Declaration on the Rights of Indigenous Peoples," *Leiden Journal of International Law* 8 (1995): 103–113.

**34.** Working Group on Indigenous Populations, 1994 Draft Declaration on the Rights of Indigenous Peoples. According to Alfredsson, the unofficial model for earlier versions of this proposal was the Danish home rule legislation for Greenland. See Alfredsson's report, "Equality and Non-discrimination: Minority Rights," Council of Europe, 7th International Colloquy on the European Convention on Human Rights, H/Coll(90)6, Strasbourg (1990), 10.

**35.** The Nuuk Conclusions and Recommendations on Indigenous Autonomy and Self-Government, Report of the Meeting of Experts to review the experience of countries in the operation of schemes of internal self-government for indigenous peoples, Nuuk, 24–28 September 1991, UN Doc. E/CN.4/1992/42, 25 November 1991, 12.

**36.** *Statutes of Canada,* 1993, 41 Eliz. 2, c. 28 (adopted 10 June 1993). See also Thomas Isaac, "The Nunavut Agreement-in-Principle and Section 35 of the Constitution Act, 1982," *Manitoba Law Journal* 21 (1992): 390–405; Kevin R. Gray, "The Nunavut Land Claims Agreement and the Future of the Eastern Arctic: The Uncharted Path to Effective Self-Government," *Toronto Faculty of Law Review* 52 (1994): 300–344. See also the 1986 Act Relating to Self-Government for the Sechelt Indian Band, *Statutes of Canada* 1986, 34 Eliz. 2, c. 27 (adopted 17 June 1986). The author wishes to express her gratitude to Professor Anne Bayefsky and Ms. Mary D. Temple for having provided her the relevant texts.

**37.** The deal was a constitutional reform package intended to increase Quebec's powers and its recognition as a "distinct society," as well as to reorganize the federal Senate in accordance with the wishes of the less populous western provinces. The objections to the deal related mainly to these matters, but there were also some doubts about the provision on the recognition of an "inherent right to self-government" by the indigenous groups. Most interestingly, it seems that although the deal was supported by their leaders, some of the indigenous people themselves were not satisfied with the relevant provisions, since they considered those articles not to be far-reaching enough. See "Canada's Aboriginals: Unfinishable Business," *The Economist,* 14 November 1992, 54; Dalee Sambo, "Indigenous Peoples and International Standard-Setting Processes: Are State Governments Listening?" *Transnational Law and Contemporary Problems* 3 (1993): 13–47 at 32–45.

**38.** Natan Lerner, *Group Rights and Discrimination in International Law* (Dordrecht, The Netherlands: Nijhoff, 1990).

**39.** The literature on this subject is abundant. We will mention only a few sources here: Karl Renner, *Das Selbstbestimmungsrecht der Nationen, in besonderer Anwendung auf Österreich* (Leipzig and Vienna: Franz Deutlicke, 1918); Rupert Emerson, "Self-Determination," *American Journal of International Law* 65 (1971): 459–475; Michla Pomerance, *Self-Determination in Law and Practice* (Dordrecht, The Netherlands: Nijhoff, 1982); Hannum, *Autonomy, Sovereignty, and Self-Determination,* 27–49; Antonio Cassese, "The Self-Determination of Peoples," in Henkin, *International Bill of Rights,* 92–113; Alexandre Kiss, "The Peoples' Right to Self-Determination," *Human Rights Journal* 7 (1986): 165–175; Daniel Thürer, "Self-Determination," in Bernhardt, *Encyclopedia of Public International Law,* vol. 8 (1985), 470–476; Thomas M. Franck, "Postmodern Tribalism and the Right to

Secession," in Brölmann et al., *Peoples and Minorities in International Law,*
3–35; Rosalyn Higgins, *Problems and Process: International Law and How We
Use It* (Oxford: Clarendon Press, 1994), 111–128; Antonio Cassese, *Self-
Determination of Peoples: A Legal Reappraisal* (Cambridge: Cambridge University Press, 1995); Christian Tomuschat, ed., *Modern Law of Self-Determination* (Dordrecht, The Netherlands: Nijhoff, 1993); Hurst Hannum,
"Rethinking Self-Determination," *Virginia Journal of International Law* 34
(1993): 1–69; Daniel Thürer, *Das Selbstbestimmungsrecht der Völker* (Bern:
Stämpfli, 1976); S. Calogeropoulos-Stratis, *Le Droit des peuples à disposer
d'eux-mêmes* (Brussels: Bruyland, 1973); W. Ofuatey-Kodjoe, "Self-Determination," in Oscar Schachter and Christopher C. Joyner, eds., *United Nations
Legal Order* (Washington, D.C.: American Society of International Law;
Cambridge: Cambridge University Press, 1995), 349–389.

**40.** For example, Pomerance, *Self-Determination in Law and Practice,* 67,
73–76. The legal validity of the right to self-determination has also been
denied by J. H. W. Verzijl, *International Law in Historical Perspective,* vol. 1
(Leiden: Sijthoff, 1968), 321–336 at 321 and 324; and by Sir Gerald Fitz-
maurice, "The Future of Public International Law and of the International
Legal System in the Circumstances of Today," in Institut de Droit International, *Livre du Centenaire 1873–1973* (Basel: Editions Korger, 1973),
196–328 at 233.

**41.** See, for example, Joseph S. Nye, Jr., "The Self-Determination
Trap," *Washington Post,* 15 December 1992, A3; David Binder and Barbara
Crossette, "New Peace Threat Is an Old Enemy: Emerging Ethnic Conflicts Preoccupy World Leaders," *International Herald Tribune,* 8 February
1993; and Amitai Etzioni, "The Evils of Self-Determination," *Foreign Policy* 89 (winter 1992–93): 21–35.

**42.** *Case Concerning East Timor* (Portugal v. Australia), ICJ, *Reports,*
1995, 90, at 102.

**43.** Thomas M. Franck, *The Power of Legitimacy among Nations* (London: Oxford University Press, 1990), 154–169.

**44.** Report of the International Committee of Jurists Entrusted by the
Council of the League of Nations with the Task of Giving an Advisory
Opinion upon the Legal Aspects of the Aaland Islands Question, October
1920, League of Nations, *Official Journal,* Special Supplement, no. 3, 5; *The
Aaland Islands Question,* Report Submitted to the Council of the League of
Nations by the Commission of Rapporteurs, 16 April 1921, League of
Nations Council Doc. B.7 21/68/106, 27. It appears that there is a certain
difference in the approaches of the two committees. See Nathaniel Berman,
"Sovereignty in Abeyance: Self-Determination and International Law,"
*Wisconsin International Law Journal* 7 (1988): 51–105.

**45.** Report of the International Committee of Jurists, 5; Report of the Commission of Rapporteurs, 28.

**46.** Some authors are of the opinion that the principle of self-determination was already a binding rule under the charter. See, for example, Ofuatey-Kodjoe, "Self-Determination."

**47.** For example, the 1960 United Nations Declaration on Granting of Independence to Colonial Countries and Peoples, General Assembly Resolution 1514 (XV) of 14 December 1960; the 1962 Resolution on Permanent Sovereignty over Natural Resources, General Assembly Resolution 1803 (XVII) of 14 December 1962; and the 1970 Declaration on Principles of International Law concerning Friendly Relations and Cooperation among States, General Assembly Resolution 2625 (XXV) of 24 October 1970.

**48.** For example, Principle VIII of the 1975 Helsinki Final Act of the Conference on Security and Cooperation in Europe, reproduced in *International Legal Materials* 14 (1975): 1292–1325 at 1295.

**49.** United Nations Treaty Series, 999: 171, and 993: 3.

**50.** Cassese, *Self-Determination of Peoples: A Legal Reappraisal*, 67–140.

**51.** Ernest Renan, "Qu'est-ce qu'une nation?" English translation reprinted in John Hutchinson and Anthony D. Smith, eds., *Nationalism* (Oxford: Oxford University Press, 1994), 17–18. On the other hand, it seems that among African governments "a people is the sum total of the citizens of an independent state which has liberated itself from colonialism or racism"—see Asbjorn Eide, "Minority Situations: In Search of Peaceful and Constructive Solutions," *Notre Dame Law Review* 66 (1991): 1311–1346 at 1331. Similarly, according to Adeno Addis, "it is not quite clear that the word 'peoples' . . . refers to anything other than the entire inhabitants of the nation state"—see Addis, "Individualism, Communitarianism, and the Rights of Ethnic Minorities," *Notre Dame Law Review* 66 (1991): 1219–1280 at 1264.

**52.** On the relationship between minorities' right and peoples' right to self-determination, see Patrick Thornberry, "Self-Determination, Minorities, Human Rights: A Review of International Instruments," *International and Comparative Law Quarterly* 38 (1989): 867–889; Yadhi Ben Achour, "Souveraineté étatique et protection internationale des minorités," *Recueil des Cours de l'Académie de Droit International* 245 (1994-I): 321–461 at 375. Some authors are of the opinion that the definition of a people includes both territorial and historical aspects: see Hurst Hannum, "Synthesis of Discussions," in Brölmann et al., eds., *Peoples and Minorities in International Law*, 333–339 at 334; Ofuatey-Kodjoe, "Self-Determination," 358, 374; others mention the quantitative difference between a people and an ethnic group. See also Gilbert, "The Legal Protection Accorded to Minority Groups in Europe," 73–74. The lack of a proper distinction has led some writers to the conclusion that "[p]eoples are recognized as such when they have asserted and forced upon the world the recognition of peoplehood. . . . State practice since the end of World War Two has been to recognize the right of self-determination outside the decolonization context only of peoples or nations that have succeeded in separating themselves from a controlling power, most often by the use of force. . . ." See M. C. van Walt van Praag, "The Position of UNPO in the International Legal Order," in Brölmann et al., *Peoples and Minorities in International Law*, 313–329 at 317.

**53.** Franck, *The Power of Legitimacy among Nations*, 153, 162–165.

**54.** See, for example, Higgins, *Problems and Processes*, 113–114, 115–116, 124; Cassese, *Self-Determination of Peoples: A Legal Reappraisal*, 59–60, 326. It seems that the inhabitants of a nonindependent territory have the right to self-determination irrespective of whether they constitute a "people." See Hannum, *Autonomy, Sovereignty, and Self-Determination*, 36.

**55.** *International Legal Materials* 31 (1992): 1498.

**56.** See, for example, Hannum, *Autonomy, Sovereignty, and Self-Determination*, 46; Hannum, "Rights of Minorities," 1457; Hannum, "Rethinking Self-Determination," 41–57, 67; Michla Pomerance, "Self-Determination: The Metamorphosis of an Ideal," *Israel Law Review* 19 (1984): 310–339 at 320; Cassese, *Self-Determination of Peoples: A Legal Appraisal*, 339; Allan Rosas, "Internal Self-Determination," in Tomuschat, *Modern Law of Self-Determination*, 225–252 at 228; Max M. Kampelman, "Secession and the Right of Self-Determination: An Urgent Need to Harmonize Principle and Pragmatism," *Washington Quarterly* 16 (1993): 5–12. (According to Kampelman, secession should be achieved only peacefully, through negotiation.) Hector Gros Espiell, *Implementation of United Nations Resolutions Relating to the Right of Peoples under Colonial and Alien Domination to Self-Determination*, UN Doc. E/CN.4/Sub.2/405/Rev.1 (1980), paragraph 90; Aureliu Cristescu, *The Right to Self-Determination: Historical and Current Developments on the Basis of United Nations Instruments*, UN Doc. E/CN.4/Sub.2/404/Rev.1, Sales No. E.80.XIV.3 (1981), 41, paragraph 279; Peter Malanczuk, "The Kurdish Crisis and Allied Intervention," *European Journal of International Law* 2 (1991): 114–132 at 124; Philippe Cahier, "Changements et continuité du droit international," *Recueil des Cours de l'Académie de Droit International* 195 (1985-VI): 9–374 at 48; Thürer, "Self-Determination," 474.

**57.** For example, Daniel Turp, "Le droit de sécession en droit international public," *Canadian Yearbook of International Law* 20 (1982): 24–78;

Yoram Dinstein, "Collective Human Rights of Peoples and Minorities," *International and Comparative Law Quarterly* 25 (1976): 102–120 at 108; and Dinstein, "Multinational, Federal and Confederal Arrangements" (in Hebrew), *Tel Aviv Studies in Law* 17 (1992): 231–285 at 237–238. In the second article, Dinstein tends to limit slightly the right to secession.

**58.** Lee C. Buchheit, *Secession: The Legitimacy of Self-Determination* (New Haven: Yale University Press, 1978), 222. Buchheit talks about "remedial secession" as a last resort in the case of oppression.

**59.** Lea Brilmayer, "Secession and Self-Determination: A Territorial Interpretation," *Yale Journal of International Law* 16 (1991): 177–202. For a political-moral perspective on secession, see Allen Buchanan, *Secession: The Morality of Political Divorce from Fort Sumter to Lithuania and Quebec* (Boulder, Colo.: Westview, 1991); Buchanan, "Self-Determination and the Right to Secede," *Journal of International Affairs* 45/2 (winter 1992): 347–366. For other attempts to strike a balance between the right to self-determination, including secession on the one hand, and the territorial integrity of the state on the other, see Alexis Heraclides, "Secession and Third-Party Intervention," *Journal of International Affairs* 45/2 (winter 1992): 399–420 at 409–415; Lung-Chu Chen, "Self-Determination and World Public Order" *Notre Dame Law Review* 66 (1991): 1287–1297 at 1294–1297; Hannum, *Autonomy, Sovereignty, and Self-Determination,* 469–473; Jan Klabbers and René Lefeber, "Africa: Lost between Self-Determination and *uti possidetis,*" in Brölmann et al., *Peoples and Minorities in International Law,* 37–76 at 53–54; Lawrence S. Eastwood, Jr., "Secession: State Practice and International Law after the Dissolution of the Soviet Union and Yugoslavia," *Duke Journal of Comparative and International Law* 3 (1993), 299–349. According to Thomas M. Franck, the interpretation of the right to self-determination may be undergoing a change, leading to the recognition of a right to democracy. See Thomas M. Franck, "The Emerging Right to Democratic Governance," *American Journal of International Law* 86 (1992): 46–91 at 57–77.

**60.** See note 31, chapter 1.

**61.** See, for example, UN General Assembly Resolution 2625 (XXV) of 24 October 1970. One may of course doubt whether the General Assembly has the authority to define the contents of self-determination; see Pomerance, *Self-Determination in Law and Practice,* 10–11.

**62.** See, for example, UN General Assembly Resolution 49/46 of 9 December 1994, Part A, paragraphs 2 and 4.

**63.** On this commission, see text accompanying notes 14–20, chapter 1.

**64.** Pellet, "Opinions of the Badinter Arbitration Committee," 184; *International Legal Materials* 31 (1992): 1498.

**65.** Klabbers and Lefeber, "Africa," 39.

**66.** The questions and peculiarities are discussed, inter alia, in Pomerance, *Self-Determination in Law and Practice;* Ruth Lapidoth, "Sovereignty in Transition," *Journal of International Affairs* 45/2 (winter 1992): 325–346; Franck, "Postmodern Tribalism" (with special reference to the crisis in the former Yugoslavia).

**67.** UN General Assembly Resolution 2625 (XXV) of 24 October 1970. See also the 1993 Vienna Declaration on Human Rights, UN Doc. A/CONF.157/23, 12 July 1993, Article 2.

**68.** Gidon Gottlieb, *Nation Against State: A New Approach to Ethnic Conflicts and the Decline of Sovereignty* (New York: Council on Foreign Relations Press, 1993), 3–5. David J. Elkins too envisages "a greater role for non-territorial organizations and identities" in the next century. See David J. Elkins, *Beyond Sovereignty: Territory and Political Autonomy in the Twenty-First Century* (Toronto: University of Toronto Press, 1995), 6. See also Thomas Fleiner, "State without Nation: Reconsidering the Nation-State Concept" (paper presented at the Law Faculty of the Hebrew University of Jerusalem, 14 December 1994).

**69.** Kiss, "Peoples' Right to Self-determination," 173; Ian Brownlie, "The Rights of Peoples in Modern International Law," in James Crawford, ed., *The Rights of Peoples* (Oxford: Clarendon Press, 1988), 1–16. Malanczuk, "The Kurdish Crisis and Allied Intervention," 124; Buchanan, "Self-Determination and the Right to Secede," 351–352; Heraclides, "Secession and Third-Party Intervention," 400; Chen, "Self-Determination and World Public Order," 1288, 1291; Hannum, *Autonomy, Sovereignty, and Self-Determination,* 473–475; Hannum, "Rethinking Self-Determination," 34, 64–65; Cassese, *Self-Determination of Peoples: A Legal Reappraisal,* 124, 352–359; Henry Schermers, "The Bond between Man and State," in *Recht zwischen Umbruch und Bewahrung: Festschrift für Rudolf Bernhardt* (Berlin: Springer, 1995), 187-198 at 189 (Schermers recommended autonomy for minorities); Luzius Wildhaber, *Menschen und Minderheitenrechte in der modernen Demokratie,* Basler Universitätsreden 88. Heft (Basel: Hilbing & Lichtenhahn, 1992), 21; Christian Tomuschat, "Self-Determination in a Post-Colonial World," in Tomuschat, *Modern Law of Self-Determination,* 1–20 at 13–17; Asbjorn Eide, "In Search of Constructive Alternatives to Secession," in ibid., 139–176 at 170–173; Guyora Binder, "The Kaplan Lecture on Human Rights: The Case for Self-Determination," *Stanford Journal of International Law* 29 (1993): 223–270 at 248–249.

For additional means to deal with similar situations, see, for example, Donald L. Horowitz, *Ethnic Groups in Conflict* (Berkeley: University of California Press, 1989); Arend Lijphart, *Democracy in Plural Societies* (New

Haven: Yale University Press, 1977); Claire Palley, "The Role of Law in Relation to Minority Groups," in Antony E. Alcock et al., eds., *The Future of Cultural Minorities* (New York: St. Martin's Press, 1979), 120–160; Claire Palley, "Possible Ways and Means to Facilitate the Peaceful and Constructive Resolution of Situations Involving Racial, National, Religious and Linguistic Minorities," UN Doc. E/CN.4/Sub.2/1989/43, 4 July 1989; Claire Palley, introduction to *Minorities and Autonomy in Western Europe* (London: Minority Rights Group, 1991), 5. Palley deals with minorities, but the same considerations are valid for peoples.

## 2. OTHER REASONS FOR ESTABLISHING AUTONOMY

**1.** A. D. Hughes, "Hong Kong," in Rudolf Bernhardt, ed., *Encyclopedia of Public International Law,* vol. 2 (1995), 870–873; Georg Ress, "The Legal Status of Hong Kong after 1997," *Zeitschrift für ausländisches öffentliches Recht und Völkerrecht* 46 (1986): 647–699. The two most important documents—the 1984 Joint Declaration of Britain and China and the 1990 Basic Law for the Hong Kong Special Administrative Region of China—have been reprinted in Hurst Hannum, ed., *Documents on Autonomy and Minority Rights* (Dordrecht, The Netherlands: Nijhoff, 1993), 219–272.

**2.** Walter Rudolf, "Macau," in Bernhardt, *Encyclopedia of Public International Law,* vol. 12 (1990), 223–225; Lazar Focsaneanu, "La déclaration conjointe Sino-Portugaise sur Macao," *Revue Générale de Droit International Public* 91 (1987): 1279–1303.

**3.** UN General Assembly Resolution 181 (II) on the future government of Palestine of 29 November 1947, Part III, Chapter C, Article 3, UN General Assembly Official Records, 2nd session, 1947, 131–151.

## 3. THE CONCEPT OF AUTONOMY

**1.** Martin Ostwald, *Nomos and the Beginnings of Athenian Democracy* (London: Oxford University Press, 1969); Ostwald, *Autonomia: Its Genesis and Early History,* American Classical Studies, vol. 11 (Chico, Calif.: Scholars Press, 1982). The author wishes to express her thanks to Professor John Van Sickle for his helpful comments.

**2.** Sir Isaiah Berlin, *Four Essays on Liberty* (London: Oxford University Press, 1969), 131; Richard Lindley, *Autonomy* (Atlantic Highlands, N.J.: Humanities Press, 1969), 131; Gerald Dworkin, *The Theory and Practice of Autonomy* (Cambridge: Cambridge University Press, 1988), 20.

**3.** *Oxford English Dictionary,* 2d ed., s.v. "autonomy."

**4.** John Rawls, *A Theory of Justice* (Cambridge, Mass.: Harvard University Press, Belknap Press, 1971), 5. Speaking of the idea of justice, Rawls expresses the opinion that "it seems natural to think of the concept of justice as distinct from the various conceptions of justice and as being specified by the role which these different sets of principles, these different conceptions, have in common."

**5.** Georg Jellinek, *Allgemeine Staatslehre*, 3rd ed. (Bad Homburg, Germany: Hermann Gentner Verlag, 1928; reprinted 1960), 493.

**6.** Paul Laband, *Das Staatsrecht des Deutschen Reiches*, 5th ed., vol. 1 (Tübingen, Germany: Mohr, 1911), 106–107.

**7.** R. Carré de Malberg, *Contribution à la Théorie générale de l'Etat spécialement d'après les données fournies par le Droit constitutionnel français*, vol. 1 (Paris: Sirey, 1920), 169–170.

**8.** Léon Duguit, *Traité de droit constitutionnel*, vol. 2 (Paris: Fontemoing-Boccard, 1921), paragraph 55, p. 478 et seq. (quoted from Heinrich Dörge, *Der Autonome Verband im geltenden Staats- und Völkerrecht* [Vienna and Leipzig: Brämüller, 1931], 26).

**9.** Henry Berthélémy, *Traité élémentaire de droit administratif*, 11th ed. (Paris: Rousseau, 1926), 174–177.

**10.** Maurice Hauriou, *Précis de droit administratif et de droit public*, 11th ed., vol. 1 (Paris: Sirey, 1927), 345–346.

**11.** Dörge, *Der Autonome Verband*, 18.

**12.** Ibid., 74, note 16.

**13.** Jacob Robinson, *Kommentar der Konvention über das Memelgebiet vom 8 Mai 1924*, vol. 1 (Kaunas, Lithuania: Verlag "Spaudos Fondas," 1934), 254, 256.

**14.** *Dictionnaire de la terminologie du droit international* (Paris: Sirey, 1960), 74–75.

**15.** Louis Sohn, "The Concept of Autonomy in International Law and the Practice of the United Nations," *Israel Law Review* 15 (1980): 58–68.

**16.** *Encyclopaedia Britannica*, 11th ed., s.v. "autonomy"; and *Encyclopaedia Britannica*, 13th ed., s.v. "autonomy."

**17.** *Encyclopedia of the Social Sciences*, vol. 1 (in Hebrew) (Tel Aviv: Sifriyat Po'alim, 1962), 43. See also *Encyclopaedia Hebraica*, vol. 1 (in Hebrew) (Jerusalem: Encyclopaedia Publishing Company, 1953), 780–792; *Encyclopaedia Judaica*, vol. 3 (Jerusalem: Keter, 1971), 921–931.

**18.** Rudolf Bernhardt, "Federalism and Autonomy," in Yoram Dinstein, ed., *Models of Autonomy* (New Brunswick, N.J.: Transaction Books, 1981), 23–28 at 25–26.

**19.** James Crawford, *The Creation of States in International Law* (Oxford: Clarendon Press, 1979), 211.

**20.** Hurst Hannum and Richard B. Lillich, "The Concept of Autonomy in International Law," *American Journal of International Law* 74 (1980): 858–889 at 859.

**21.** Hurst Hannum, *Autonomy, Sovereignty, and Self-Determination: The Accommodation of Conflicting Rights* (Philadelphia: University of Pennsylvania Press, 1990), 4.

**22.** Heinrich Oberreuter, "Autonomie," in *Staatslexikon,* vol. 1 (Freiburg, Basel, and Vienna: Verlag Herder, 1985), 490–493 at 491.

**23.** Henry J. Steiner, "Ideals and Counter-Ideals in the Struggle over Autonomy Regimes for Minorities," *Notre Dame Law Review* 66 (1991): 1539–1555.

**24.** Oberreuter, "Autonome," 492.

**25.** UN General Assembly Resolution 390 (V) of 2 December 1950.

**26.** Convention of Paris of 8 May 1924 concerning the Memel Territory (published in London by H. M. Stationery Office, Cmd. 2235, 1924).

**27.** League of Nations, Minutes of the 17th Meeting of the Council, 27 June 1921 (Minutes of the 13th Session of the League of Nations, Geneva, 17–28 June 1921), 52.

**28.** United Nations Treaty Series, vol. 49 (1950), 3, at 184 (Article 10 and Annex IV).

## 4. TERRITORIAL AUTONOMY AND PERSONAL (OR CULTURAL) AUTONOMY

**1.** Not to be confused with individual autonomy, a term used in philosophy. See Lindley, *Autonomy,* 6 (see note 2, chapter 3).

**2.** Robert Redslob, "Le principe des nationalités," *Recueil des Cours de l'Académie de Droit International* 37 (1931–III): 1–82 at 48–49.

**3.** See, for example, Louis Finkelstein, *Jewish Self-Government in the Middle Ages* (1924; reprint, Westport, Conn.: Greenwood Press, 1972); *Encyclopaedia Judaica,* vol. 3 (Jerusalem: Keter, 1971), 921–931; Kurt Stillschweig, "Nationalism and Autonomy among Eastern European Jewry," *Historica Judaica* 6 (1944): 27–68.

**4.** Kemal Karpat, "The Ottoman Ethnic and Confessional Legacy in the Middle East," in Milton J. Esman and Itamar Rabinovich, eds., *Ethnicity, Pluralism, and the State in the Middle East* (Ithaca and London: Cornell University Press, 1988), 35–53; Kemal Karpat, *An Inquiry into the Social Foun-*

*dations of Nationalism in the Ottoman State: From Social Estates to Classes, from Millets to Nations,* Research Monograph no. 39 (New Haven: Center for International Studies, Princeton University, 1973), 31–39, 87–97, 109–116; Benjamin Braude and Bernard Lewis, eds., *Christians and Jews in the Ottoman Empire: The Functioning of a Plural Society* (New York: Holmes and Meier, 1982); Stanford J. Shaw and Ezel Kural Shaw, *History of the Ottoman Empire and Modern Turkey,* vol. 1 (Cambridge: Cambridge University Press, 1976), 151–155; 163–167; 283–284; Sir Harry Luke, *The Old Turkey and the New: From Byzantium to Ankara* (London: Geoffrey Bles, 1955), 7–9, 66–101. The author wishes to express her thanks to Professor Dorothy Willner for having guided her with the bibliography on the *millets*.

5. Article 21 of the Estonian constitution of 1920, followed by a 1925 statute on the Cultural Self-Administration of National Minorities in Estonia, quoted in Dörge, *Der Autonome Verband,* 44–45 (see note 8, chapter 3); Redslob, "Le principe des nationalités," 53–54; Eugen Maddison, *Die Nationalen Minderheiten Estlands und ihre Rechte,* 2d ed. (Tallinn [Reval], Estonia: Verlag von A. Keiserman, 1930). See also Max M. Laserson, "Das Minoritätenrecht der Baltischen Staaten," *Zeitschrift für ausländisches öffentliches Recht und Völkerrecht* 2 (1931): 14. In the opinion of Simon Dubnow and Jacob Robinson, the autonomy in Estonia was the most consistent one: see Simon Dubnow and Jacob Robinson, "Autonomie," in *Encyclopaedia Judaica,* vol. 3 (Berlin: Verlag Eschkol, 1928), 749–764 at 762. After Estonia regained its independence, it again adopted a law granting cultural autonomy to national minorities—see note 142, chapter 8.

6. The 1919 Statute on the School System for National Minorities. See Dörge, *Der Autonome Verband,* 45–46. See also Laserson, "Das Minoritätenrecht der Baltischen Staaten."

7. Dörge, *Der Autonome Verband,* 46–47; Laserson, "Das Minoritätenrecht der Baltischen Staaten"; Jakob Robinson, "Der Litauische Staat und seine Verfassungsentwicklung," *Jahrbuch des öffentlichen Rechts* 16 (1928): 295–326, comments at 304–305, text of the relevant sections at 320. On Jewish personal autonomy in Lithuania, see Natan Feinberg, "Memories from the Jewish Autonomy in Lithuania," in *Essays on Jewish Issues of Our Time* (in Hebrew) (Jerusalem: Dvir, 1980), 88–95.

8. "Law on the Unrestricted Development and Right to Cultural Autonomy of Latvia's Nationalities and Ethnic Groups" (English translation of text supplied by the Legation of Latvia in Washington, D.C.). The author hereby expresses her thanks to the Legation (now an Embassy).

9. According to the "Document of the Copenhagen Meeting of the Conference on the Human Dimension of the CSCE" (see note 7, chapter 1), "[t]o belong to a national minority is a matter of a person's individ-

ual choice and no disadvantage may arise from the exercise of such choice" (Article 32). But it seems that in practice this freedom of choice is not always recognized. See Steiner, "Ideals and Counter-Ideals," 1551, 1552, 1553 (see note 23, chapter 3). The 1992 UN Declaration on the Rights of Persons Belonging to National or Ethnic, Religious and Linguistic Minorities (see note 2, chapter 1) states that "[n]o disadvantage shall result for any person belonging to a minority as the consequence of the exercise or non-exercise of the rights set forth in the present Declaration" (Article 3[2]), but freedom of choice is not mentioned.

**10.** Karl Renner, *Das Selbstbestimmungsrecht der Nationen in besonderer Anwendung auf Österreich* (Leipzig and Vienna: Franz Deuticke, 1918), 149.

**11.** Ibid., 41, 43.

**12.** Ibid., 69.

**13.** Atle Grahl-Madsen, "Introduction," and "Draft of a Sami Convention," *Nordic Journal of International Law* 55 (1986): 2–11.

**14.** For a favorable discussion of personal autonomy, see Otto Kimminich, "Die personale Autonomie: Relikt einer vergangenen Zeit oder Modell für die Zukunft?" in Wilfried Fiedler and Georg Ress, eds., *Verfassungsrecht und Völkerrecht: Gedächtnisschrift für Wilhelm Karl Geck* (Berlin: Carl Heymanns Verlag, 1989), 431–499. ("Theoretically it has been shown long ago, that the problems of a mixed multinational state can be solved only through the application of the principle of personal autonomy." Ibid., 449.)

## 5. AUTONOMY AND SOVEREIGNTY

**1.** Louis Henkin, "The Mythology of Sovereignty," *Newsletter of the American Society of International Law,* March–May 1993, 1–7 at 6. See also Louis Henkin, "International Law: Politics, Values, and Functions," *Recueil des Cours de l'Académie de Droit International* 216 (1989-IV): 9–416 at 24–26. Shlomo Avineri distinguishes between sovereignty as a legal-constitutional concept that can be dealt with on a reasonable basis, on the one hand, and the meaning the term has for the layman—a conception with a strong, symbolic, and emotional effect; see Shlomo Avineri, "Beyond Sovereignty? Some Historical and Theoretical Problems," in Werner Weidenfeld and Moshe Zimmermann, eds., *Beyond Sovereignty? The European Integration* (in Hebrew) (Jerusalem: Academon, 1996), 207–212.

**2.** For the history of the notion of sovereignty, see Jellinek, *Allgemeine Staatslehre,* 435–474 (see note 5, chapter 3); Francis Harry Hinsley, *Sovereignty,* 2d ed. (Cambridge: Cambridge University Press, 1986), 27–213;

Helmut Steinberger, "Sovereignty," in R. Bernhardt, ed., *Encyclopedia of Public International Law,* vol. 10 (1987), 397–418; Paul Guggenheim, "La souveraineté dans l'histoire du droit des gens," in *Mélanges Henri Rolin* (Paris: Pedone, 1964), 134–146; Ruth Lapidoth, "Sovereignty in Transition," *Journal of International Affairs* 45 (1992): 325–346; Ruth Lapidoth, "Redefining Authority: The Past, Present, and Future of Sovereignty," *Harvard International Review* 17, no. 3 (1995): 8–11, 70–71.

**3.** On this point, see Advisory Opinion no. 41, *Customs Regime between Germany and Austria,* PCIJ, ser. A/B, no. 41 (1931).

**4.** Although Alexander Hamilton says in *The Federalist Papers* (no. 31) that "the State governments by their original constitutions are invested with complete sovereignty" (*The Federalist Papers,* ed. Clinton Rossiter [New York: Mentor, 1961], 196), he also mentions (no. 9) that they are "constituent parts of the national sovereignty" (ibid., 76). He spoke of "rights of sovereignty" (no. 32, 198), and James Madison mentioned "attributes of sovereignty" (no. 45, 289), "portion of sovereignty," and "residual sovereignty" (no. 62, 378), expressions that imply partial or limited sovereignty.

**5.** That division of powers and its theoretical basis are still discussed in the decisions of the U.S. Supreme Court.

**6.** An expression coined by Chief Justice Marshall in *Cherokee Nation v. Georgia,* 30 US (5 Pet.) 1 (1831) at 17. See, however, James A. Casey, "Sovereignty by Sufferance: The Illusion of Indian Tribal Sovereignty," *Cornell Law Review* 79 (1994): 404–451.

**7.** Alfred Verdross et al., "Territoriale Souveränität und Gebietshoheit," *Österreichische Zeitschrift für öffentliches Recht und Völkerrecht* 31 (1980): 223–245.

**8.** See *Report of the Commission on the Political and Constitutional Future of Quebec* (Belanger-Campeau Commission, March 1991), 28.

**9.** *La Presse,* 1 October 1991.

**10.** Robert H. Jackson, *Quasi-States: Sovereignty, International Relations, and the Third World* (Cambridge: Cambridge University Press, 1990), 26–31.

**11.** See Nathaniel Berman, "Sovereignty in Abeyance: Self-Determination and International Law," *Wisconsin International Law Journal* 7 (1988): 51–105. According to the author, in normal times international law safeguards sovereignty, but in extraordinary times of transformation, sovereignty may be suspended in favor of self-determination, as happened after World War I when Finland was born and the future of the Åland Islands was considered (ibid., 74–75).

**12.** Amos J. Peaslee, ed., *Constitutions of Nations,* 3rd ed. by Dorothy Peaslee Xydis, vol. 3 (The Hague: Nijhoff, 1968), 1184–1193.

**13.** Article 2 of the 1958 Convention on the Continental Shelf and Article 77 of the 1982 United Nations Convention on the Law of the Sea with regard to the continental shelf; Article 56(1)(a) of the 1982 Convention with regard to the exclusive economic zone, UN Sales no. E.83.V.5 (1983). See also Willem Riphagen, "Some Reflections on 'Functional Sovereignty,'" *Netherlands Yearbook of International Law* 6 (1975): 121–165.

**14.** Harold Joseph Laski, "The Sovereignty of the State," in *Studies in the Problem of Sovereignty* (New Haven, Conn.: Yale University Press, 1924), 1–26.

**15.** Article 91(3) of the Constitution of The Netherlands; Article 23 of the Basic Law of Germany, as amended in 1992. On the situation in other countries that are members of the European Community and the European Union, see Finn Laursen and Sophie Vanhoonacker, eds., *The Ratification of the Maastricht Treaty: Issues, Debates, and Future Implications* (Dordrecht, The Netherlands: Nijhoff, 1994).

**16.** Advisory Opinion, *Customs Regime* (see note 3, this chapter).

**17.** For a recent analysis of the question of sovereignty and the European Union, see Eivind Smith, "A Higher Power: Supranationality in the European Union," *Harvard International Review* 17, no. 3 (1995): 12–14, 71–72. See also Jean-Victor Louis, *L'ordre juridique communautaire,* 6th ed. (Brussels and Luxembourg: Commission des Communautés Européennes, 1993), 13–27.

**18.** Horst Dreier, "Souveränität," in *Staatslexikon,* vol. 4 (Freiburg, Basel, and Vienna: Verlag Herder, 1988), 1203–1209 at 1208. Yadhi Ben Achour spoke of *souveraineté assiégée* (besieged sovereignty). See his "Souveraineté etatique et protection internationale des minorités," *Recueil des Cours de l'Académie de Droit International* 245 (1994-I): 321–461 at 383.

**19.** Luzius Wildhaber, "Sovereignty and International Law," in R. St. J. Macdonald and Douglas M. Johnston, eds., *The Structure and Process of International Law: Essays in Legal Philosophy, Doctrine, and Theory* (Dordrecht, The Netherlands: Nijhoff, 1986), 425–452 at 440, 441. According to W. Michael Reisman, due to the development of human rights, the notion of sovereignty must be reinterpreted by a process of "updating," "contemporization," or *actualisation*; see W. Michael Reisman, "Sovereignty and Human Rights in Contemporary International Law," *American Journal of International Law* 84 (1990): 866–876 at 873. See also the discussions on sovereignty in *88th Annual Meeting of the American Society of International Law, Proceedings for 1994* (1995), 1–87. A study of sovereignty from the point of view of the theory of international relations led its authors to the conclusion that "a reconceptualization of sovereignty is necessary, timely and possible"; see Joseph A. Camilleri and Jim Falk, *The End of Sovereignty?*

*The Politics of a Shrinking and Fragmenting World* (Aldershot, England: Edward Edgar Publishing, 1992), 237.

**20.** Ted Robert Gurr and James R. Scarritt, "Minorities Rights at Risk: A Global Survey," *Human Rights Quarterly* 11 (1989): 375–405 at 375.

### 6. TERRITORIAL AUTONOMY AND OTHER ARRANGEMENTS FOR DIFFUSION OF POWER

**1.** Daniel Elazar cites a long list of concepts: federations, confederations, decentralized unions, transformed feudal arrangements, federacies, home rule, cultural home rule, autonomous provinces or national districts, regional arrangements (intranational or transnational), customs unions, leagues based on common national or cultural ties, state-diaspora ties, extraterritorial arrangements or enclaves, condominiums, state structures functioning through autonomous tribes, and consociational arrangements. See Daniel J. Elazar, ed., *Federal Systems of the World: A Handbook of Federal, Confederal and Autonomy Arrangements,* 2d ed. (London: Longman, 1994), xvii–xviii. See also Elazar's *Exploring Federalism* (Tuscaloosa: University of Alabama Press, 1987), 38–64.

**2.** For example, Hans Kelsen, *General Theory of Law and State* (Cambridge, Mass.: Harvard University Press, 1949), 308–317.

**3.** Daniel J. Elazar, "Federalism v. Decentralization: The Drift from Authenticity," *Publius: The Journal of Federalism* 6 (1976): 9–19 at 12.

**4.** However, in the Soviet Union the autonomous republics, regions, and areas were represented in the Council of Nationalities of the Supreme Soviet (section 110 of the 1977 constitution), and in Yugoslavia the autonomous provinces of Kosovo and Vojvodina were represented in the Council of the Presidency as well as in the Chamber of Republics and Provinces (Sections 284 and 321 of the 1974 constitution and Amendment IV).

**5.** "L'Etat autonomique se distingue donc du fédéralisme par l'autonomie des parties, en l'absence de toute co-détermination de celles-ci sur le tout qui, de ce fait, jouit d'une liberté d'action plus grande. . . . Etat autonomique et Etat fédéral se fondent sur l'autonomie des parties, mais règlent autrement les rapports de ces dernières avec le centre" ["The autonomist state differs from federalism since the parties are autonomous, yet there is no co-determination of the latter on the whole. . . . The autonomist state and the federal state are based on the autonomy of the parties, but they deal differently with the relations between the parties and the center"]; see Daniel Louis Seiler, "L'Etat autonomique et la science politique: Centre, périphérie et territorialité," in Christian Bidegaray, ed.,

*L'Etat autonomique: Forme nouvelle ou transitoire en Europe?* (Paris: Economica, 1994), 11–35 at 34–35.

**6.** See chapter 8, the section on autonomy in the Soviet Union.

**7.** Kosovo is an 11,000-square-kilometer area that, since 1913, has been a part of Serbia, and later of Yugoslavia. The area has great historical and symbolic significance for Serbs due to a battle that took place there in 1389 and as a result of which the medieval Serbian Empire was overthrown by the Turks. In modern times about 90 percent of the population has been ethnic Albanian, and the remaining 10 percent mainly Serbian. In 1968 Kosovo was granted the status of an autonomous province within the Republic of Serbia, and under the 1974 Constitution of Yugoslavia Kosovo's autonomy was increased. However, after the death of Marshal Tito (1980), relations between the two communities deteriorated, and in 1989, in the wake of the Serbian nationalist revival, Kosovo's autonomy was abolished. Tensions were heightened due to the imposition of the Serbian curriculum in schools, and to mass firing of ethnic Albanians from their jobs on the one hand, and to the Kosovars' attempt to declare their independence and their quiet wish to be part of Albania on the other hand. See Elazar, *Federal Systems*, 307, 347; Janusz Bugajski, *Nations in Turmoil: Conflict and Cooperation in Eastern Europe*, 2d ed. (Boulder, Colo.: Westview Press, 1995), 133–141.

**8.** The prosperous area of Vojvodina has been an autonomous province within Serbia since the dismemberment of the Austro-Hungarian Empire. Fifty-four percent of the population has been Serbian, while 19 percent has been ethnic Hungarian. Under the 1974 Constitution of Yugoslavia, the area's autonomy was enhanced. However, the rise of extreme Serbian nationalism led to the erosion of Vojvodina's autonomy. Due to the fighting that followed the dismemberment of Yugoslavia, many ethnic Hungarians fled to Hungary, and large numbers of Serbian refugees arrived in the province. The remaining Hungarians have been trying to get at least limited personal autonomy. See Elazar, *Federal Systems of the World*, 307–308; Bugajski, *Nations in Turmoil*, 144–150.

**9.** For a statement of the grievances and aspirations of the Parti Quebecois, see, for example, Bill Respecting the Future of Quebec, introduced by Prime Minister Jacques Parizeau, in preparation for the referendum that took place on 30 October 1995.

**10.** Kelsen, *General Theory of Law and State*, 316.

**11.** Mark O. Rousseau and Raphael Zariski, *Regionalism and Regional Devolution in Comparative Perspective* (New York: Praeger, 1987), 3, 32; *Encyclopaedia Britannica*, 15th ed., s.v. "federalism."

**12.** Another related term is home rule. According to Isi Foighel, home rule is "a particularly qualified type of self-government"; see Isi Foighel, "A Framework for Local Autonomy: The Greenland Case," in Dinstein, *Models of Autonomy,* 31–52 at 37 (see note 18, chapter 3).

**13.** These provisions have been discussed, inter alia, in the following books: Leland Matthew Goodrich et al., *Charter of the United Nations: Commentary and Documents,* 3rd revised ed. (New York: Columbia University Press, 1969), 448–462; Crawford, *Creation of States in International Law,* 356–384, in particular 367–370 (see note 19, chapter 3). The legislative history of the provisions is reviewed in Louis B. Sohn, "Models of Autonomy within the United Nations Framework," in Dinstein, *Models of Autonomy,* 5–22 at 6–9 (see note 18, chapter 3).

**14.** The deliberations on this matter were reviewed in Emil John Sady, *The United Nations and Dependent Peoples* (Washington, D.C.: Brookings, 1956), 81–83.

**15.** One list was temporarily adopted in 1952, by UN General Assembly Resolution 648 (VII) of 10 December 1952; a second list was approved in 1953, by Resolution 742 (VIII) of 27 November 1953; a third list was included in Resolution 1541 (XV) of 15 December 1960.

**16.** Report of the Sub-Committee of the Fourth Committee, UN Doc. A/C.4/L.180 and Corr. 2, 22 December 1951, and UN General Assembly Res. 567 (VI), Annex II of 18 January 1952. See also Appendix to Resolution 648 (VII), 10 December 1952.

**17.** Sohn, "Concept of Autonomy," 58, 61 (see note 15, chapter 3).

**18.** Yoram Dinstein, "Autonomy," in Dinstein, *Models of Autonomy,* 291–303 at 291 (see note 18, chapter 3).

**19.** Statement by Augusto Willemsen Diaz at the morning session of 28 September 1991. Because of Diaz's opinion, the term autonomy was added next to the word self-government in all relevant provisions of the Conclusions and Recommendations of the Meeting. See UN Doc. E/CN.4/1992/42, 25 November 1991.

**20.** UN General Assembly Resolution 742 (VIII) of 27 November 1953, paragraph 6; Resolution 1541 (XV) of 15 December 1960, Principle VI; Declaration on Principles of International Law Concerning Friendly Relations and Co-operation among States in Accordance with the Charter of the United Nations, Resolution 2625 (XXV) of 24 October 1970.

**21.** W. Michael Reisman, *Puerto Rico and the International Process: New Roles in Association,* The American Society of International Law, Studies in Transnational Legal Policy, no. 6 (St. Paul, Minn.: West, 1975), 10.

**22.** Menachem Mautner, "The West Bank and Gaza: The Case for Associate Statehood," *Yale Studies in World Public Order* 6 (1980): 297–360 at 305.

**23.** See Reisman, *Puerto Rico;* Marcel Korn, "Free Association: Political Integration as a Trade-Off," in Daniel J. Elazar, ed., *Constitutional Design and Power-Sharing in the Post-Modern Epoch* (Lanham, Md.: University Press of America, 1991), 185–217. For a detailed analysis of the various territories linked to the United States, see Arnold H. Leibowitz, *Defining Status: A Comprehensive Analysis of United States Territorial Relations* (Dordrecht, The Netherlands: Nijhoff, 1989), 127–232 (Puerto Rico); 520–593 (The Commonwealth of the Northern Mariana Islands); 595–703 (The Freely Associated States of Micronesia, including the Marshall Islands, Micronesia, and Palau). On the main differences between the latter and Puerto Rico, see ibid., 44. See also Roger S. Clark, "Self-Determination and Free Association: Should the United Nations Terminate the Pacific Islands Trust?" *Harvard International Law Journal* 21 (1980): 1–86; Manuel Rodriguez-Orellana, "In Contemplation of Micronesia: The Prospects for the Decolonization of Puerto Rico under International Law," *Inter-American Law Review* 18 (1987): 457–503; David Isenberg, "Reconciling Independence and Security: The Long-Term Status of the Trust Territory of the Pacific Islands," *Pacific Basin Law Journal* 4 (1985): 210–243; Raymond Goy, "La fin de la dernière tutelle," *Annuaire Français de Droit International* 40 (1994): 356–370. For earlier cases, see Mautner, "West Bank and Gaza," 324–326; and Margaret Broderick, "Associated Statehood: A New Form of Decolonisation," *International and Comparative Law Quarterly* 17 (1968): 368–403. The Broderick article deals with six islands in the southeast Caribbean that were formerly British colonies and in 1967 became "States in Association with Britain." On these islands, see also George Abbott, "The Associated States and Independence," *Journal of Interamerican Studies and World Affairs* 23 (1981): 69–94.

**24.** See UN General Assembly Resolution 1541 (XV) of 15 December 1960, Principle no. VII; compare with Resolution 648 (VII) of 10 December 1952, Annex, and Resolution 742 (VIII) of 27 November 1953, Annex, Third Part. See also Reisman, *Puerto Rico;* Crawford, *Creation of States in International Law,* 12 (see note 19, chapter 3). The need for the population's consent, in contrast to the mere decision of the rulers, distinguishes associate statehood from the status of protectorates that existed in the past. See Reisman, *Puerto Rico,* 12.

**25.** Request for the inclusion of an item in the provisional agenda of the forty-eighth session, Effective Realization of the Right of Self-Determination through Autonomy, UN Doc. A/48/147, 16 July 1993;

Statement by H.S.H. Prince Hans-Adam II of Liechtenstein at the Plenary Meeting of the General Assembly on 25 October 1993, UN General Assembly Offical Records, 48th session, 30th Plenary Meeting; Statement by Ambassador Claudia Fritsche at the Third Committee on 3 November 1993, UN General Assembly Official Records, Third Committee, Summary Records, UN Doc. A/C.3/48/SR.22, 30 November 1993; Statement by Fritsche in the Third Committee to agenda item 94, 17 October 1994. The author wishes to thank Nomi Bar-Yaacov, who was the first to draw her attention to the Liechtenstein initiative.

**26.** For a summary, see UN Doc. A/48/147/Add.1, 29 September 1993, and UN Doc. A/50/492, 2 October 1995.

**27.** Permanent Mission of the Principality of Liechtenstein to the United Nations, Draft Convention on Self-Determination through Self-Administration and Comments (New York, April 1994).

**28.** Draft Convention, Article 1(a).

**29.** Draft Convention, Articles 5 and 6.

**30.** Draft Convention, Article 4.

**31.** Ibid.

**32.** Draft Convention, Article 5.

**33.** Draft Convention, Article 6.

**34.** Draft Convention, Article 7.

**35.** Draft Convention, Article 8(3).

**36.** Draft Convention, Article 8(4).

**37.** Draft Convention, Articles 9–16.

**38.** See references in note 25 for text and statements of 1993.

### 7. SOME EARLIER CASES

**1.** There is an ample bibliography for most of the examples discussed in this part. The references, however, will be limited to short lists. For many of the territories to be discussed, two general publications may be consulted: Daniel J. Elazar, ed., *Federal Systems of the World: A Handbook of Federal, Confederal, and Autonomy Arrangements,* 2d ed. (London: Longman, 1994); and *The Europa World Year Book* (London: Europa Publications Ltd., issued annually). The constitutional texts have been reproduced in: Albert P. Blaustein and Gisbert H. Flanz, eds., *Constitutions of the Countries of the World* (Dobbs Ferry, N.Y.: Oceana, 1971–; regular new releases ); Albert P. Blaustein and Phyllis M. Blaustein, eds., *Constitutions of Dependencies and Special Sovereignties* (Dobbs Ferry, N.Y.: Oceana, 1975–; new releases published periodically); and Hurst Hannum, ed., *Documents on Autonomy and Minority Rights* (Dordrecht, The Netherlands: Nijhoff, 1993).

**2.** Dietrich Schindler, "Andorra," in Rudolf Bernhardt, ed., *Encyclopedia of Public International Law*, vol. 1 (1992), 164–165; James Crawford, "The International Legal Status of the Valleys of Andorra," *Revue de Droit International, de Sciences Diplomatiques et Politiques* 55 (1977): 258–272; Pierre Raton, *Le Statut Juridique de l'Andorre* (Andorra: Casa de la Vall, 1983); Daniel J. Elazar, "Andorra," in *Federal Systems*, 8–10; *The Europa World Year Book, 1995*, 1: 346–349.

**3.** Schindler, "Andorra," 9.

**4.** Charles Rousseau, *Droit International Public*, vol. 2 (Paris: Sirey, 1974), 342–347 at 342.

**5.** *The Europa World Year Book, 1991*, 1: 328. In 1919, two experts described Andorra as a "protected independent State"; see W. W. Willoughby and C. G. Fenwick, *Types of Restricted Sovereignty and of Colonial Autonomy* (Washington, D.C.: Government Printing Office, 1919), 15.

**6.** Jean-Claude Colliard, "L'Etat d'Andorre," *Annuaire Français de Droit International* 39 (1993): 377–392.

**7.** Dietrich Schindler, "Liechtenstein," in Bernhardt, *Encyclopedia of Public International Law*, vol. 12 (1990), 220–222; Walter S. G. Kohn, "The Sovereignty of Liechtenstein," *American Journal of International Law* 61 (1967): 547–557; Bernd M. Malunat, *Der Kleinstaat im Spannungsfeld von Dependenz und Autonomie: Eine Fallstudie über das Fürstentum Liechtenstein* (Frankfurt: Lang, 1987); Daniel Elazar, "Liechtenstein," in *Federal Systems*, 132–134; *The Europa World Year Book, 1995*, 2: 1914–1917.

**8.** Schindler, "Liechtenstein," 220.

**9.** See also Elazar, "Liechtenstein," 132, who describes Liechtenstein as "a *de facto* associated state of Switzerland." See also Marcel Korn, "Free Association: Political Integration as a Trade-Off," in Daniel J. Elazar, ed., *Constitutional Design and Power-Sharing in the Post-Modern Epoch* (Lanham, Md.: University Press of America, 1991), 185–217 at 191–193.

**10.** Dietrich Schindler, "Monaco," in Bernhardt, *Encyclopedia of Public International Law*, vol. 12 (1990), 227–228; Jean Pierre Gallois, *Le régime international de la Principauté de Monaco* (1964); Jean Pillon and Jean-François Vilotte, "Les institutions politiques de la Principauté de Monaco," *Revue du droit public et de la science politique en France et à l'étranger* 98 (1982): . 355–376; Daniel Elazar, "Monaco," in *Federal Systems*, 155–156; *The Europa World Year Book, 1995*, 2: 2105–2108. For the constitutional documents, see Gisbert H. Flanz in Blaustein and Flanz, *Constitutions of Countries*, binder 12, issued December 1986.

**11.** According to Schindler, it is a sovereign state. See Schindler, "Monaco," 227. Schindler also quotes a different opinion, according to which Monaco is a "quasi protectorate." According to Willoughby and Fenwick, Monaco was a "protected independent State"; see Willoughby and Fenwick, *Types of Restricted Sovereignty*, 59.

**12.** According to Korn, the relationship established by a treaty between France and Monaco was "a precursor of contemporary models of free association"; see Korn, "Free Association," 190.

**13.** Dietrich Schindler, "San Marino," in Bernhardt, *Encyclopedia of Public International Law*, vol. 12 (1990), 340–341; T. Veiter, "Die Republik San Marino: Staats- und völkerrechtliche Entwicklung," in Dietrich Wilke and Horst Weber, eds., *Gedächtnisschrift für F. Klein* (1977), 535–541; *The Europa World Year Book, 1995*, 2: 2624–2627.

**14.** Schindler, "San Marino," 340. This is also the opinion expressed by Ambassador S. Lewis in a personal interview (1991). According to Willoughby and Fenwick, San Marino was a "protected independent State"; see Willoughby and Fenwick, *Types of Restricted Sovereignty*, 79.

**15.** Hazel Fox, "United Kingdom of Great Britain and Northern Ireland: Dependent Territories," in Bernhardt, *Encyclopedia of Public International Law*, vol. 12 (1990), 384–388; Elazar, "United Kingdom," in *Federal Systems*, 262–274; *The Europa World Year Book, 1995*, 2: 3125–3197; Elizabeth W. Davies, *The Legal Status of British Dependent Territories: The West Indies and North Atlantic Region* (Cambridge: Cambridge University Press, 1995). For the various constitutional documents and their analysis, see Blaustein and Blaustein, *Constitutions of Dependencies*, binders 4, 5, and 6.

**16.** Michael Charles Wood, "Channel Islands and Isle of Man," in Bernhardt, *Encyclopedia of Public International Law*, vol. 1 (1992), 560–561; Fox, "United Kingdom," 385; *The Europa World Year Book, 1995*, 2: 3188–3191; Elazar, "United Kingdom," 271–272. For the constitutional documents and their analysis, see Simon A. Horner, "Isle of Man," in Blaustein and Blaustein, *Constitutions of Dependencies*, binder 4, issued February 1987.

**17.** Ibid., 9.

**18.** Ibid., 10.

**19.** Wood, "Channel Islands," 560; Fox, "United Kingdom," 385; *The Europa World Year Book, 1995*, 2: 3192–3197; Elazar, "United Kingdom," 272–274. For the constitutional documents, see St. John A. Robilliard and T. J. Kennedy, "Bailiwick of Guernsey, Alderney, and Sark" (1990), and St. John A. Robilliard, "Bailiwick of Jersey," in Blaustein and Blaustein, *Constitutions of Dependencies*, binder 5, issued October 1986.

**20.** Robilliard, "Bailiwick of Jersey," 9.

**21.** Ibid., 11.

**22.** Ibid., 21.

**23.** Article 227(5)(c) of the 1992 Maastricht Treaty, and the Treaty of Accession of 22 January 1972, Protocol 3.

**24.** Arthur Berriedale Keith, *Letters on Imperial Relations, Indian Reform, Constitutional and International Law, 1916–1935* (London: Oxford University Press, 1935); Keith, *Constitutional History of the First British Empire* (Oxford: Clarendon Press, 1930); Keith, *The Constitutional Law of the British Dominions* (London: Macmillan, 1932); Keith, *Imperial Unity and the Dominions* (Oxford: Clarendon Press, 1916); James Brown Scott, *Autonomy and Federation within Empire: The British Self-Governing Dominions* (Washington, D.C.: Carnegie Endowment, 1920); P. J. Noel Baker, *The Present Juridical Status of the British Dominions in International Law* (London: Longmans, 1929).

**25.** *Imperial Conference 1926, Summary of Proceedings,* Cmd. 2768 (1926), reproduced in Baker, *The Present Juridical Status,* 385–402 at 386.

**26.** Heinrich Dörge, *Der Autonome Verband im geltenden Staats- und Völkerrecht* (Vienna and Leipzig: Braumüller, 1931), 74. For his analysis of the status of the dominions, see ibid., 31–33, 58–63. For a critical comment on Dörge's opinion, see Jacob Robinson, *Kommentar der Konvention über das Memelgebiet vom 8 Mai 1924* (Kaunas, Lithuania: Verlag "Spaudos Fondas," 1934), 309–310.

**27.** Dörge, *Der Autonome Verband,* 31, note 53.

**28.** See Willoughby and Fenwick, *Types of Restricted Sovereignty,* 19, 22, 37, 76, 77, 80.

**29.** See references cited in chapter 4, note 4.

**30.** *British Foreign and State Papers,* 1: 338.

**31.** It seems that "matters of internal policy and legislation described as common interests" were also excluded from the powers of Finland. See Report of the International Committee of Jurists Entrusted by the Council of the League of Nations with the Task of Giving an Advisory Opinion upon the Legal Aspects of the Aaland Islands Question, October 1920, League of Nations, *Official Journal,* Special Supplement no. 3, 7.

**32.** League of Nations, *The Aaland Islands Question,* Report Submitted to the Council of the League of Nations by the Commission of Rapporteurs, 16 April 1921, League of Nations Council Doc. B.7 21/68/106.

**33.** Quoted in Dörge, *Der Autonome Verband,* 5. Jellinek had mainly Alsace-Lorraine in mind.

**34.** Ibid., 8–9.

## 8. AUTONOMIES ESTABLISHED AFTER WORLD WAR I

**1.** Article 81 of the Treaty of Versailles of 28 June 1919 had also fore-seen autonomy for the Ruthenian Territory, south of the Carpathians. See Clive Parry, ed., *Consolidated Treaty Series* (Dobbs Ferry, N.Y.: Oceana, 1981), 225: 189–395 at 233–234. Specific provisions to this effect had been included in the Convention on the Protection of Minorities (Articles 10–14) concluded on 10 September 1919 by the Allied and Associated Powers on the one hand, and Czechoslovakia on the other hand. Ibid., 226: 170–181. For the relevant Czechoslovak implementing enactments, see Robinson, *Kommentar der Konvention,* 2: 696 (see note 26, chapter 7). How-ever, according to Dörge these provisions were hardly implemented. See Dörge, *Der Autonome Verband,* 51–53 (see note 26, chapter 7).

**2.** Articles 10 and 11 of the Peace Treaty of Dorpat of 14 October 1920 between the Russian Socialist Federal Soviet Republic and Finland, and the Declaration of the Russian Delegation with regard to the Auton-omy of Eastern Karelia, League of Nations Treaty Series, 3: 5; see also Pub-lications of the Permanent Court of International Justice, Ser. C, no. 3, vol. 2, 4, 26-27 (1923).

**3.** Decision adopted by the Conference of Ambassadors Regarding the Eastern Frontiers of Poland, Paris, 15 March 1923, (League of Nations Treaty Series, 15: 261) and the Polish law of 26 September 1922.

**4.** Article 14 of the Treaty of Lausanne of 24 July 1923 between the Allied and Associated Powers on the one hand, and Turkey on the other hand, League of Nations Treaty Series, 28: 11.

**5.** Poland's Organic Law of 15 July 1920, reproduced in Robinson, *Kommentar der Konvention,* 2: 712.

**6.** Spain's law of 15 September 1932, reproduced in Robinson, *Kom-mentar der Konvention,* 2: 728.

**7.** See chapter 4, text accompanying notes 5, 6, and 7.

**8.** Article 11 of the Minorities Treaty between the Principal Allied and Associated Powers and Roumania, 9 December 1919, League of Nations Treaty Series, 5: 335–347.

**9.** Article 12 of the Treaty Concerning the Protection of Minorities in Greece, of 10 August 1920 (revised on 24 July 1923), League of Nations Treaty Series, 28: 243.

**10.** Article 10 of the Treaty Concerning the Protection of Minorities in the Serb-Croat-Slovene State, 10 September 1919 (Parry, *Consolidated Treaty Series,* 226: 182); Article 2 of the Declaration Concerning the Pro-tection of Minorities in Albania, 2 October 1921, League of Nations Treaty Series, 9: 173 (Article 2 of the declaration assured equality to all minorities as well as the right to use their languages and practice their religions; in addition, it provided "for regulating family law and personal status in accordance with Mussulman usage," a right granted only to Muslims); Article 14 of the Treaty concerning Greece (see note 9, chapter 8). On the autonomy of the monks on Mount Athos, see Charalambos Papastathis, *Mount Athos and the European Community* (Thessaloniki: Institute of Balkan Studies, 1993), 55–75.

**11.** Article 42 of the 1923 Treaty of Lausanne (see note 4, chapter 8).

**12.** *Åland in Brief* (Åland: Ålands landskapsstyrelse and Ålands landsting, 1989); Tore Modeen, "Aaland Islands," in Rudolf Bernhardt, ed., *Encyclopedia of Public International Law,* vol. 1 (1992), 1–3; Elazar, *Federal Systems,* 85–87 (see note 1, chapter 7). For a detailed description of the islands, see the Report Submitted to the Council of the League of Nations by the Commission of Rapporteurs (see note 32, chapter 7).

**13.** Report (cited in note 12, above), 7–21; and Tore Modeen, "The International Protection of the National Identity of the Åland Islands," *Scandinavian Studies in Law* 17 (1973): 177–210; Modeen, *De Folkraettsliga garantierna foer bevarandet av Ålandsoearnas nationella karaktaer* (Mariehamn, Finland: Skrifter utgivna av Ålands kulturstiftelse VII, 1973) (French summary, 217–232); Modeen, "The Åland Islands Question," in Paul Smith, ed., *Ethnic Groups in International Relations,* Comparative Studies on Governments and Non-Dominant Ethnic Groups in Europe, 1850–1940, vol. 5 (New York: New York University Press, 1991), 153–168; E. Menzel, "Aland-Inseln," in Strupp-Schlochauer, ed., *Wörterbuch des Völkerrechts,* vol. 1 (Berlin: De Gruyter, 1960), 21; Hurst Hannum, *Autonomy, Sovereignty, and Self-Determination: The Accommodation of Conflicting Claims* (Philadelphia: University of Pennsylvania Press, 1990), 370–375; James Barros, *The Aland Islands Question: Its Settlement by the League of Nations* (New Haven: Yale University Press, 1968). In the literature the name Åland is sometimes rendered as Aland or Aaland.

**14.** The Peace of Fredrikshamn, 1809 (see note 30, chapter 7).

**15.** Georg Friedrich de Martens, *Nouveau Recueil Général de Traités,* série 1, vol. 15, 788. For an analysis, see Eckart Klein, *Statusverträge im Völkerrecht: Rechtsfragen territorialer Sonderregime—Treaties Providing for Objective Territorial Regimes* (Berlin, Heidelberg, and New York: Springer-Verlag, 1980), English summary, 2–6.

**16.** The 1908 Baltic Declaration was intended to preserve the status quo in the Baltic area. See *British Foreign and State Papers,* 101: 974.

**17.** League of Nations, *Official Journal,* vol. 21 (1921 II), 699, reproduced in Hannum, *Documents,* 141 (see note 1, chapter 7).

**18.** Text in Modeen, "International Protection of the National Identity of the Åland Islands," 206–207; and in Hannum, *Documents,* 142.

**19.** Martens, *Nouveau Recueil Général de Traités,* série 3, vol. 12, 65. For later developments, see Modeen, "Aaland Islands," 2.

**20.** The Council approved the agreement on 27 June 1921. Minutes of the 13th Session of the League of Nations, Geneva, 17–28 June 1921, 52, reproduced in Tore Modeen, "The International Protection of National Minorities in Europe," *Acta Academiae Aboensis,* Ser. A, Humaniora, vol. 37, no. 1 (Turku, Finland: Åbo Akademi, 1969), 161–162. On the question of the validity of the agreement, see Modeen, "International Protection of the National Identity of the Åland Islands," 184–187.

**21.** Modeen, "International Protection of the National Identity of the Åland Islands," 186.

**22.** Ibid., 190; and Hannum, *Documents,* 117–140.

**23.** Modeen, "International Protection of the National Identity of the Åland Islands," 189.

**24.** Study of the Legal Validity of the Undertakings Concerning Minorities, Memorandum by the Secretary-General, UN Doc. E/CN.4/367 (1950), and Add. 1 (1951). While the memorandum concluded that most of the minorities commitments had lost their validity, it expressed the view that Finland's obligations toward Sweden were still valid. See also Modeen, "International Protection of the National Identity of the Åland Islands," 191–202, and Modeen, "Aaland Islands," 3. It seems that Finland's obligation to respect the autonomy of the Åland Islands derives also from international customary law. See Lauri Hannikainen, *Cultural, Linguistic, and Educational Rights in the Åland Islands: An Analysis in International Law* Publications of the Advisory Board for International Human Rights Affairs, no. 5 (Helsinki: Advisory Board for International Human Rights Affairs, 1993), 10–11.

**25.** For an English translation, see Hannum, *Documents,* 117–140; and Hannikainen, *Cultural Rights in the Åland Islands,* 68–97. See also Oluf Erland, "Some of the Main Points in the Proposed New Law of Autonomy for Åland," *Nordic Journal of International Law* 57 (1988): 251–255; Finland Ministry of Foreign Affairs, "Reform of the Autonomy Act of the Åland Islands," *Finnish Features,* May 1991.

**26.** An English translation of the 1951 act was published in 1978 by Ålands Tidnings-Tryckeri Ab, Mariehamn, Åland Islands.

**27.** In addition to the already quoted sources, see Christer Janson, "The Autonomy of Åland: A Reflexion of International and Constitutional Law," *Nordisk Tidsskrift for International Ret* 51 (1982): 15–22; Finn Seyersted, "The Åland Autonomy and International Law," *Nordisk Tidsskrift for International Ret* 51 (1982): 23–28; Tore Modeen, "Völkerrechtliche Probleme der Åland-Inseln," *Zeitschrift für ausländisches öffentliches Recht und*

*Völkerrecht* 37 (1977): 604–619; Antony Alcock, "Finland: The Swedish-Speaking Community," in *Minorities and Autonomy in Western Europe: A Minority Rights Group Report* (London: Minority Rights Group, 1991), 12–15; Hannikainen, *Cultural Rights in the Åland Islands;* Rainer Hofmann, "Die rechtliche Stellung der Minderheiten in Finnland," in Jochem A. Frowein et al., eds., *Das Minderheitenrecht europäischer Staaten,* vol. 1 (Berlin: Springer, 1993), 108–125 at 121–125. The author wishes to express her thanks to Ms. Lotta Nygard for the most helpful material on Åland that she has kindly sent her.

**28.** Either it is adopted by a simple majority in Parliament, followed by a two-thirds majority vote in a newly elected one, or Parliament decides by a five-sixths majority that the matter is urgent, and then a two-thirds majority may adopt the amendment, with no need to await new elections.

**29.** For the reasons behind this complexity, see Janson, "Autonomy of Åland," 20.

**30.** Modeen, "Åland Islands," 1–3. See also Göran Lindholm, "The Right of Autonomous Regions to Participate in Nordic Co-operation," *Nordisk Tidsskrift for International Ret* 54 (1985): 79–84.

**31.** Erland, "Some of the Main Points," 255.

**32.** According to Modeen, the province does not have such a personality. See Modeen, "International Protection of the National Identity of the Åland Islands," 203. Seyersted, however, is of the opposite opinion. See Seyersted, "Åland Autonomy and International Law," 27.

**33.** Articles 18(27) and 27(42) of the 1991 act.

**34.** See Articles 23, 28, 30(7), 30(17), 30(18), 30(20), 30(21), 30(22), 33, and 58.

**35.** For a discussion of how the various provisions function in practice, see Hannikainen, *Cultural Rights in the Åland Islands.*

**36.** Section 14 of the 1919 Constitutional Act, quoted and analyzed in Jan-Magnus Jansson, "Language Legislation," in Jaakko Uotila, ed., *The Finnish Legal System,* 2d ed. (Helsinki: Finnish Lawyers Publishing Company, 1985), 77–87.

**37.** This is similar to the situation of the Swedish-speaking individuals in a unilingual Finnish-speaking area on the mainland of Finland under the 1922 Language Act. On this, see Jansson, "Language Legislation," 84. In 1992 the percentage of Swedish-speaking inhabitants of the Åland Islands was nearly 95 percent, while only 4.5 percent spoke Finnish. See Hannikainen, *Cultural Rights in the Åland Islands,* 14.

**38.** *Official Journal of the European Communities,* C 241, vol. 37, 29 August 1994, 352 (Protocol no. 2); and no. L 75/18, 4 April 1995 (Information from the Council). The author expresses her thanks to Ms. Alexandra Meir, of the Delegation of the European Commission in Tel Aviv, for having provided her the relevant texts.

**39.** See Hannikainen, *Cultural Rights in the Åland Islands,* 9.

**40.** Chapter 5 of the 1951 act. See also Janson, "Autonomy of Åland," 20–21.

**41.** Under the 1920 act, there was another ground for invalidating a provincial act: if it was contrary to the general interest of Finland; see Janson, "Autonomy of Åland," 20. According to Janson, security as a cause for vetoing a provincial act was referred to only once—when it was thought that the proposed Åland flag resembled the Swedish one too much. Ibid., note 1.

**42.** Modeen, "International Protection of the National Identity of the Åland Islands," 189.

**43.** Robinson, *Kommentar der Konvention über das Memelgebiet;* Hannum, *Autonomy, Sovereignty, and Self-Determination,* 379–384; H. Joachim Hallier, *Die Rechtslage des Memelgebiets* (Leipzig: R. Noske, 1933); Ernst-Albrecht Plieg, *Das Memelland 1920–1939* (Würzburg, Germany: Holzner, 1962); Dörge, *Der Autonome Verband,* 48–51.

**44.** Lithuanian Ministry of Foreign Affairs, *The Question of Memel* (London: Eyre and Spottiswoode, 1924), 62.

**45.** League of Nations Treaty Series, 29: 87. The convention was also published in various other places, including *Lithuania No. 1,* Cmd. 2235 (London, 1924); and Hannum, *Documents,* 663–681.

**46.** See references cited in note 43, chapter 8. For a detailed article-by-article commentary, see Robinson, *Kommentar der Konvention,* vol. 1.

**47.** Robinson, *Kommentar der Konvention,* vol. 2, 273–298, 483–501.

**48.** Hannum, *Autonomy, Sovereignty, and Self-Determination,* 382.

**49.** *Interpretation of the Statute of the Memel Territory,* PCIJ, ser. A/B, no. 49 (1932).

**50.** Ibid., 325.

**51.** Ibid., 318.

**52.** Ibid., 323.

**53.** Ibid., 332.

**54.** Ibid., 336.

**55.** Ibid., 318 and 319.

**56.** Ibid., 314 and 316.

**57.** Ibid., 320.

**58.** Bohdan Nahaylo and Victor Swoboda, *Soviet Disunion: A History of the Nationalities Problem in the USSR* (New York: Free Press, 1990), xi and 360; Minority Rights Group, ed., *World Directory of Minorities,* (Chicago: St. James Press, 1989), 141–175. The author expresses her thanks to Mr. Yossi Perlov for having drawn her attention to some of the articles dealing with autonomy in the Soviet Union.

**59.** V. Kozlov, *The Peoples of the Soviet Union* (Bloomington: Indiana University Press, 1988), 83–98 (tables on 86–88 and 94–96); and Gerhard Simon, *Nationalism and Policy toward the Nationalities in the Soviet Union: From Totalitarian Dictatorship to Post-Stalinist Society* (Boulder, Colo.: Westview, 1991), 376–389.

**60.** See Ilya Levkov, "Self-Determination in Soviet Politics," in Yona Alexander and Robert A. Friedlander, eds., *Self-Determination: National, Regional, and Global Dimensions* (Boulder, Colo.: Westview, 1980), 133–190 at 167.

**61.** The term *nation* is sometimes used as a synonym of *people* or *ethnic group,* and at other times as a designation of the population of a certain state. (See references cited in chapter 1, note 51, and accompanying text.) In the present context it is used as a synonym of *ethnic group.*

**62.** On these terms, see Zvi Magen, "Jews in the USSR: A Minority at Crossroads," *Israel Yearbook on Human Rights* 20 (1991): 319–350 at 320, note 4.

**63.** According to Stalin, "[a] nation is a historically evolved stable community of language, territory, economic life and psychological make-up, manifested in a community of culture." Quoted in Alfred Cobban, *The Nation State and National Self-Determination* (London: Collins, 1969), 192. See also Levkov, "Self-Determination in Soviet Politics," 158–161.

**64.** Simon, *Nationalism and Policy,* 14.

**65.** Levkov, "Self-Determination in Soviet Politics," 145.

**66.** On these changes, see Simon, *Nationalism and Policy,* 147; Kozlov, *Peoples of the Soviet Union,* 32–35 (table 2 on p. 33); Levkov, "Self-Determination in Soviet Politics," 140–146.

**67.** Cobban, *Nation State,* 187.

**68.** On the development of the attitude of the Marxist leaders, see Walter Connor, *The National Question in Marxist-Leninist Theory and Strategy* (Princeton: Princeton University Press, 1984), 5–66; Cobban, *Nation State,* 187–218; Simon, *Nationalism and Policy,* 1–24; Erich Hula, "The Nationalities Policy of the Soviet Union: Theory and Practice," in Erich Hula, ed., *Nationalism and Internationalism: European and American Perspectives* (Lanham, Md.: University Press of America, 1984), 19–43; Victor

Shevtsov, *The State and Nations in the USSR* (Moscow: Progress Publishers, 1982); John N. Hazard, *The Soviet System of Government,* 5th ed. (Chicago: University of Chicago Press, 1980), 93–97.

**69.** Vladimir Ilich Lenin, *Critical Remarks on the National Question: The Right of Nations to Self-Determination* (Moscow: Foreign Languages Publishing House, translated from the 1954 Russian edition), 20.

**70.** For a detailed analysis, see, for example, Hula, "Nationalities Policy," 21–30.

**71.** Quotation from Cobban, *Nation State,* 192.

**72.** Opinions differ on the origin of this motto. See Connor, *The National Question,* 202, 240–241, note 7.

**73.** "Both Marx and Lenin condoned the manipulation of national aspirations as a means of furthering the world revolutionary movement. They felt, however, that there was no place for nationalism in a post-revolutionary society governed by the principles of scientific socialism"; Connor, *The National Question,* xiii.

**74.** Section 70 of the 1977 constitution. For an English translation, see Ferdinand Joseph Maria Feldbrugge, *The Constitutions of the USSR and the Union Republics: Analysis, Texts, Reports* (Alphen, The Netherlands: Sijthoff and Nordhoff, 1979), 71–171.

**75.** Carl J. Friedrich, *Trends of Federalism in Theory and Practice* (New York: Praeger, 1968), 162–169. According to Boris Meissner, it is "ein in föderative Formen gekleideter Einheitsstaat mit beschränkter Verwaltungsdezentralisation auf einzelnen Sondergebieten, insbesondere auf dem Gebiet der Kultur und der Volksbildung" [It is a unitary state cloaked in federal forms with limited administrative decentralization in a few special areas, in particular in the area of culture and education]. See Boris Meissner, *Sowjetunion und Selbstbestimmungsrecht* (Cologne: Verlag für Wissenschaft und Politik, 1962), 60.

**76.** Daniel Elazar, "The Soviet Union," in *Federal Systems,* 344 (see note 1, chapter 7).

**77.** Cobban, *Nation State,* 200–201.

**78.** Sections 35 and 37 of the 1936 Constitution of the USSR; Sections 109 and 110 of the 1977 Constitution.

**79.** Simon, *Nationalism and Policy,* 147–148.

**80.** They have been enumerated in Section 71 of the 1978 Constitution of the Russian Soviet Federated Socialist Republic (RSFSR).

**81.** Section 35 of the 1936 Constitution of the USSR; Section 110 of the 1977 Constitution.

**82.** Section 87 of the 1977 Constitution of the USSR; Section 71 of the 1978 Constitution of the RSFSR; Section 78 of the 1978 Constitution of Azerbaijan; Section 71 of the 1978 Constitution of Georgia; and Section 70 of the 1978 Constitution of Tajikistan.

**83.** Section 110 of the 1977 Constitution of the USSR.

**84.** Section 82 of the Constitution of the RSFSR; Section 79 of the Constitution of Tajikistan; Section 84 of the Constitution of Armenia; and Section 84 of the Constitution of Georgia.

**85.** Stephan M. Weiner, "Autonomous Province," in Ferdinand Joseph Maria Feldbrugge, *Encyclopedia of Soviet Law*, vol. 1 (Alphen, The Netherlands: Sijthoff; New York: Oceana, 1973), 69–71.

**86.** Shevtsov, *State and Nations in the USSR*, 73–74.

**87.** Section 87 of the 1977 Constitution of the USSR; Section 71 of the 1978 Constitution of the RSFSR; Section 71 of the Constitution of Georgia; Section 73 of the Constitution of Uzbekistan; Section 78 of the Constitution of Azerbaijan.

**88.** Section 110 of the 1977 Constitution of the USSR.

**89.** Under Section 60(b) of the 1936 Constitution of the USSR such approval was needed.

**90.** Sections 74 and 82 of the 1977 Constitution of the USSR; Sections 78 and 81 of the Constitution of the RSFSR; Sections 78 and 81 of the Constitution of Uzbekistan; Sections 79 and 82 of the Constitution of Azerbaijan; and Sections 79 and 82 of the Constitution of Georgia.

**91.** Section 114 of the 1978 Constitution of the RSFSR; Sections 111 and 120 of the 1978 Constitution of Uzbekistan; Sections 113 and 123 of the 1978 Constitution of Azerbaijan; and Sections 114 and 123 of the 1978 Constitution of Georgia.

**92.** Section 108 of the 1978 Constitution of the RSFSR; Section 105 of the 1978 Constitution of Uzbekistan; Section 108 of the 1978 Constitution of Azerbaijan; and Section 108 of the 1978 Constitution of Georgia.

**93.** Sections 109 and 110 of the 1977 Constitution of the USSR.

**94.** Section 73(1) of the 1977 Constitution of the USSR.

**95.** This was an innovation of the 1977 Constitution of the USSR (Section 84). Before 1977 this principle was included only in the constitutions of the autonomous republics themselves.

**96.** S. G. Batyev, "Problems in the Development of the Legal Status of the Autonomous Republic," *Soviet Law and Government: A Journal of Translations* 21, no. 4 (1982): 51–70 at 60 and 63. When this article was written, the author was chairman of the Presidium of the Supreme Soviet of the Tatar ASSR.

**97.** It is, however, doubtful whether this principle has been fully implemented in the various autonomous republics. See Simon, *Nationalism and Policy*, 38; Ellsworth Raymond, *The Soviet State*, 2d ed. (New York: New York University Press, 1978), 256.

**98.** Sections 36 (2d paragraph),45 and 159 of the 1977 Constitution of the USSR. The quotations are from the translation in Feldbrugge, *Constitutions of the USSR*, 74.

**99.** Section 36 (1st paragraph) of the Constitution of the USSR.

**100.** Hannum, *Autonomy, Sovereignty, and Self-Determination*, 364; Raymond, *The Soviet State*, 257.

**101.** Connor, *The National Question*, 254–263.

**102.** Section 73 of the 1977 Constitution of the USSR. For an analysis of the various powers, see Hans Georg Belz, "Das Prinzip des Föderalismus in der Sowjetunion," *Jahrbuch des öffentlichen Rechts der Gegenwart, neue Folge* 12 (1963): 249–293. This commentary relates to the parallel provisions in the 1936 Constitution of the USSR.

**103.** Section 76 of the 1977 Constitution of the USSR.

**104.** Batyev's description gives the impression that the autonomous republics had authority in a number of areas, but a closer look reveals that most of the powers mentioned by him in fact boiled down to the implementation of policies established by the center. See Batyev, "Problems," 64–66.

**105.** Hazard, *Soviet System of Governments*, 101–102.

**106.** Asbjorn Eide, "Minority Situations: In Search of Peaceful and Constructive Solutions," *Notre Dame Law Review* 66 (1991): 1311–1346 at 1327; Anatole Goldstein, *The Soviet Attitude toward Territorial Minorities and the Jews* (New York: Institute of Jewish Affairs, 1953), 1–2, 5.

**107.** Goldstein, *Soviet Attitude toward Minorities*, 5–7. According to Igor Grazin, the proper expression is "Sovietization," not "Russification," since in his opinion the Russian culture was also subdued; see *Notre Dame Law Review* 66 (1991): 1352; and Eide, "Minority Situations," 1328, note 46.

**108.** In 1987 the Soviet Union transferred more powers to the union republics in the sphere of economics. See G. E. Schroeder, "Nationalities and the Soviet Economy," in Lubomyr Hajda and Mark Beissinger, eds., *The Nationalities Factor in Soviet Politics and Society* (Boulder, Colo.: Westview, 1990), 43–71 at 62. On 3 April 1990 the Soviet Union adopted a law on the Procedure for Deciding Questions Connected with the Secession of a Union Republic from the USSR, which is published in Albert P. Blaustein et al., "Union of Soviet Socialist Republics, Union Republics, Autonomous Republics, and Autonomous Regions: Documents Relating to State Sovereignty," in Albert P. Blaustein, Bruce Fein, and Jay A. Sigler, eds., *Constitutions of Dependencies and Special Sovereignties* (Dobbs Ferry, N.Y.: Oceana), issued April 1991, binder 4, 9–14. On 26 April 1990 the Law on the Delimitation of Powers between the USSR and Subjects of the Federation was adopted. Ibid., 1.

**109.** Albert P. Blaustein and Gisbert H. Flanz, eds., *Constitutions of the Countries of the World* (Dobbs Ferry, N.Y.: Oceana, 1971), binder 16, issued May 1994, 107–127. One text was signed with the "Sovereign Republics" belonging to the Russian Federation (p. 107), another one with the smaller entities (p. 113), and a third one with the autonomous *oblasti* and *okruga* (p. 121).

**110.** Ibid., 1.

**111.** For the list, see Section 65 of the Constitution of the Russian Federation. Some of those units are supposed to have a special national character, while others are merely administrative units. See Margareta Mommsen, *Wohin treibt Russland? Eine Grossmacht zwischen Anarchie und Demokratie* (Munich: Beck, 1996), 179.

**112.** Section 5(4) of the Constitution of the Russian Federation. Sections cited in notes 113–116 and 118–129 also refer to the Constitution of the Russian Federation.

**113.** Section 95(2).

**114.** Section 11(3).

**115.** Part 2, Section 1.

**116.** Sections 4 and 76(5).

**117.** Irina Busygina, "Russia: Difficulties in Establishing a Federation," *Aussenpolitik* 46 (1995): 253–262 at 261.

**118.** Section 77.

**119.** Sections 68(1) and 68(2).

**120.** Section 68(3).

**121.** Section 69.

**122.** Section 71.

**123.** Section 72.

**124.** Section 76(2).

**125.** Sections 73 and 76(4).

**126.** Section 72(n).

**127.** Sections 134-136.

**128.** Section 125.

**129.** Section 85.

**130.** Busygina, "Russia: Difficulties in Establishing a Federation," 257–259.

**131.** "Russia's Riddle of the Regions: A Big Shift of Power to Russia's Regions over the Past Few Years May Help Boris Yeltsin Hold on to His Presidency at the Centre," *The Economist,* 23-29 March 1996, 29–30. For an analysis of the attitude of the subjects at the time of the tension between President Yeltsin and the Parliament before the adoption of the Constitution, see Mommsen, *Wohin treibt Russland?* 128–203.

**132.** "Russia's Riddle," *The Economist.*

**133.** See text accompanying note 3, chapter 1, and text following note 4, chapter 4.

**134.** See text accompanying notes 5–7, chapter 4.

**135.** Estonia's declaration of 17 September 1923, Latvia's declaration of 7 July 1923, and Lithuania's declaration of 12 May 1922 (League of Nations, *Official Journal,* November 1923, p. 1311; August 1923, p. 932; June 1922, p. 524).

**136.** House Select Committee on Communist Aggression, *Report of the Select Committee to Investigate Communist Aggression and the Forced Incorporation of the Baltic States into the U.S.S.R* (3rd interim report), 83rd Cong., 2d sess., 1954, 94. Reprinted as *Baltic States: A Study of Their Origin and National Development, Their Seizure and Incorporation into the USSR,* vol. 4 of the International Military Law and History Reprint Series, ed. Igor I. Kavass and Adolph Spruzz (Buffalo, N.Y.: William S. Hein, 1972). See also Eugen Maddison, *Die Nationalen Minderheiten Estlands und ihre Rechte,* 2d ed. (Tallinn, Estonia: Verlag von A. Keiserman, 1930), 7.

**137.** Maddison, *Die Nationalen Minderheiten Estlands,* 7. See also Section 23 of the 1920 Constitution of Estonia.

**138.** Maddison, *Die Nationalen Minderheiten Estlands,* 6, 8.

**139.** Ibid., 8–34. The law was supplemented by regulations for its implementation adopted in 1925.

**140.** Ibid., 15, 24; Dörge, *Der Autonome Verband,* 105.

**141.** This follows from Section 1 of the 1925 Statute, which compared the institutions of self-administration to local authorities. It was also expressly stated in Section 2 of the implementing regulations of 1925; see Dörge, *Der Autonome Verband,* 45; and Maddison, *Die Nationalen Minderheiten Estlands,* 14.

**142.** The authorization by the government of Estonia was granted in 1925 to the German minority and in 1926 to the Jewish minority. See Maddison, *Die Nationalen Minderheiten Estlands,* 26–33. As mentioned, according to Dubnow and Robinson, the autonomy in Estonia was the most consistent one. See Dubnow and Robinson, *Encyclopaedia Judaica* (1928), s.v. "autonomie."

In 1993 Estonia again adopted a law that permitted national minorities to acquire cultural autonomy. The possibility was given to "persons belonging to German, Russian, Swedish and Jewish minorities and persons belonging to national minorities with a membership of more than 3,000" to establish "national minority cultural autonomy." The right was given only to citizens of Estonia who reside in Estonia and "maintain longstanding, firm and lasting ties with Estonia." See Riigi Teataja Part I 1993, no. 71, Article 1001. The law was adopted on 26 October 1993 and came into force on 28 November 1993.

**143.** For references, see note 6, chapter 4.

**144.** See note 8, chapter 4.

**145.** House Select Committee, *Communist Aggression,* 124, and references in note 7, chapter 4.

**146.** Natan Feinberg, "Memories from the Jewish Autonomy in Lithuania," in *Essays on Jewish Issues of Our Time* (in Hebrew) (Jerusalem: Dvir, 1980), 93.

**147.** Reproduced in Hannum, *Documents,* 325–327.

**148.** A. Seidman, "The Jewish National Autonomy in the Independent Ukraine in the Years 1917-1918" (Ph.D. diss., Tel Aviv University, 1982); Solomon I. Goldelman, *Jewish National Autonomy in Ukraine 1917–1920* (Chicago: Ukrainian Research and Information Institute, 1968). For a collection of documents on this autonomy (translated into German), see Marcel Kaleff, "Das Nationalitätenproblem (Ein Beitrag zum Nationalitätenrecht)" (Ph.D. diss., University of Göttingen, 1923), 154–183.

**149.** Lenin, *Critical Remarks on the National Question.*

## 9. Autonomies Established after World War II

**1.** Milton J. Esman, "Political and Psychological Factors in Ethnic Conflict," in Joseph V. Montville, ed., *Conflict and Peacemaking in Multiethnic Societies* (Lexington, Mass.: Lexington Books, 1990), 53–64 at 57–58.

**2.** Donald L. Horowitz, *Ethnic Groups in Conflict* (Berkeley and Los Angeles: University of California Press, 1985), 4–5.

**3.** This section on South Tyrol/Alto Adige draws from the following sources: Dietrich Schindler, "South Tyrol," in R. Bernhardt, ed., *Encyclopedia of Public International Law,* vol. 12 (1990), 348–350; F. Gunther Eyck, "South Tyrol and Multiethnic Relations," in Montville, ed., *Conflict and Peacemaking,* 219–238; Antony E. Alcock, *The History of the South Tyrol Question* (London: Michael Joseph, for the Graduate Institute of International Studies, Geneva, 1970); Alain Fenet, *La Question du Tyrol du Sud: Un prob-*

lème de droit international (Paris: Librairie générale de droit et de jurisprudence, 1968); Herbert Miehsler, Südtirol als Völkerrechtsproblem (Graz,
Vienna, and Cologne: Verlag Styria, 1962); Pietro Pastorelli, "I rapporti italo-
austriaci dall'accordo De Gasperi–Gruber alle intese piu recenti (1946–
1969)," in La politica estera italiana del dopoguerra (Bologna: Il Mulino,
1987), 73–105; Christoph Schreuer, "Autonomy in South Tyrol," in Yoram
Dinstein, ed., Models of Autonomy (New Brunswick, N.J.: Transaction
Books, 1981), 53–65; Federico Guiglia, Alto Adige: Volti e risvolti di un 'golpe'
perfetto (Merano, Italy: Hauger, 1983); Dieter Blumenwitz, "Völkerrechtliche Grundlagen der Südtirol-Frage," in Die Friedenswarte (1986), 91;
Mario Toscano-Carbone, Alto Adige-South Tyrol: Italy's Frontier with the Ger-
man World (English edition by George A. Carbone) (Baltimore: Johns Hop-
kins University Press, 1975); Antony Alcock, "Italy: The South Tyrol," in
Minorities and Autonomy in Western Europe: A Minority Rights Group Report
(London: Minority Rights Group, 1991), 6–12; Antony Alcock, Südtirol
seit dem Paket (Vienna: Braumüller, 1982); Felix Ermacora, Südtirol und das
Vaterland Österreich (1984); Otto Triffterer, "The Rights of the German
Speaking Population in the South Tyrol," in Israel Yearbook on Human Rights
21 (1991): 15–42; Alain Fenet, "La fin du litige italo-autrichien sur le Haut
Adige–Tyrol du Sud," Annuaire Français de Droit International 39 (1993):
357–376. The author wishes to express her thanks to Simonetta della Seta
for her assistance in locating articles that describe Italy's position. The
author also thanks Mr. Federico Guiglia, Professor Christoph Schreuer,
and Professor Waldemar Hummer for the material they have most kindly
sent her.

   4. On the procedure by which the dispute was declared settled, see
Fenet, "La fin du litige."

   5. Provincial Government of South Tyrol, Statistisches Jahrbuch für
Südtirol, Annuario Statistico (1987), 74–75, quoted in Hurst Hannum, Auton-
omy, Sovereignty, and Self-Determination: The Accommodation of Conflicting
Rights (Philadelphia: University of Pennsylvania Press, 1990), 433.

   6. Clive Parry, ed., The Consolidated Treaty Series (Dobbs Ferry, N.Y.:
Oceana, 1981), 226: 9–169 (Article 27, p. 14). For the legislative history
of this provision, see Nina Almond and Ralph Haswell Lutz, eds., The
Treaty of St. Germain: A Documentary History of Its Territorial and Political
Clauses (Stanford: Stanford University Press, 1935), 335–359. For the ear-
lier history, see Alcock, History of the South Tyrol Question, 3–18.

   7. British and Foreign State Papers, 112: 973.

   8. Alcock, History of the South Tyrol Question, 52–53; Toscano-
Carbone, Alto Adige-South Tyrol, 35–51; Triffterer, "Rights of the German
Speaking Population," 23–25.

**9.** United Nations Treaty Series, vol. 49, 3 and 184 (Article 10 and Annex IV). For the various opinions about the nature and effect of this agreement, see Miehsler, *Südtirol als Völkerrechtsproblem,* 161–171; Waldemar Hummer, "Zum Rechtscharakter des Gruber–De Gasperi-Abkommens 1946, Völkerrechtlicher Vertrag, einseitige Verpflichtungserklärung oder blosses 'gentlemen's agreement'?" in *Südtirol und der Pariser Vertrag, Geschichte und Perspektiven* (Bolzano, Italy: Tiroler Landesinstitut and the Bundesländerhaus Tirol, 1988), 137; Toscano-Carbone, *Alto Adige-South Tyrol,* 113–120.

**10.** See, for example, Miehsler, *Südtirol als Völkerrechtsproblem,* 246–248; Eyck, *South Tyrol and Multiethnic Relations,* 226; Toscano-Carbone, *Alto Adige-South Tyrol,* 121–128, 136–138.

**11.** For an English translation of the text, see Alcock, *History of the South Tyrol Question,* 475–492.

**12.** Schreuer, "Autonomy in South Tyrol," 55.

**13.** UN General Assembly Resolution 1497 (XV) of 31 October 1960, and UN General Assembly Resolution 1661 (XVI) of 28 November 1961.

**14.** On the 1959 debate in the Consultative Assembly of the Council of Europe, see Alcock, *History of the South Tyrol Question,* 308–312; for the opinion of the Commission on Human Rights, see European Commission on Human Rights, Report of 30 March 1963, in *Yearbook of the European Convention on Human Rights,* vol. 4 (1963), 138.

**15.** For an English translation of the Package, see Alcock, *History of the South Tyrol Question,* 434–448. According to Triffterer, the "Paket" was not formally signed, and there existed various slightly differing German translations of the document. See Triffterer, "Rights of the German Speaking Population," 32. Ermacora, in *Südtirol und das Vaterland Österreich,* 157, describes it as a "stratified text. It consists of the results of the Austrian-Italian negotiations, of the results of the talks between Moro [at the time the foreign minister of Italy] and Magnago [at the time the president of the main German party in South Tyrol, the SVP], of 'footnotes,' the Italian version of the 'footnotes,' and the Austrian-South Tyrolean version of the 'footnotes.'" See also Heinrich Siegler, *Die österreichisch-italienische Einigung über die Regelung des Südtirolkonflikts* (Bonn, Vienna, and Zurich: Verlag für Zeitarchive, 1970). On the legal nature and effect of the Package, see Waldemar Hummer et al., *Völkerrechtliche und Europarechtliche Probleme der Südtirolautonomie* (an opinion prepared for the provincial government of South Tyrol, Innsbruck, Austria, 1988), 48–104; Triffterer, "Rights of the German Speaking Population," 33; Fenet, "La fin du litige," 373–376. On the implementation of the Package, see Waldemar Hummer and Karl Zeller, "Der Abschluss der Durchführung des 'Südtirol-Pakets': Chronologie und aktuelle Probleme," *Österreichisches Jahrbuch für internationale Politik* 5 (1988): 57–101: and Fenet, "La fin du litige," 362–373.

**16.** For an English translation of the Operational Calendar, see Alcock, *History of the South Tyrol Question,* 448–449. On its legal nature, see Hummer et al., *Völkerrechtliche und Europarechtliche Probleme der Südtirolautonomie,* 106–118.

**17.** Schreuer, "Autonomy in South Tyrol," 57. See also Triffterer, "Rights of the German Speaking Population," 34.

**18.** An English translation, by Mario G. R. Oriani-Ambrosini and Sacha B. Knop, has been published in Albert P. Blaustein and Phyllis M. Blaustein, eds., *Constitutions of Dependencies and Special Sovereignties,* binder 1 (Dobbs Ferry, N.Y.: Oceana, 1988); for another translation, see Hurst Hannum, ed., *Documents on Autonomy and Minority Rights* (Dordrecht, The Netherlands: Nijhoff, 1993), 462–495. However, at some points the author has used her own translation.

**19.** See Title V of the 1948 Constitution of Italy, Sections 114–133; for an English translation of the constitution, see Gisbert H. Flanz and Albert P. Blaustein, eds., *Constitutions of the Countries of the World,* binder 8 (Dobbs Ferry, N.Y.: Oceana, March 1987); Fabio Lorenzoni, "Italian Accommodation of Cultural Differences," in Daniel Elazar, ed., *Governing Peoples and Territories* (Philadelphia: Institute for the Study of Human Issues, 1982), 89–99.

**20.** Section 115 of the Constitution.

**21.** Section 116 of the Constitution.

**22.** Sections 4 and 5 of the 1972 New Autonomy Statute.

**23.** Sections 24–35 of the 1972 New Autonomy Statute.

**24.** Sections 36–46 of the 1972 New Autonomy Statute.

**25.** Section 45 of the 1972 New Autonomy Statute.

**26.** Section 40 of the 1972 New Autonomy Statute.

**27.** Section 4 of the 1972 New Autonomy Statute.

**28.** Section 5 of the 1972 New Autonomy Statute.

**29.** Section 55 of the 1972 New Autonomy Statute.

**30.** Sections 55 and 56 of the 1972 New Autonomy Statute.

**31.** Section 57 of the 1972 New Autonomy Statute.

**32.** Section 58 of the 1972 New Autonomy Statute.

**33.** Sections 8 and 9 of the 1972 New Autonomy Statute.

**34.** Sections 8(23) and 9(5) of the 1972 New Autonomy Statute.

**35.** Section 10 of the 1972 New Autonomy Statute.

**36.** Section 8(10) of the 1972 New Autonomy Statute.

**37.** Section 8(22) of the 1972 New Autonomy Statute.

**38.** Sections 8(25) and 9(10–11) of the 1972 New Autonomy Statute.

**39.** Sections 8(2–4) and 8(26–29) of the 1972 New Autonomy Statute.

**40.** Hannum, *Autonomy, Sovereignty, and Self-Determination,* 438.

**41.** Section 20 of the 1972 New Autonomy Statute.

**42.** Sections 20 and 22 of the 1972 New Autonomy Statute.

**43.** Sections 8(26–29), 9(2), and 19 of the 1972 New Autonomy Statute. See also Schreuer, "Autonomy in South Tyrol," 59.

**44.** Section 8(28) of the 1972 New Autonomy Statute.

**45.** Section 99 of the 1972 New Autonomy Statute.

**46.** Section 19 of the 1972 New Autonomy Statute.

**47.** Section 29, 2d paragraph of the 1972 New Autonomy Statute.

**48.** Section 19, 3d paragraph of the 1972 New Autonomy Statute.

**49.** Section 100 of the 1972 New Autonomy Statute.

**50.** Section 94, 4th paragraph of the 1972 New Autonomy Statute.

**51.** Section 100, last paragraph of the 1972 New Autonomy Statute.

**52.** Section 100, 4th paragraph of the 1972 New Autonomy Statute.

**53.** Section 50, 4th paragraph of the 1972 New Autonomy Statute.

**54.** Section 61 of the 1972 New Autonomy Statute.

**55.** Section 19, 12th paragraph of the 1972 New Autonomy Statute.

**56.** Section 91, 1st paragraph of the 1972 New Autonomy Statute.

**57.** Section 49 of the 1972 New Autonomy Statute. No similar obligation has been included with regard to the government of the province. See Section 50 of the 1972 New Autonomy Statute.

**58.** Section 89 of the 1972 New Autonomy Statute.

**59.** Ibid., last paragraph.

**60.** Ibid., 3d paragraph.

**61.** Hannum, *Autonomy, Sovereignty, and Self-Determination,* 437, note 1176.

**62.** Eyck, "South Tyrol and Multiethnic Relations," 230–231, and 236, note h.

**63.** See Alcock, "Italy: The South Tyrol," 11; and Alcock, "Proportional Representation in Public Employment as a Technique for Diminishing Conflict in Culturally Divided Communities: The Case of South Tyrol," in *Regional Politics and Policy* 1 (1991): 74–86.

**64.** See Alcock, "Italy: The South Tyrol," 10.

**65.** Sections 47, 48, and 49 of the 1972 New Autonomy Statute.

**66.** Sections 33 and 49 of the 1972 New Autonomy Statute; see text accompanying note 23, chapter 9.

**67.** Although the province of Bolzano has two vice-presidents, none are foreseen for the province of Trento. See Section 50, 1st and 3rd paragraphs of the 1972 New Autonomy Statute.

**68.** Section 52, last paragraph of the 1972 New Autonomy Statute.

**69.** Section 87 of the 1972 New Autonomy Statute.

**70.** Section 91, 8th paragraph of the 1972 New Autonomy Statute.

**71.** Section 91, 1st paragraph of the 1972 New Autonomy Statute.

**72.** Section 92 of the 1972 New Autonomy Statute.

**73.** Section 93 of the 1972 New Autonomy Statute.

**74.** Title VI, Sections 69–86 of the 1972 New Autonomy Statute.

**75.** Alcock, "Italy: The South Tyrol," 10.

**76.** Sections 97 and 98 of the 1972 New Autonomy Statute.

**77.** Section 103 of the 1972 New Autonomy Statute.

**78.** Rudolf Hrbek and Sabine Weyand, *Betrifft: Das Europa der Regionen: Fakten, Probleme, Perspektiven* (Munich: Verlag C. H. Beck, 1994), 53–57.

**79.** Arni Olafsson, "International Status of the Faroe Islands," *Nordic Journal of International Law* 51 (1982): 29–38; Erlendur Patursson, "Some Critical Observations on the Political Development of the Faroe Islands and Their Present Political Situation," *Nordic Journal of International Law* 54 (1985): 52–58; Halgir Winther Poulsen, "Self-Government and Natural Resources–The Faroese Case I," *Nordic Journal of International Law* 57 (1988): 338–341; Arni Olafsson, "Self-Government and Natural Resources–The Faroese Case II," *Nordic Journal of International Law* 57 (1988): 342–344; Erlendur Patursson, "Some Critical Observations on the Faroese-Danish Financial Relations," *Nordic Journal of International Law* 55 (1986): 41–45; Frederick Harhoff, "Faroe Islands," in Bernhardt, *Encyclopedia of Public International Law,* vol. 2 (1995), 357–358; Hans Jacob Debes, "On the Formation of a Nation: The Faroe Islands" (manuscript, 1991); Halgir Winther Poulsen, "Faroe Islands Home Rule" (manuscript, 1979). The author wishes to express her thanks to Dr. Debes and to Mr. Poulsen for having allowed her to study their manuscripts.

**80.** Olafsson, "International Status of the Faroe Islands," 32–39.

**81.** Article 227(5) of the 1957 Treaty of Rome and the 1992 Maastricht Treaty.

**82.** Olafsson, "International Status of the Faroe Islands," 34 and 37; Goeran Lindholm, "The Right of Autonomous Regions to Participate in Nordic Cooperation," *Nordic Journal of International Law* 54 (1985): 79–84.

**83.** Olafsson, "International Status of the Faroe Islands," 31.

**84.** Ibid., 31.

**85.** Patursson, "Some Critical Observations on the Political Development," 55.

**86.** The historical introduction in the following section will be limited to those developments relevant to the system of self-government of the city.

**87.** U.S. Department of State, *Documents on Germany 1944–1985*, Department of State Publication 9446 (Washington, D.C.: Department of State, 1985), 33.

**88.** Protocol between the United States, the United Kingdom, and the USSR on Zones of Occupation in Germany and Administration of the "Greater Berlin" Area, Appproved by the European Advisory Commission, London, 12 September 1944, United Nations Treaty Series, 227: 279; and U.S. Department of State, *Documents on Germany*, 1, Articles 1 and 5. The European Advisory Commission had been established by the 1943 Moscow Conference of Foreign Ministers, and was dissolved at the Potsdam Conference in August 1945. It consisted originally of representatives of the Soviet Union, the United Kingdom, and the United States; France joined in 1944; see I. D. Hendry and M. C. Wood, *The Legal Status of Berlin* (Cambridge: Grotius Publications, 1987), 3, note 5. The above protocol was amended twice: on 14 November 1944 (U.S. Department of State, *Documents on Germany*, 4), an amendment that was not relevant to Berlin; and on 26 July 1945, in order to include France among the occupying powers and to establish a French zone of occupation in Germany and Berlin, in areas that had been part of the U.S. and British zones. See U.S. Department of State, *Documents on Germany*, 44–48.

**89.** Agreement on Control Machinery in Germany, adopted by the European Advisory Commission, 14 November 1944, United Nations Treaty Series, 236: 359; and U.S. Department of State, *Documents on Germany*, 6, Articles 3(b)(iv), and 7. See also the Allied Agreement on the Quadripartite Administration of Berlin, adopted by the Conference of the Representatives of the Allied Commands held in Berlin on 7 July 1945; see U.S. Department of State, *Documents on Germany*, 43–44.

**90.** Senate Committee on Foreign Relations, communiqué issued at the end of the Crimea (Yalta) Conference, 11 February 1945, *Documents on Germany 1944–1971*, 92nd Cong., 1st sess, 1971, 8.

**91.** Protocol of the Proceedings of the Berlin (Potsdam) Conference, 1 August 1945, Part II, sec. A, paragraph 9(iv), and sec. B, paragraph 14, U.S. Department of State, *Documents on Germany*, 54–65 at 57 and 58.

**92.** For an English translation, see U.S. Department of State, *Documents on Germany*, 221–258.

**93.** Ibid., 278–306.

**94.** Ernst R. Zivier, *The Legal Status of the Land Berlin: A Survey after the Quadripartite Agreement,* translated by Paul S. Ulrich (Berlin: Berlin-Verlag, 1980), 14.

**95.** Letter from the Military Governors of the Three Western Zones of Occupation to the President of the West German Parliamentary Council Approving, with Reservations, the Basic Law for the Federal Republic of Germany, 12 May 1949; U.S. Department of State, *Documents on Germany,* 260–262 at 261, paragraph 4.

**96.** Ibid., 324–340 at 324, Section 1(3), and at 340, Section 87(3).

**97.** Occupation Statute Defining the Powers to Be Retained by the Occupation Authorities, Signed by the Three Western Foreign Ministers, 8 April 1949, U.S. Department of State, *Documents on Germany,* 212–214. On the same day they also agreed on the Basic Principles for Merger of the Three Western German Zones of Occupation and Creation of an Allied High Commission; ibid., 215–216.

**98.** U.S. Department of State, *Documents on Germany,* 262–264.

**99.** Ibid., 263, Section 3(a).

**100.** Constitution of the German Democratic Republic of 7 October 1949, Section 2; U.S. Department of State, *Documents on Germany,* 278.

**101.** Joint Resolution to Terminate the State of War between the United States and the Government of Germany: Public Law 181, 82nd Congress, Approved 19 October 1951; U.S. Department of State, *Documents on Germany,* 356.

**102.** U.S. Department of State, *Documents on Germany,* 425–438; United Nations Treaty Series, 231: 327.

**103.** Proclamation by the Allied High Commission Revoking the Occupation Statute and Abolishing the Allied High Commission and the Offices of the Land Commissioners in the Federal Republic of Germany, Signed at Bonn, 5 May 1955; U.S. Department of State, *Documents on Germany,* 444.

**104.** Sections 2 and 4(2), U.S. Department of State, *Documents on Germany,* 425–438.

**105.** Section 6, ibid.

**106.** Declaration by the Federal Republic of Germany on Relations with Berlin, 26 May 1952, as amended on 23 October 1954; ibid., 436–437; and letter from the Allied High Commissioners to Chancellor Adenauer on Relations between the Federal Republic of Germany and Berlin, 26 May 1952, as amended on 23 October 1954; ibid., 437–438.

**107.** Treaty on Relations between the Soviet Union and the German Democratic Republic, Signed at Moscow, 20 September 1955. Ibid., 458–460, Preamble; United Nations Treaty Series, 226: 208–212.

**108.** U.S. Department of State, *Documents on Germany,* 379–382. This declaration had been drafted on 26 May 1952, and came into force on 5 May 1955.

**109.** Agreement between France, the United Kingdom, and the United States on the Exercise of Retained Rights in Germany, signed in Paris on 23 October 1954, entered into force on 5 May 1955. U.S. Department of State, *Documents on Germany,* 431–432, Article 1.

**110.** For a historical overview, see Hendry and Wood, *Legal Status of Berlin,* 10–11.

**111.** United Nations Treaty Series, 880: 115-148; U.S. Department of State, *Documents on Germany,* 1135–1187. This agreement was concluded in the wake of the 1970 Moscow Treaty between the Soviet Union and the Federal Republic of Germany (for an unofficial English translation, see ibid., 1103–1105). The conclusion of the 1971 Quadripartite Agreement was accompanied by the conclusion of agreements between the Federal Republic of Germany and the German Democratic Republic on telecommunications and on transit, as well as by agreements between the Senat of Berlin and the German Democratic Republic on visiting arrangements and on the exchange of some territory. For an analysis of the 1971 Quadripartite Agreement, see, for example, Honore M. Catudal, Jr., *The Diplomacy of the Quadripartite Agreement on Berlin: A New Era in East-West Politics* (Berlin: Berlin-Verlag, 1978); Hendry and Wood, *Legal Status of Berlin,* 44–54; Zivier, *Legal Status of the Land Berlin,* 149–228.

**112.** Treaty on the Final Settlement with Respect to Germany, concluded by the Federal Republic of Germany, the German Democratic Republic, France, the USSR, the United Kingdom, and the United States, in Moscow on 12 September 1990, *International Legal Materials* 29 (1990): 1186–1193, Article 1(1). See also the Unification Treaty, concluded by the Federal Republic of Germany and the German Democratic Republic in Berlin on 31 August 1990, *International Legal Materials* 30 (1991): 457–503, Articles 1, 3, 4, 16, Protocol re: Articles 1, 9(5), 16, and Statement for the Record; Agreement on the Settlement of Certain Matters Relating to Berlin, concluded by France, the Federal Republic of Germany, the United Kingdom, and the United States in Bonn on 25 September 1990, *International Legal Materials* 30 (1991): 445–449; Exchange of Notes between France, the Federal Republic of Germany, the United Kingdom and the United States Concerning the Presence in Berlin of Armed Forces, Bonn, 25 September 1990, *International Legal Materials* 30 (1991): 450–453.

**113.** Treaty on the Final Settlement with Respect to Germany, of 12 September 1990, Article 7 (see note 112).

**114.** Statement of Principles (1949) (see note 98), and Instrument of Revision of the Statement of Principles for Berlin, Promulgated by the Allied (Western) *Kommandatura* of 7 March 1951, U.S. Department of State, *Documents on Germany,* 262, 348.

**115.** Ingo von Münch, *Dokumente des geteilten Deutschland,* 2d ed. (Stuttgart: Alfred Kröner, 1976), 158–171, sections 25–39. For an English translation, see U.S. Department of State, *Documents on Germany,* 324–340. The 1950 Constitution replaced a temporary one adopted in 1946.

**116.** Constitution, Sections 40–44.

**117.** Ibid., Section 41.

**118.** Ibid., Sections 62–72.

**119.** Ibid., Sections 50–61.

**120.** Ibid., Section 44. On the special status of the police force and its relations to the *Kommandatura,* see Hendry and Wood, *Legal Status of Berlin,* 288–289.

**121.** The 1955 declaration on Berlin, Section IV (see note 108). On the extent and modalities of the application of federal legislation to Berlin, see Hendry and Wood, *Legal Status of Berlin,* 156–167.

**122.** The 1971 Quadripartite Agreement on Berlin, Part II, Article B (see note 111). The Western Allies were consistent on this matter, and suspended the operation of provisions of the 1949 Basic Law of the Federal Republic of Germany (Section 23) and of the 1950 Constitution of Berlin (Section 1, paragraphs 2 and 3, and Section 87), which purported to establish that Berlin was a part of the Federal Republic of Germany; see letters from the Military Governors of the Three Western Zones of Occupation to the President of the West German Parliamentary Council Approving, with Reservations, the Basic Law for the Federal Republic of Germany, 12 May 1949, U.S. Department of State, *Documents on Germany,* 260–262, paragraph 4; BK/O (49) 139 by the Allied (Western) *Kommandatura* Berlin on the Decisions of the (West) Berlin City Assembly Concerning the Representation of Berlin in the Bundestag, 30 June 1949, ibid., 272; Letter from the Allied (Western) *Kommandatura* to the West Berlin Authorities Approving, with Reservations, the West Berlin Constitution, 29 August 1950, ibid., 340–341. The Allies either suspended or gave a restrictive interpretation to the doubtful provisions.

**123.** The 1971 Quadripartite Agreement, Annex II, Section 3 (see note 111).

**124.** Zivier, *Legal Status of the Land Berlin,* 83–92.

**125.** The 1971 Quadripartite Agreement, Annex IV, U.S. Department of State, *Documents on Germany,* 1140–1141; for the implementation of these provisions, see Hendry and Wood, *Legal Status of Berlin,* 189–231; and Zivier, *Legal Status of the Land Berlin,* 194–205.

**126.** See Hendry and Wood, *Legal Status of Berlin,* 235–240; Zivier, *Legal Status of the Land Berlin,* 132–138.

**127.** This limited participation was possible in view of Sections 38, 50, and 144 of the Basic Law of the Federal Republic of Germany, which permit a Land or part of a Land in which the application of the Basic Law is restricted, to send representatives to the *Bundestag* and the *Bundesrat.* The *Kommandatura* objected to the holding of general elections in Berlin in order to elect representatives to the *Bundestag.* U.S. Department of State, *Documents on Germany,* 272, paragraph 5. See also Zivier, *Legal Status of the Land Berlin,* 105–107.

**128.** Zivier, *Legal Status of the Land Berlin.*

**129.** Ibid., 106–107.

**130.** The 1955 Declaration on Berlin, Section IX (see note 108).

**131.** Ibid.

**132.** Ibid., Section VII. The right of repeal applied to all cases of "inconsistency with Allied legislation, or with other measures of the Allied authorities, or with the rights of the Allied authorities under" the 1955 Declaration. See also Hendry and Wood, *Legal Status of Berlin,* 88–90, on the implementation of this provision. The *Kommandatura* decreed that "even in those cases where no reservations are laid down expressly by the Allied Kommandatura, such laws and treaties do not affect the rights and responsibilities of the Allies or Allied legislation." Ibid., 89.

**133.** Zivier, *Legal Status of the Land Berlin,* 59.

**134.** The 1955 Declaration on Berlin, Section III (see note 108).

**135.** Articles 7 and 10 of the Allied *Kommandatura* Berlin Law no. 7, quoted in the judgment discussed below (note 140).

**136.** The 1955 Declaration on Berlin, Section II (see note 108).

**137.** Ibid., Section V.

**138.** Ibid., Section VII.

**139.** Ibid., Section VI.

**140.** *United States v. Tiede and Ruske,* U.S. Court for Berlin, 86 F.R.D. 227 (1979). See also Herbert Z. Stern, *Judgment in Berlin* (New York: Universe Books, 1984).

**141.** Law No. 46 of the U.S. High Commissioner for Germany of 28 April 1955, quoted extensively in an appendix to the judgment, 86 F.R.D. at 261–265.

**142.** It will be remembered that as of 1955 the respective ambassadors in the Federal Republic of Germany were in charge of the rights and responsibilities of the Western Allies in Berlin (see note 109).

**143.** 86 F.R.D. at 260. The conclusion of the court was based both on the U.S. constitutional right to a trial by jury and on the provisions of the 1963 Tokyo Convention on Offenses and Certain Other Acts Committed on Board Aircraft, which requires that foreign defendants be accorded treatment that is no less favorable for their protection than that accorded to nationals.

**144.** 86 F.R.D. at 238.

**145.** 86 F.R.D. at 245.

**146.** *Dostal et al. v. Alexander Haig et al.,* U.S. Court of Appeals for the District of Columbia Circuit, 652 F.2d 173 (1981).

**147.** 652 F.2d at 175.

**148.** 652 F.2d at 176.

**149.** See, for example, Jochen A. Frowein, "Berlin," in Bernhardt, *Encyclopedia of Public International Law,* vol. 1 (1992), 382–387; Robert R. Bowie et al., *The Issues in the Berlin-German Crisis,* The Hammerskjold Forums, no. 1 (Dobbs Ferry, N.Y.: Oceana, 1963), 19–29, 37–39; Hans von Mangoldt, "Zur Rechtslage Berlins," *Recht in Ost und West* 34 (1990): 1–12; Stanley D. Metzger et al., *West Berlin: The Legal Context,* ed. Roland J. Stanger (Columbus: Ohio State University Press, 1966); Rupert Scholz, "Der Status Berlins," in Joseph Isensee and Paul Kirchhoff, eds., *Handbuch des Staatsrechts der Bundesrepublik Deutschland,* vol. 1 (Heidelberg: Müller, 1987), 352–386 at 366–374.

**150.** A situation similar to that of Memel-Klaipeda (see chapter 8).

**151.** This section on the historical background of Eritrea is drawn from the following sources: Ethiopiawi, "The Eritrean-Ethiopian Conflict," in Astri Suhrke and Lela Garner Noble, eds., *Ethnic Conflict in International Relations* (New York: Praeger, 1977), 127–145; Hannum, *Autonomy, Sovereignty, and Self-Determination,* 337–338; Haggai Erlich, "The Eritrean Autonomy 1952–1962: Its Failure and Its Contribution to Further Escalation," in Dinstein, *Models of Autonomy,* 171–182. For a legal analysis, see J. Klabbers and Rene Lefeber, "Africa: Lost between Self-Determination and *uti possidetis,*" in Catherine Brölmann et al., eds., *Peoples and Minorities in International Law* (Dordrecht, The Netherlands: Nijhoff, 1993), 37–76 at 70–74; G. H. Tesfagiorgis, "Self-Determination: Its Evolution and Practice in the United Nations and Its Application to the Case of Eritrea," *Wisconsin International Law Journal* 6 (1987): 75–127; Raymond Goy, "L'Indépendance de l'Erythrée," *Annuaire Français de Droit International* 39 (1993): 337–356.

**152.** Clive Parry, ed., *Consolidated Treaty Series* (Dobbs Ferry, N.Y.: Oceana, 1978), 172: 95–102.

**153.** United Nations Treaty Series, 49: 3–507, at page 139, Article 23.

**154.** Ibid., 215, Annex XI, paragraph 3.

**155.** General Assembly Resolution 390A (V), reproduced in Final Report of the United Nations Commissioner in Eritrea, 17 October 1952, General Assembly Official Records, seventh session, supplement no. 15 (A/2188), 74–75. On the question of whether this was the right solution, see Goy, "L'Indépendance de l'Erythrée," 340.

**156.** Dr. Eduardo Anze Matienzo of Bolivia. On the various steps leading to the adoption of the constitution, see Goy, "L'Indépendance de l'Erythrée," 4–42.

**157.** This procedure had been foreseen by the above General Assembly Resolution, paragraph 13. For the relevant texts, see Final Report of the United Nations Commissioner in Eritrea, 43–46 (see note 155).

**158.** Ibid., 70–71.

**159.** UN General Assembly Resolution 617 (VII), of 17 December 1952, General Assembly Official Records, Supplement 20 (A/2361), 9.

**160.** Erlich, "Eritrean Autonomy 1952–1962," 179.

**161.** For an analysis of the illegality of the dissolution of the special regime, see Theodor Meron and Anna Mamalakis Pappas, "The Eritrean Autonomy: A Case Study of a Failure," in Dinstein, *Models of Autonomy,* 183–212 at 210–212; and Goy, "L'Indépendance de l'Erythrée," 341.

**162.** On the question whether this development constituted decolonization or secession, see Goy, "L'Indépendance de l'Erythrée," 341–343.

**163.** Federal Act, paragraph 1, and the Constitution, Section 3; see in Final Report of the United Nations Commissioner in Eritrea, 74, 79.

**164.** The text of the constitution is reproduced in ibid., 76–89. According to the Federal Act, the constitution was supposed to "contain provisions adopting and ratifying the Federal Act on behalf of the people of Eritrea" and was to be "consistent with the provisions of the Federal Act." Ibid., 75, paragraph 12.

**165.** Federal Act, paragraph 3, ibid., 74; Constitution, Section 6, ibid., 79.

**166.** Constitution, Section 5(2), ibid., 79.

**167.** Final Report of the United Nations Commissioner in Eritrea, 47, paragraph 499. See also Preamble to the Federal Act, paragraph (c), ibid., 74.

**168.** Federal Act, paragraph 2, ibid., 74.

**169.** Constitution, Sections 14 and 58(3), ibid., 80, 84.

**170.** Constitution, Sections 20, 39–66, ibid., 80, 82–85.

**171.** Constitution, Sections 91–93, ibid., 88.

**172.** Constitution, Sections 65, 68, 66, ibid., 85.

**173.** Constitution, Sections 59–64, ibid., 84–85.

**174.** Constitution, Sections 67–79, ibid., 85–87.

**175.** Final Report of the United Nations Commissioner in Eritrea, 52, paragraph 565.

**176.** Constitution, Sections 85–90, ibid., 87–88.

**177.** Constitution, Section 85, ibid., 87.

**178.** Constitution, Section 90(3), ibid., 88.

**179.** Constitution, Sections 1–15, 58, 73, ibid., 80, 84, 86. The question has been raised whether certain powers of the emperor's representative in Eritrea could be reconciled with the Federal Act. See Meron and Pappas, "Eritrean Autonomy," 207–209.

**180.** Federal Act, paragraph 5; Constitution, Section 7(1), Final Report of the United Nations Commissioner in Eritrea, 74, 79.

**181.** Federal Act, paragraph 7; Resolution 390A (V), paragraph 12 (paragraph 12 of the resolution was not part of the Federal Act, since the latter consisted only of the first seven paragraphs of the Resolution); Constitution, Sections 16, 17, 19, 23–35, ibid., 75, 80–82.

**182.** Federal Act, paragraph 6, and Constitution, Section 8, ibid., 74–75, 79–80.

**183.** Constitution, Section 21, ibid., 80.

**184.** Constitution, Section 38, ibid., 82.

**185.** Constitution, Section 36, ibid.

**186.** Federal Act, paragraph 5; Constitution, Section 7(2), ibid., 74, 79.

**187.** Federal Act, paragraph 4, Constitution, Section 6(3), ibid., 74, 79.

**188.** This fact was also mentioned with regret by the UN Commissioner in Eritrea. Final Report of the United Nations Commissioner in Eritrea, 50, paragraphs 544 and 545.

**189.** On the distinction, see chapter 6.

**190.** See note 180.

**191.** Constitution, Section 38, Final Report of the United Nations Commissioner in Eritrea, 82.

**192.** Constitution, Section 36, ibid., 82.

**193.** Constitution, Section 37, ibid.

**194.** This is reminiscent of the situation of democratic Finland, which had autonomy from autocratic Russia in the nineteenth century. See chapter 7.

**195.** The author wishes to express her warm thanks to Pedro A. Malavet, Esq., J.D., LL.M., whose oral explanations, bibliographical advice, and memorandum of 17 December 1993 have helped her understand the special situation and problems of Puerto Rico.

**196.** In the final tally, 48.4 percent voted for continued commonwealth status, while 46.2 percent voted for statehood, and 4.4 percent for independence. See *Washington Post,* 15 November 1993. These results, however, represented a decline in the percentage of those who favored commonwealth status.

**197.** For the historical background, one may consult Arnold H. Leibowitz, *Defining Status: A Comparative Analysis of United States Territorial Relations* (Dordrecht, The Netherlands: Nijhoff, 1989), 127–185; W. Michael Reisman, *Puerto Rico and the International Process: New Roles in Association* (Washington, D.C.: American Society of International Law, 1975), 2–35; Juan R. Torruella, *The Supreme Court and Puerto Rico: The Doctrine of Separate and Unequal* (Puerto Rico: Editorial de la Universidad de Puerto Rico, 1985), 7–160; Raymond Carr, *Puerto Rico: A Colonial Experiment* (New York: New York University Press, 1984), 17–72; Natan Lerner, "Puerto Rico: Autonomy, Statehood, Independence?" in Dinstein, *Models of Autonomy,* 125–134.

**198.** Office of the Commonwealth of Puerto Rico, ed., *Documents on the Constitutional History of Puerto Rico,* 2d ed. (Washington, D.C.: 1964), 22–46 (hereinafter, *Documents on Puerto Rico*).

**199.** Parry, *Consolidated Treaty Series,* vol. 187 (1979), 100–105.

**200.** *Documents on Puerto Rico,* 64–80.

**201.** *De Lima v. Bidwell,* 182 U.S. 1 (1901); *Downes v. Bidwell,* 182 U.S. 244 (1901); *Dooley v. United States,* 182 U.S. 222 (1901); *Armstrong v. United States,* 182 U.S. 243 (1901). The first three judgments mentioned here have also been partly reprinted in *Documents on Puerto Rico,* 117–134. These decisions have been discussed, inter alia, in Leibowitz, *Defining Status,* 17–29; Torruella, *Supreme Court and Puerto Rico,* 40–83; Jon M. Van Dyke, "The Evolving Legal Relationships between the United States and Its Affiliated U.S.-Flag Islands," *University of Hawai'i Law Review* 14 (1992): 445–517 at 455–459.

**202.** U.S. Constitution, Article 4, Section 3, 2d paragraph.

**203.** On the scope of this power, see Van Dyke, "Evolving Legal Relationships," 453–459. The term *state* is generally used in this study with its international meaning, but in the chapter on Puerto Rico it is also used with the meaning it has in the United States, i.e., the states that constitute the United States.

**204.** *Downes v. Bidwell,* 182 U.S. 244 at 311–312 (1901).

**205.** Torruella, "Supreme Court and Puerto Rico." According to Torruella, the *Insular* cases doctrine had severe political consequences in Puerto Rico. It led to the establishment of a party that demanded full independence and to the radicalization of the nationalists. Ibid., 117–133.

**206.** U.S. Constitution, Article 1, Section 8, first paragraph.

**207.** *Documents on Puerto Rico,* 81–112.

**208.** See, for example, Jose A. Cabranes, *Citizenship and the American Empire: Notes on the Legislative History of the United States Citizenship of Puerto Ricans* (New Haven: Yale University Press, 1979).

**209.** *Balzac v. People of Puerto Rico,* 258 U.S. 298 (1922).

**210.** *Rassmussen v. United States,* 197 U.S. 516 (1905).

**211.** *Elective Governor Act of 5 August 1947, Statutes at Large* 61 (1947): 772; *Documents on Puerto Rico,* 113–116.

**212.** *Act of 3 July 1950,* ch. 446, *Statutes at Large* 64 (1950): 319; *Documents on Puerto Rico,* 153–154. The text has also been reproduced in Reisman, *Puerto Rico and the International Process,* 124–125. On the legislative history of this law, see Torruella, "The Supreme Court and Puerto Rico," 133–159.

**213.** Opinions differ on the value and impact of this "compact." See Pedro A. Malavet, mimeographed memorandum addressed to the author, 17 December 1993, 2.

**214.** The following changes were requested: (1) the addition of a provision according to which any amendment to the constitution has to be consistent with certain U.S. texts; (2) the deletion of a provision recognizing the right to work and obtain an adequate standard of living as well as social protection in old age or sickness; and (3) the addition of a provision ensuring continuance of private elementary schools. See Reisman, *Puerto Rico and the International Process,* 33.

**215.** *Documents on Puerto Rico,* 155–163. Also reproduced in Reisman, *Puerto Rico and the International Process,* 126–136.

**216.** *Documents on Puerto Rico,* 168–192. Text also reproduced in Reisman, *Puerto Rico and the International Process,* 137–169. The constitution was also approved by the U.S. Congress; see *Statutes at Large* 66 (1952): 327; *Documents on Puerto Rico,* 194–195.

**217.** On the deliberations at the United Nations, see Torruella, "The Supreme Court and Puerto Rico," 160–166; Leibowitz, *Defining Status,* 228–231.

**218.** UN General Assembly Resolution 748 (VIII), of 27 November 1953, 8 UN General Assembly Official Record, supplement 17, 25.

**219.** See the section on autonomy and self-government in chapter 6.

**220.** UN General Assembly Resolution 1514 (XV), of 14 December 1960, 15 UN General Assembly Official Records, supplement 16, 66.

**221.** See, for example, resolutions adopted on 28 August 1972 and 30 August 1973 by the Special Committee established in order to make recommendations regarding the implementation of Resolution 1514 (XV), UN Doc. A/AC.109/419 (1972), and UN Doc. A/AC.109/438 (1973).

**222.** See, for example, Carr, *Puerto Rico: A Colonial Experiment,* 339–367.

**223.** See Reisman, *Puerto Rico and the International Process,* 43 (President Eisenhower); Leibowitz, *Defining Status,* 231 (President Carter); *Washington Post,* 15 November 1993 (President Clinton).

**224.** In June 1951, 76.5 percent of those who voted approved Public Law 600, and later 58 percent supported the adoption of the constitution. In 1967, the results were 60.41 percent for commonwealth, 38.98 percent for statehood, and 0.6 percent for independence (many of the independence partisans boycotted this referendum). In 1993, the results were 48.4 percent for commonwealth, 46.2 percent for statehood, and 4.4 percent for independence.

**225.** Reisman, *Puerto Rico and the International Process,* xii; Leibowitz, *Defining Status,* 178, note 172.

**226.** Puerto Rican Federal Relations Act, Section 9.

**227.** 758 F. 2d 40 (1st Cir. 1985).

**228.** "While the creation of the Commonwealth granted Puerto Rico authority over its own local affairs, Congress maintains similar powers over Puerto Rico as it possesses over the federal states." See *United States v. Quiñones,* 758 F. 2d 40, 43 (1st Cir. 1985).

**229.** *Califano v. Torres,* 435 U.S. 1 (1978); *Harris v. Rosario,* 446 U.S. 651 (1980). The first case dealt with Social Security benefits to the elderly, blind, and handicapped who live in Puerto Rico. The second case dealt with the program of Aid to Families with Dependent Children. The justifications for this unequal treatment have been: (1) the fact that Puerto Ricans do not pay federal taxes; (2) the cost of granting Puerto Rico the full benefits of the programs would be very high; and (3) increasing the benefits in Puerto Rico might seriously disrupt the Puerto Rican economy (causing inflation and increasing unemployment).

**230.** Constitution of Puerto Rico, Article 4, Section 1.

**231.** Ibid., Article 3.

**232.** Ibid., Article 5, Section 8.

**233.** Ibid., Article 3, Section 19.

**234.** Ibid., Article 6, Section 16.

**235.** *Bonet v. Texas Co. of Puerto Rico,* 308 U.S. 463, 471 (1940).

**236.** Puerto Rican Federal Relations Act, Section 41.

**237.** Ibid., Section 8.

**238.** Reisman, *Puerto Rico and the International Process,* 37.

**239.** Ibid., 21.

**240.** Puerto Rican Federal Relations Act, Section 42.

**241.** Constitution of Puerto Rico, Article 3, Section 5.

**242.** Puerto Rican Federal Relations Act, Section 5a.

**243.** Van Dyke, "Evolving Legal Relationships," 469–470.

**244.** Leibowitz, *Defining Status,* 196–197.

**245.** Ibid., 198–199.

**246.** U.S. Constitution, Article 1, Section 10.

**247.** Leibowitz, *Defining Status,* 196, note 265. On the general question of the participation of federal units in international affairs, see Hans J. Michelmann and Panayotis Soldatos, eds., *Federalism and International Relations: The Role of Subnational Units* (Oxford: Clarendon Press, 1990).

**248.** Reisman has explored the various possibilities. See Reisman, *Puerto Rico and the International Process,* 39–123.

**249.** See, for example, Leibowitz, *Defining Status,* 199–203; Carr, *Puerto Rico: A Colonial Experiment,* 201–230; Francisco A. Catala, "General Overview of the Economy of Puerto Rico," in Pamela S. Falk, ed., *The Political Status of Puerto Rico* (Lexington, Mass.: Lexington Books, 1986), 43–47.

**250.** Until 1976 it was a Possessions Corporation Exemption, under Section 931 of the Internal Revenue Code. For the gradual development of this provision, see Leibowitz, *Defining Status,* 204–212.

**251.** Ibid., 205–206.

**252.** Carr, *Puerto Rico: A Colonial Experiment,* 208.

**253.** Jeffrey Puryear, "Puerto Rico: An American Dilemma," in Falk, *Political Status of Puerto Rico,* 3–14 at 8.

**254.** Constitution of Puerto Rico, Article 7, Section 3.

**255.** Reisman, *Puerto Rico and the International Process,* 33.

**256.** See note 223.

**257.** *Rodriguez v. Popular Democratic Party,* 457 U.S. 1 at 8 (1982).

**258.** *Alcoa Steamship Co. v. Perez,* 295 F. Supp. 187 at 197 (D.P.R. 1968), affirmed, 424 F. 2d 433 (1st Cir. 1970).

**259.** *Ortiz v. Hernandez-Colon,* 475 F. 2d 135 (1st Cir. 1975).

**260.** See, for example, *Americana of Puerto Rico, Inc. v. Kaplus,* 368 F. 2d 431 at 436 (3d Cir. 1966). For a survey of the various court decisions that dealt with the status of Puerto Rico after the establishment of the commonwealth, see Van Dyke, "Evolving Legal Relationships," 473–479; Torruella, *The Supreme Court and Puerto Rico,* 166–200.

**261.** Van Dyke, "Evolving Legal Relationships," 480.

**262.** Reisman, *Puerto Rico and the International Process,* 1.

**263.** Resolution 22 of the Constitutional Convention of Puerto Rico, 1952, *Documents on Puerto Rico,* 164–165; also quoted in Reisman, *Puerto Rico and the International Process,* 39–40.

**264.** Van Dyke, "Evolving Legal Relationships," 451.

**265.** See the section on autonomy and associate statehood in chapter 6.

**266.** Reisman, *Puerto Rico and the International Process,* 42–45.

**267.** Daniel J. Elazar, ed., *Federal Systems of the World: A Handbook of Federal, Confederal, and Autonomy Arrangements,* 2d ed. (London: Longman, 1994), 292.

**268.** See the section on autonomy and federalism in chapter 6.

**269.** The opinion has been expressed that many of these exemptions benefit mainly the U.S. investors, and not the Puerto Rican workers. See Charles A. Rodriguez, "The State of Puerto Rico," *Washington Post,* 20 December 1995. The writer signed as majority leader of the Puerto Rico Senate.

**270.** Ibid.

**271.** See Isi Foighel, "Home Rule in Greenland 1979," *Nordisk Tidsskrift for International Ret* 48 (1979): 4–14; Foighel, "Home Rule in Greenland: A Framework for Local Autonomy," *Common Market Law Review* 17 (1980): 91–108; Foighel, "Home Rule in Greenland," in Meddelelser om Gronland, *Man and Society* (1980), 3–18; Foighel, "A Framework for Local Autonomy: The Greenland Case," in Yoram Dinstein, *Models of Autonomy* (New Brunswick, N.J.: Transaction Books, 1981), 31–52; Lars Adam Rehof, "Effective Means of Planning for and Implementing Autonomy Including Negotiated Constitutional Arrangements and Involving Both Territorial and Personal Autonomy," background paper to United Nations Meeting of Experts to Review the Experience of Countries in the Operation of Schemes of Internal Self-Government for Indigenous Populations UN Doc. HR/NUUK/1991/SEM.1, BP.2, 17 September 1991, 10–17; Emil Abelsen, "Home Rule in Greenland," UN Doc. HR/NUUK/1991/SEM.1, BP.4, 16 September 1991; Hans Engell (Minister of Justice of Denmark), Transcript of Opening Speech at the Nuuk Conference, 20 September 1991; Daniel J. Elazar, "Greenland," in Elazar, *Federal Systems,* 79–81; Hurst Hannum, *Autonomy, Sovereignty, and Self-Determination: The Accommodation of Conflicting Rights* (Philadelphia: University of Pennsylvania Press, 1990), 341–346.

**272.** UN General Assembly Resolution 849(IX) of 22 November 1954, *Yearbook of the United Nations,* 1954, 319–323.

**273.** Engell, Opening Speech, 5–6.

**274.** Act No. 577 of 29 November 1978. For an English translation, see *Nordisk Tidsskrift for International Ret* 48 (1979): 10–14; Foighel, *Man and Society* (1980), 15–18; Hurst Hannum, ed., *Documents on Autonomy and Minority Rights* (Dordrecht, The Netherlands: Nijhoff, 1993), 213–218.

**275.** Rehof, "Effective Means," 12–13; Frederik Harhoff, "Greenland's Withdrawal from the European Communities," *Common Market Law Review* 20 (1983): 13–33.

**276.** Rehof, "Effective Means," 12, note 31; Harhoff, "Greenland's Withdrawal," 23–26. The association of the Overseas Countries and Territories with the European Community is regulated by Part Four of the amended Treaty of Rome, Articles 131–136a. According to Article 131, "the purpose of association shall be to promote the economic and social development of the countries and territories and to establish close economic relations between them and the Community as a whole." Article 136a, added in 1985, expressly refers to Greenland: "The provisions of Articles 131 to 136 shall apply to Greenland, subject to the specific provisions for Greenland set out in the Protocol on special arrangements for Greenland, annexed to this Treaty"; *Official Journal of the European Communities,* no. L 29/1, 1 February 1985.

**277.** See the section on the Faroe Islands in chapter 9.

**278.** Foighel, "Home Rule in Greenland 1979," 6, paragraph 4.

**279.** Foighel, *Man and Society,* 6.

**280.** For references, see note 274.

**281.** Section 4(1) of the Home Rule Act.

**282.** Section 4(3) of the Home Rule Act.

**283.** Section 4(4) of the Home Rule Act.

**284.** Section 5(1) of the Home Rule Act.

**285.** Foighel "Home Rule in Greenland 1979," 7; Abelsen, "Home Rule in Greenland," 4.

**286.** Foighel, "A Framework for Local Autonomy: The Greenland Case," 42.

**287.** Section 5(2) of the Home Rule Act; Foighel, "A Framework for Local Autonomy: The Greenland Case," 43–44.

**288.** Abelsen, "Home Rule in Greenland," 3–4.

**289.** Section 7(1) of the Home Rule Act.

**290.** Section 7(2) of the Home Rule Act.

**291.** Sections 4(2), 4(3), and 5(1) of the Home Rule Act.

**292.** "About Greenland: Its Legal System and Constitution" (paper submitted to the Nuuk Conference, 1991), 7–9 (based on a paper by Agnethe Weis Bentzon presented to the 12th International Congress of Comparative Law in Sydney/Melbourne, Australia, 1986).

**293.** Engell, Opening Speech, 4.

**294.** Foighel, "Home Rule in Greenland 1979," 7.

**295.** Foighel, "A Framework for Local Autonomy: The Greenland Case," 41; Foighel, *Man and Society*, 7.

**296.** Section 11 of the Home Rule Act.

**297.** Section 12(1) of the Home Rule Act.

**298.** Section 12(2) of the Home Rule Act.

**299.** Section 12(3) of the Home Rule Act.

**300.** Engell, Opening Speech, 4.

**301.** Ibid.

**302.** Section 11(1) of the Home Rule Act.

**303.** Section 10 of the Home Rule Act.

**304.** Section 11(2) of the Home Rule Act.

**305.** Section 13 of the Home Rule Act.

**306.** Abelsen, "Home Rule in Greenland," 5–6.

**307.** Section 16(1) of the Home Rule Act.

**308.** Section 16(2) of the Home Rule Act.

**309.** Section 16(3) of the Home Rule Act.

**310.** Rehof, "Effective Means," 12.

**311.** Treaty amending, with regard to Greenland, the treaties establishing the European Communities of 13 March 1984, *Official Journal of the European Communities,* no. L 29/1, 1 February 1985. The author wishes to thank Alexandra Meir for having provided her with this text. See also references in notes 275 and 276.

**312.** Rehof, "Effective Means," 13.

**313.** Engell, Opening Speech, 8–9.

**314.** ICJ, *Reports,* 1993, 38.

**315.** Section 9(1) of the Home Rule Act.

**316.** Abelsen, "Home Rule in Greenland," 9.

**317.** Section 9(1) of the Home Rule Act.

**318.** Section 9(2) of the Home Rule Act.

**319.** Section 8 of the Home Rule Act.

**320.** Abelsen, "Home Rule in Greenland," 8–9.

**321.** Engell, Opening Speech, 7.

**322.** Ibid.

**323.** Section 1(2) of the Home Rule Act.

**324.** Section 2(1) of the Home Rule Act.

**325.** Sections 2(2) and 2(3) of the Home Rule Act.

**326.** "General and Practical Information about Greenland," prepared for the Nuuk Conference (1991), 3.

**327.** Section 3 of the Home Rule Act.

**328.** Section 17 of the Home Rule Act.

**329.** See chapter 9, text following note 85.

**330.** Section 18 of the Home Rule Act.

**331.** Rehof, "Effective Means," 11.

**332.** Abelsen, "Home Rule in Greenland," 6.

**333.** Engell, Opening Speech, 10; Rehof, "Effective Means," 15, 16.

**334.** Foighel, *Man and Society*, 6; Foighel, "A Framework for Local Autonomy: The Greenland Case," 37.

**335.** Central Bureau of Statistics, *Statistical Abstract of Israel*, (1995), 46: 43. For the 1948 and 1950 numbers, see Susan Hattis Rolef, ed., *Political Dictionary of the State of Israel* (New York: Macmillan, 1987), 259. See also Don Peretz, *Palestinians, Refugees, and the Middle East Peace Process* (Washington, D.C.: United States Institute of Peace Press, 1993), 11–17.

**336.** League of Nations, *Official Journal*, August 1922, 1007–1012, reproduced in Ruth Lapidoth and Moshe Hirsch, *The Arab-Israel Conflict and Its Resolution: Selected Documents* (Dordrecht, The Netherlands: Nijhoff, 1992), 25–32. The provisions of the Mandate for Palestine were inspired by the 1917 Balfour Declaration of the British government. See Lapidoth and Hirsch, *Arab-Israel Conflict: Documents*, 20.

**337.** Article 6 of the Terms of the Mandate.

**338.** Article 7 of the Terms of the Mandate.

**339.** *Statistical Yearbook of Jerusalem*, no. 13, *1994/95* (Jerusalem: Jerusalem Institute for Israel Studies, 1996), 25.

**340.** Memorandum by the British Representative under Article 25 of the Palestine Mandate, approved by the Council on 16 September 1922, reproduced in Terms of League of Nations Mandates, UN Doc. A/70, October 1946, 2–7.

**341.** For example, Agreement between the Emir Faisal of Hedjaz and Dr. Chaim Weizmann of the Zionist Organization, 3 January 1919, reproduced in Lapidoth and Hirsch, *Arab-Israel Conflict: Documents*, 21–22.

**342.** UN General Assembly Resolution 181(II) on the Future Government of Palestine, of 29 November 1947, General Assembly Official Records, 2d session, 1947, 131–151.

**343.** UN General Assembly Official Records, 2d session 1947, Ad Hoc Committee on the Palestinian Question, 12–19.

**344.** Ibid., 5–11; and Plenary Meetings, vol. II, 1425, 1426, 1427.

**345.** For an English translation, see *Laws of the State of Israel, Authorized Translation,* vol. 1, 5708–1948, 3.

**346.** Hashemite Jordan Kingdom–Israel: General Armistice Agreement, signed at Rhodes, on 3 April 1949, United Nations Treaty Series, vol. 42, no. 656, 304–320.

**347.** Egyptian-Israeli General Armistice Agreement, signed at Rhodes, on 24 February 1949, ibid., no. 654, 252–270.

**348.** Marjorie M. Whiteman, *Digest of International Law,* vol. 2, Department of State publication 7553(Washington, D.C.: Department of State, 1963), 1164–1168.

**349.** For English translation, see Lapidoth and Hirsch, *Arab-Israel Conflict: Documents,* 136–141.

**350.** UN General Assembly Resolution 3237 (XXIX) of 22 November 1974.

**351.** United Nations Treaty Series, vol. 1138, no. 17853, 39–45.

**352.** Ibid., no. 17855, 72–75.

**353.** See, for example, Ruth Lapidoth, "The Autonomy Negotiations: A Stocktaking," *Middle East Review* 15 (1983): 35–43; Harvey Sicherman, *Palestinian Self-Government (Autonomy): Its Past and Its Future* (Washington, D.C.: Washington Institute for Near East Policy, 1991).

**354.** *International Legal Materials* 21 (1982): 1199.

**355.** Lapidoth and Hirsch, *Arab-Israel Conflict: Documents,* 337–338.

**356.** For an English translation, see ibid., 357–360.

**357.** For an English translation, see *International Legal Materials* 27 (1988): 1637.

**358.** Political Communiqué and Declaration of Independence by Palestine National Council, 15 November 1988; for an English translation, see UN Doc. A/43/827; S/20278, 18 November 1988.

**359.** For the text of the invitation, see Lapidoth and Hirsch, *Arab-Israel Conflict: Documents,* 384–386.

**360.** *International Legal Materials* 32 (1993): 1525–1544; UN Doc. A/48/486–S/26560 (Annex), 11 October 1993. On this declaration, see Joel Singer, "The Declaration of Principles on Interim Self-Government

Arrangements," *Justice* 1 (1994): 4–21; Eyal Benvenisti, "The Israel-Palestinian Declaration of Principles: A Framework for Future Settlement," *European Journal of International Law* 4 (1993): 542–554; Antonio Cassese, "The Israel-PLO Agreement and Self-Determination," *European Journal of International Law* 4 (1993): 564–571; Raja Shihadeh, "Can the Declaration of Principles Bring About a 'Just and Lasting Peace'?" *European Journal of International Law* 4 (1993): 555–563; Karin Calvo-Goller, "Le régime d'autonomie prévu par la déclaration de principes du 13 Septembre 1993," *Annuaire Français de Droit International* 39 (1993): 435; K. W. Meighan, "The Israel-PLO Declaration of Principles: Prelude to a Peace?" *Virginia Journal of International Law* 34 (1994): 435–468.

**361.** Article 14 and Annex 2 of the Declaration of Principles.

**362.** Agreement on the Gaza Strip and the Jericho Area, 4 May 1994, UN Doc. A/49/180-S/1994/727 (Annex), 20 June 1994, *International Legal Materials* 33 (1994): 622–720 (henceforth 1994 Cairo Agreement).

**363.** Article 6 and Agreed Minutes to Article 6 of the Declaration of Principles.

**364.** *International Legal Materials* 34 (1995): 457–481.

**365.** Protocol on Further Transfer of Powers and Responsibilities, signed in Cairo on 27 August 1995.

**366.** Articles 1, 3, 4, 7, 13, and Annex 1 of the Declaration of Principles. The agreement (henceforth 1995 Interim Agreement) was signed in Washington on 28 September 1995, and was published by the Ministry of Foreign Affairs of Israel. See Joel Singer, "The West Bank and Gaza Strip: Phase Two," *Justice* 7 (December 1995): 1–12; Rotem M. Giladi, "The Practice and Case Law of Israel in Matters Related to International Law," *Israel Law Review* 29 (1995): 506–553 at 506–534.

**367.** Articles 4, 5(3) and Agreed Minutes to Article 4 of the Declaration of Principles.

**368.** Article 5 of the Declaration of Principles.

**369.** Security Council Official Records, 22nd year, Resolutions and Decisions, 8–9. This resolution has been the subject of differing interpretations by the parties, and of a great number of scholarly articles. Among the more recent ones are: Adnan Abu Odeh et al., *U.N. Security Council Resolution 242: The Building Blocks of Peacemaking* (Washington, D.C.: Washington Institute for Near East Policy, 1993); Ruth Lapidoth, "Security Council Resolution 242 at Twenty Five," *Israel Law Review* 26 (1992): 295–318.

**370.** Security Council Official Records, 28th year, Resolutions and Decisions, 10.

**371.** Article 5(4) of the Declaration of Principles.

**372.** Articles 1 and 5(1) of the Declaration of Principles.

**373.** Article 8 of the Declaration of Principles.

**374.** Agreed Minutes to Article 8 of the Declaration of Principles; see Karin Calvo-Goller "Legal Analysis of the Security Arrangements between Israel and the PLO," *Israel Law Review* 28 (1994): 236–267.

**375.** Annex 2, Article 3(d) of the Declaration of Principles.

**376.** Annex 3 of the Declaration of Principles.

**377.** Annex 4 of the Declaration of Principles.

**378.** Article 10; Annex 3 of the Declaration of Principles; Agreed Minutes to article 7(2) and Agreed Minutes to Article 8 of the Declaration of Principles.

**379.** Article 15 of the Declaration of Principles.

**380.** Article 12 of the Declaration of Principles.

**381.** Article 5(3) of the Declaration of Principles.

**382.** Preamble, last paragraph, and Article 31(2) of the 1995 Interim Agreement (see note 366).

**383.** Article 2 and Annex 1 of the 1994 Cairo Agreement. See Calvo-Goller, "Legal Analysis of the Security Arrangements."

**384.** Article 8 of the Declaration of Principles.

**385.** Annex 1, Article 3 of the 1994 Cairo Agreement; Articles 12 and 14 and Annex 1, Article 4 of the 1995 Interim Agreement.

**386.** Annex 1, Article 3(4) of the 1994 Cairo Agreement; Annex 1, Article 6(4) of the 1995 Interim Agreement; map no. 2, annexed to the 1995 Interim Agreement.

**387.** Annex 1, Article 3(2) of the 1994 Cairo Agreement; Annex 1, Article 6(2) of the 1995 Interim Agreement, and map no. 2, annexed to the 1995 Interim Agreement.

**388.** Annex 1, Articles 2(3) and 2(4) of the 1994 Cairo Agreement; Annex 1, Articles 3(4) and 3(5) of the 1995 Interim Agreement.

**389.** Annex 1, Article 12 of the 1994 Cairo Agreement; Annex 1, Article 13 of the 1995 Interim Agreement.

**390.** Annex 1, Article 11 of the 1994 Cairo Agreement; Annex 1, Article 14 of the 1995 Interim Agreement; map no. 8 annexed to the 1995 Interim Agreement.

**391.** Annex 1, Article 10 of the 1994 Cairo Agreement; Article 30 and Annex 1, Article 8, and Appendix 5 of the 1995 Interim Agreement.

**392.** Article 11 and Annex 1, Article 9 of the 1994 Cairo Agreement; Article 29 and Annex 1, Article 10 of the 1995 Interim Agreement; map no. 6 annexed to the 1995 Interim Agreement.

**393.** Article 20 of the 1994 Cairo Agreement; Article 16 and Annex 7 of the 1995 Interim Agreement.

**394.** Map no. 1 annexed to the 1995 Interim Agreement.

**395.** Article 10(1) of the 1995 Interim Agreement.

**396.** Articles 10(2) and 11(2)(d) of the 1995 Interim Agreement.

**397.** Article 12(1) of the 1995 Interim Agreement.

**398.** Article 13(2)(a) and Annex 1, Article 5(3)(a) of the 1995 Interim Agreement.

**399.** Article 13(2)(b)(8), and Annex 1, Article 5(3)(8) of the 1995 Interim Agreement.

**400.** Article 11(2)(b) of the 1995 Interim Agreement.

**401.** Article 11(2)(c) of the 1995 Interim Agreement.

**402.** Articles 11(2)(e) and 13(2)(b)(8) of the 1995 Interim Agreement.

**403.** Annex 1, Articles 5(4) and (5) of the 1995 Interim Agreement.

**404.** Article 17 of the 1995 Interim Agreement.

**405.** Annex 3, Article 2 and Appendix of the 1995 Interim Agreement.

**406.** For an analysis of the parallel provisions in the 1994 Cairo Agreement, see Moshe Hirsch, "Environmental Aspects of the Cairo Agreement on the Gaza Strip and the Jericho Area," *Israel Law Review* 28 (1994): 374–401.

**407.** For additional provisions that deal with religious sites, see Annex 1, Articles 5(2)(b), 5(7), 7(9); Annex 3, Article 38(11) (a) of the 1995 Interim Agreement.

**408.** Annex 3, Appendix 1, Article 29 of the 1995 Interim Agreement.

**409.** Annex 3, Appendix 1, Article 28 of the 1995 Interim Agreement. Some difficult matters were left to be solved by the permanent status negotiations; for example, questions of water rights and the fate of archaeological artifacts found in the autonomous areas by Israel since 1967. See Annex 3, Appendix 1, Articles 2(10) and 40 of the 1995 Interim Agreement, respectively.

**410.** Article 9(5) of the 1995 Interim Agreement. See Joel Singer, "Aspects of Foreign Relations under the Israeli-Palestinian Agreements on Interim Self-Government Arrangements for the West Bank and Gaza," *Israel Law Review* 28 (1994): 268–296. Singer's article relates to the 1994 Cairo Agreement on Gaza and Jericho, but the relevant provision is identical to Article 9(5) of the 1995 Interim Agreement.

**411.** See, for example, Articles 2 and 3 of the 1995 Interim Agreement.

**412.** Under Article 4 of the 1995 Interim Agreement, the number of the members to be elected was 82, but later the parties agreed to increase it to 87. To this one must add the chairman, or *Ra'ees*.

**413.** Article 18(4)(a) of the 1995 Interim Agreement.

**414.** Articles 18(5) and (6) of the 1995 Interim Agreement.

**415.** Article 18(4)(b) of the 1995 Interim Agreement.

**416.** Article 5 of the 1995 Interim Agreement.

**417.** Article 8 of the 1995 Interim Agreement.

**418.** Article 9(6) of the 1995 Interim Agreement.

**419.** For an analysis of the relevant provisions in the 1994 Cairo Agreement, see Celia Wasserstein-Fassberg, "Israel and the Palestinian Authority: Jurisdiction and Legal Assistance," *Israel Law Review* 28 (1994): 318–346.

**420.** Annex 4, Articles 1(1)(c), 1(2), 1(4), and 1(7) of the 1995 Interim Agreement.

**421.** Annex 4, Article 1(1).

**422.** Annex 4, Article 3.

**423.** Annex 4, Article 3(4).

**424.** Annex 4, Article 3(3).

**425.** Annex 4 of the 1994 Cairo Agreement.

**426.** Annex 5, Article 1(1) of the 1995 Interim Agreement.

**427.** See Ephraim Kleiman, "The Economic Provisions of the Agreement between Israel and the PLO," *Israel Law Review* 28 (1994): 347–373. Kleiman's article is based on the 1994 Cairo Agreement, but the relevant provisions are almost identical with those in the 1995 Interim Agreement.

**428.** Annex 5, Articles 8(1) and 9(1) of the 1995 Interim Agreement.

**429.** Annex 5, Article 8(10) of the 1995 Interim Agreement.

**430.** Annex 5, Articles 8(2)–8(9) of the 1995 Interim Agreement.

**431.** Annex 5, Articles 3(5) and (10) of the 1995 Interim Agreement.

**432.** Annex 5, Articles 3(2) and 3(3), and lists A1 (in Appendix 1) and A2 (in Appendix 2), as amended by the 1995 Supplement to the Protocol on Economic Relations, Article 6.

**433.** Annex 5, Article 3(4) and List B (in Appendix 3) of the 1995 Interim Agreement.

**434.** Annex 5, Article 3(11) of the 1995 Interim Agreement.

**435.** Annex 5, Article 3(7) of the 1995 Interim Agreement. Israel imposes a 17 percent tax.

**436.** Annex 5, Articles 8(11) and 9(6) of the 1995 Interim Agreement.

**437.** Annex 5, Articles 5 and 6 of the 1995 Interim Agreement, as amended by Appendixes 1 and 2 of the same Agreement.

**438.** Annex 5, Article 5(4) of the 1995 Interim Agreement, as amended by Appendix 1, and Supplement to the Protocol on Economic Relations.

**439.** Annex 5, Articles 5 and 6 of the 1995 Interim Agreement, as amended by Appendixes 1 and 2.

**440.** Annex 5, Article 7(1) of the 1995 Interim Agreement.

**441.** Annex 5, Article 4 of the 1995 Interim Agreement.

**442.** Annex 5, Articles 4(10) and 4(11)(b) of the 1995 Interim Agreement.

**443.** Kleiman, "Economic Provisions," 371–372.

**444.** For example, Annex 1, Articles 3(1), 3(2), and 3(3); Annex 3, Article 1; Annex 5, Article 2 of the 1995 Interim Agreement.

**445.** Article 19 of the 1995 Interim Agreement. See Eyal Benvenisti, "Responsibility for the Protection of Human Rights under the Interim Israeli-Palestinian Agreements," *Israel Law Review* 28 (1994): 297–317.

**446.** Article 22(1) of the 1995 Interim Agreement.

**447.** Article 31(7) of the 1995 Interim Agreement.

**448.** Articles 1(1) and 17(4) of the 1995 Interim Agreement.

**449.** Article 31(a) of the 1995 Interim Agreement.

**450.** Published by Israel's Ministry of Foreign Affairs.

**451.** Letter of 4 May 1994.

**452.** Amina Hess and Sami Sokol, "The PNC Has Repealed Those Provisions of the Palestinian Covenant That Deny Israel's Right to Exist" (in Hebrew), *Ha'aretz,* 25 April 1996, A1, A12.

**453.** See text accompanying notes 351–353. For a comparison between the Camp David Framework and the arrangements foreseen by the 1993 Declaration of Principles, see Yehuda Z. Blum, "From Camp David to Oslo," *Israel Law Review* 28 (1994): 211–235; Antonio Cassese, *Self-Determination of Peoples: A Legal Reappraisal* (Cambridge: Cambridge University Press, 1995), 245–247.


## 10. THE QUEST FOR AUTONOMY

**1.** See, for example, Ernest Gellner, *Nations and Nationalism* (Ithaca, N.Y.: Cornell University Press, 1983); John Hutchinson and Anthony D. Smith, eds., *Nationalism* (Oxford: Oxford University Press, 1994).

**2.** C. Geertz, "The Integrative Revolution: Primordial Sentiments and Civil Politics in the New States," in J. L. Finkle and R. W. Gable, eds., *Political Development and Social Change,* 2d ed. (New York: Wiley, 1971), 656.

**3.** Joseph V. Montville, "Epilogue: The Human Factor Revisited," in J. V. Montville, ed., *Conflict and Peacemaking in Multiethnic Societies* (Lexington, Mass.: Lexington Books, 1990), 535–541 at 536. Anthony D. Smith, "Ethnic Identity and World Order," *Millenium: Journal of International Studies* 12 (1983): 149–161.

**4.** Uri Ra'anan, "The Nation-State Fallacy," in Montville, ed., *Conflict and Peacemaking,* 5–20 at 8. The description quoted in the text is Ra'anan's definition of nationalism, a term that in his text has a connotation similar to that of ethnicity and group allegiance in the present study. Other authors also tend to use the term nationalism in a similar context. See, for example, Hans Kohn, *Nationalism: Its Meaning and History,* 2d ed. (Princeton: Van Nostrand, 1965). See also Anthony Smith, *The Ethnic Origins of Nations* (London: Oxford University Press, 1986); Gellner, *Nations and Nationalism.*

**5.** Donald L. Horowitz, *Ethnic Groups in Conflict* (Berkeley and Los Angeles: University of California Press, 1985), 4–5.

**6.** Alexander J. Motyl, "The Modernity of Nationalism," *Journal of International Affairs* 45 (1992): 307–324 at 315.

**7.** Allen Buchanan, "Self-Determination and the Right to Secede," *Journal of International Affairs* 45 (1992): 347–366 at 362.

**8.** Robert Lansing, *The Peace Negotiations: A Personal Narrative* (New York, London, and Boston: Houghton Mifflin, 1921), 97–98.

**9.** For example, Michla Pomerance, *Self-Determination in Law and Practice* (Dordrecht, The Netherlands: Nijhoff, 1982), 67, 73–76.

**10.** For example, Antonio Cassese, *Self-Determination of Peoples: A Legal Reappraisal* (Cambridge: Cambridge University Press, 1995), 59, 90, 99; Rosalyn Higgins, *Problems and Process: International Law and How We Use It* (Oxford: Clarendon Press, 1994), 115–116.

**11.** Cassese, *Self-Determination of Peoples,* 146; and Higgins, *Problems and Process,* 120.

**12.** *International Legal Materials* 31 (1992): 1498.

**13.** See chapter 1, note 68.

**14.** See, for example, Buchanan, "Self-Determination and the Right to Secede," 351–352; Hurst Hannum, *Autonomy, Sovereignty and Self-Determination: The Accommodation of Conflicting Rights* (Philadelphia: University of Pennsylvania Press, 1990), 473–475; Cassese, *Self-Determination of Peoples* 124, 351, 352, 354. For a categorization of the various regimes of minorities within a theoretical framework, see Guy Heraud, "Essai de typologie des statuts ethniques," in *La Construction Européenne: Mélanges Fernand Dehousse,* vol. 2 (Paris: Fernand Nathan; Brussels: Editions Labor, 1979), 39–44; and Otto Kimminich, "The Organization of Multinational States," *Law and State* 37 (1988): 7–28.

**15.** Arend Lijphart, *Democracy in Plural Societies* (New Haven: Yale University Press, 1977); Lijphart, "The Power-Sharing Approach," in Montville, ed., *Conflict and Peacemaking,* 491–509 at 492–494; see also the "alternative ways of coping" with the Irish problem, analyzed in R. Rose, *Northern Ireland: Time of Choice* (Washington, D.C.: American Enterprise Institute for Public Policy Research, 1976), 139–166.

**16.** Lijphart, *Democracy in Plural Societies;* and Lijphart, "Power Sharing Approach." For other proposals along somewhat similar lines, see E. A. Nordlinger, *Conflict-Regulation in Divided Societies,* Occasional Paper no. 29 (Cambridge, Mass.: Harvard University, Center for International Affairs, 1972); Kenneth D. McRae, ed., *Consociational Democracy: Political Accommodation in Segmented Societies,* Carlton Library, no. 79 (Toronto: McClelland and Stewart, 1974); M. J. Esman, "The Management of Communal Conflict," *Public Policy* 21 (winter 1973): 49–78.

**17.** Jürg Steiner, "Power-Sharing: Another Swiss 'Export Product'?" in Montville, ed., *Conflict and Peacemaking,* 107–114; Nicholas Schmitt, *Federalism: The Swiss Experience* (Pretoria, South Africa: Human Sciences Research Council, 1996).

**18.** For a different proposal, see Horowitz, *Ethnic Groups in Conflict,* 596–600.

**19.** In July 1996 the participants at a meeting of Hungarian authorities and the leaders of eleven organizations of Hungarians living in adjoining countries recommended measures promoting autonomy to enhance the preservation of the identity of the Hungarians living abroad. It was said that this aspiration is in conformity with the prevailing practice in Europe and with the spirit of international norms. However, Slovakia, which has a large Hungarian minority, denied the existence of such a right. See "Slowakisch-Ungarische Verstimmung: Umstrittener Wunsch nach Autonomie von Minderheiten," *Neue Züricher Zeitung,* 12 July 1996, 5. On the problem of Hungarian minorities, see, for example, László Vaki, "Minority Protection in Hungary–Hungarian Minorities Abroad," *Israel Yearbook on Human Rights* 21 (1991): 43–69.

**20.** Henry J. Steiner, "Ideals and Counter-Ideals in the Struggle over Autonomy Regimes for Minorities," *Notre Dame Law Review* (1991): 1539–1560 at 1547.

**21.** Nirmala Chandrahasan, "Minorities, Autonomy, and the Intervention of Third States: A droit de regard." *Israel Yearbook on Human Rights* 23 (1993): 129–145 at 129. S. James Anaya seems to derive a right to autonomy from "an emergent human rights of cultural survival and flourishment"; see "The Capacity of International Law to Advance Ethnic or Nationality Rights Claims," *Iowa Law Review* 75 (1990): 837–844 at 841.

**22.** The 1969 Vienna Convention on the Law of Treaties, Article 31 ("general rules on interpretation").

**23.** Steiner, "Ideals and Counter-Ideals," 1557.

**24.** Ibid., 1559.

**25.** Hannum, *Autonomy, Sovereignty, and Self-Determination*, 473–474. In the revised 1996 edition of his book (at p. 506) he, however, added that "it would be premature to claim that an 'international right to autonomy' has been recognized."

**26.** See the section on autonomy and self-administration in chapter 6.

**27.** See the section on autonomy and minority rights in chapter 1.

**28.** For example, the 1986 Constitution of Nicaragua, Articles 8, 89–91, and 180, and the 1987 Autonomy Statute of the Atlantic Coast Regions of Nicaragua, reproduced in Hurst Hannum, ed., *Documents on Autonomy and Minority Rights* (Dordrecht, The Netherlands: Nijhoff, 1993), 381–399; the 1987 Constitution of the Philippines, Article 2, Sections 22 and 25, Article 10, Sections 15–21, ibid., 428–459; see Ponciano L. Bennagen, Fiscal and Administrative Relations between Indigenous Governments and States, background paper for the UN Meeting of Experts to Review the Experience of Internal Self-Government for Indigenous Populations, UN Doc. HR/NUUK/1991/SEM.1, BP1, 21 August 1991, 8–15; the 1982 Constitution Act of Canada, Articles 25, 35, and 37, and the negotiations that followed them, as well as the 1986 act relating to self-government for the Sechelt Indian Band and the 1993 act to establish a territory to be known as Nunavut and provide for its government. (The text was kindly provided to the author by Professor Anne Bayefsky). On the arrangements introduced in Norway, Sweden, and Finland for the benefit of the Sami people, see Lars Adam Rehof, Effective Means of Planning for and Implementing Autonomy, Including Negotiated Constitutional Arrangements and Involving Both Territorial and Personal Autonomy, background paper for the above-mentioned UN Meeting of Experts, UN Doc. HR/NUUK/1991/SEM.1, BP2, 17 September 1991, 17–21.

**29.** See chapter 1, text accompanying note 69.

**30.** Thomas Buergenthal, conversation with author, 1990.

## 11. Establishing an Autonomous Regime: Issues to Consider

**1.** See chapter 3 and chapter 10.

**2.** Reproduced in Hurst Hannum, ed., *Documents on Autonomy and Minority Rights* (Dordrecht, The Netherlands: Nijhoff, 1993), 86–101; and in Florence Benoît-Rohmer, *The Minority Question in Europe: Texts and Commentary* (Strasbourg: Council of Europe Publishing, 1996), 152–169.

3. UN Doc. CCPR/C/21/Rev.1/Add.1 (1989), paragraph 13.

4. European Charter, Article 11.

5. See chapter 5.

6. See chapter 3 and chapter 10.

### 13. AUTONOMY: AN APPRAISAL OF THE PROS AND CONS

1. Robert A. Friedlander, "Autonomy and the Thirteen Colonies: Was the American Revolution Really Necessary?" in Yoram Dinstein, ed., *Models of Autonomy* (New Brunswick, N.J.: Transaction Books, 1981), 135–150 at 135; Yoram Dinstein, "Autonomy," in Dinstein, *Models of Autonomy*, 291–303 at 302.

2. Hurst Hannum and Richard B. Lillich, "The Concept of Autonomy in International Law, *American Journal of International Law* 74 (1980): 858–889 at 889. See also Claire Palley, "The Role of Law in Relation to Minority Groups," in Antony E. Alcock et al., eds., *The Future of Cultural Minorities* (New York: St. Martin's Press, 1979), 120–160; Claire Palley, Possible Ways and Means to Facilitate the Peaceful and Constructive Resolution of Situations Involving Racial, National, Religious and Linguistic Minorities, UN Doc. E/CN.4/Sub.2/1989/43, 4 July 1989; Claire Palley, "Introduction" to *Minorities and Autonomy in Western Europe* (London: Minority Rights Group, 1991), 5.

3. Friedlander, "Was the American Revolution Really Necessary?" 136; and Dinstein, "Autonomy," 302.

4. This was probably the reason why Spain granted a right to autonomy to all its provinces.

5. H. J. Steiner, "Ideals and Counter-Ideals," 1552–1553 (see note 20, chapter 10).

6. See chapter 5.

# INDEX

# Jennings Randolph Program for International Peace

As part of the statute establishing the United States Institute of Peace, Congress envisioned a fellowship program that would appoint "scholars and leaders of peace from the United States and abroad to pursue scholarly inquiry and other appropriate forms of communication on international peace and conflict resolution." The program was named after Senator Jennings Randolph of West Virginia, whose efforts over four decades helped to establish the Institute.

Since it began in 1987, the Jennings Randolph Program has played a key role in the Institute's effort to build a national center of research, dialogue, and education on critical problems of conflict and peace. Through a rigorous annual competition, outstanding men and women from diverse nations and fields are selected to carry out projects designed to expand and disseminate knowledge on violent international conflict and the wide range of ways it can be peacefully managed or resolved.

The Institute's Senior Fellows are individuals from a wide variety of academic and other professional backgrounds who work at the Institute on research and education projects they have proposed and participate in the Institute's collegial and public outreach activities. The Institute's Peace Scholars are doctoral candidates at American universities who are working on their dissertations.

Institute fellows and scholars have worked on such varied subjects as international negotiation, regional security arrangements, conflict resolution techniques, international legal systems, ethnic and religious conflict, arms control, and the protection of human rights, and these issues have been examined in settings throughout the world.

As part of its effort to disseminate original and useful analyses of peace and conflict to policymakers and the public, the Institute publishes book manuscripts and other written products that result from the fellowship work and meet the Institute's high standards of quality.

Joseph Klaits
Director

# AUTONOMY

This book is set in Perpetua; the display type is Albertus MT. Marti Betz designed the book's cover, and Joan Engelhardt and Day W. Dosch designed the interior. Pages were made up by Helene Y. Redmond.